Voices of Resistance

SUNY Series in Oral and Public History

Michael Frisch, Editor

Voices of Resistance

Oral Histories of Moroccan Women

Alison Baker

State University of New York Press

Published by
State University of New York Press

Printed in the United States of America

For information, address State University of New York Press,
State University Plaza, Albany, N.Y. 12246

Production by M. R. Mulholland
Marketing by Dana E. Yanulavich

Library of Congress Cataloging-in-Publication Data

Baker, Alison, 1939–
    Voices of resistance : oral histories of Moroccan women / Alison
Baker.
       p.   cm. — (SUNY series in oral and public history)
    Includes bibliographical references (p.   ) and index.
    ISBN 0-7914-3621-7 (hc : acid free). — ISBN 0-7914-3622-5 (pbk. :
acid free)
    1. Women—Morocco—Interivews.   2. Women—Morocco—Social
conditions.   3. Women—Morocco—History.   4. Women revolutionaries—
Morocco.   5. Morocco—History—Autonomy and independence movements.
6. Feminism—Morocco—History.   I. Title.   II. Series.
HQ1791.B35   1998
305.4'0964—dc21   97-2649
                                                              CIP

10 9 8 7 6 5 4 3 2 1

For my mother,
Elizabeth Fain Baker,
who first told me stories about the past.

Contents

Illustrations

Morocco under the protectorate.

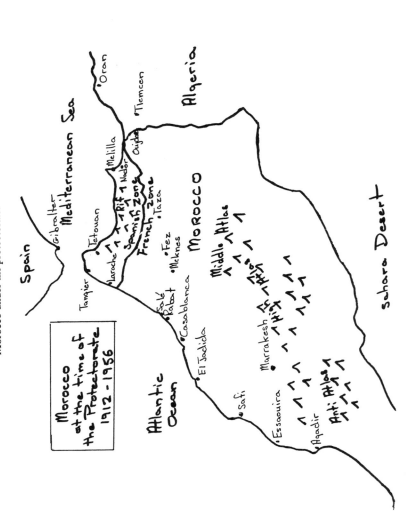

Acknowledgments

While all oral history is a collaborative venture, this project was especially so. Dr. Noufissa Benjelloun and her family (including her brother, professor Abdelmajid Benjelloun) have been involved from the very beginning. Leila Abouzeid's novel, *The Year of the Elephant*, inspired me, and Abouzeid herself translated many of the Arabic texts. Professor Soumaya Naamane-Guessous' invitation to meet with her parents and Casablanca resistance fighter Fatna Mansar launched me into the world of the armed resistance. Professor M'barek Zaki has been a constant source of advice and assistance on matters relating to the resistance. Professor Amina Leuh not only talked about her own experience in the 1940s and 1950s in Tetouan, but also about her research on women in the Rif and a whole range of other subjects. Her open mind and spirit, her thoughtful consideration of every question, and her example have encouraged and inspired me. Mohsine Rhoul and Fouzia Zaoui and their two families introduced me to the city of Oujda, and Leila Zaoui helped me get in contact with women from the Oujda resistance.

Professor Fatima Mernissi supported the project when it was at a very early stage; later, she helped me recruit students from her sociology workshop at Mohamed V University to conduct interviews with women in Rabat, Salé, and Casablanca. My thanks to these students for their excellent work: Soumia Khalfi (who also accompanied me on several interviews), Abdelfettah Ait Ayad, Merieme Chabar, Mustapha Jdiri, Mohamed Yacine Ait Ouzougagh, Khadija Sabil, and Abdelhadi Zerouaoui.

The project would not have been possible without the help of several friends and colleagues who devoted hours and hours of their time—accompanying me to interviews, working over the tapes and written transcripts, finding and translating Arabic-language archival material, and patiently answering my questions about Moroccan life and culture. I owe an enormous debt to Amina Fahim, Loubna Skalli, Najia El Hadrati, and Saadia Abenou.

Director emeritus Dr. Abdelhadi Tazi and researchers at the *Institut universitaire de la recherche scientifique* of Mohamed V University in Rabat gave me a home base, an intellectual community. The High Commission for Veterans of the Resistance and Liberation Army, High Commissioner Benjelloun and his staff, and Commission Delegations in Rabat/Salé, Casablanca, Fez, and Taza provided every facility to enable me to meet and interview women from the resistance and to consult their dossiers. At the Morrocan-American Commission for Educational and Cultural Exchange, Executive Secretary emeritus Edward H. Thomas and his staff made it possible for me to obtain necessary government permissions and provided other assistance and support, even though I never officially came under the Commission's aegis. The project has benefited from the cooperation of Istiqlal Party Women's Association (*Organisation de la femme istiqlalienne*) and the Women's Action Union (*Union d'action féminine*), their respective presidents Latifa Benani Smires and Latifa Jbabdi, and staff and party members.

Two wonderful photographers donated their time to work on the project: Ann Jones is responsible for the photos of Ghalia Moujahide and Halima Ben Moussa, and Anne White for almost all the other original photos, as well as for photographing old photographs from women's private collections.

I am pleased to acknowledge grants and in-kind support for research, travel to Morocco, and time and space to write the book, as follows: The American Institute of Maghrebi Studies (AIMS), 1992; The Ucross Foundation, 1994; Cottages at Hedgebrook, 1994 and 1996; Royal Air Maroc, 1995; The Camargo Foundation (Cassis, France), 1995; The Blue Mountain Center, 1996.

Anthropologist Eva Evers Rosander and writer Jenny Offill have each read and critiqued the manuscript at several stages in the writing process. The book is much better than it would have been without their comments; whatever deficiencies of content or style persist are my own responsibility.

My children, Eleanor, Caroline, and Ted, have not only tolerated my frequent absences without complaint, but have actively encouraged me and promoted the project. Eleanor took on the entire responsibility and the painstaking detail of getting the manuscript ready for the press.

Most of all, I am profoundly grateful to the women of the nationalist movement and armed resistance in Morocco who shared their stories and let me into their lives. Without them, none of this would have been possible.

Preface

There aren't many foreigners who know anything about Morocco, not even other Arabs. People don't study Moroccan history. Even tourist attractions are not well known; nor do people know about the great Moroccan cities. . . . And no foreigner knows anything about the Moroccan woman. Even in Morocco, hardly anyone knows about the Moroccan woman. . . .

These are the words of Oum Keltoum El Khatib, a Moroccan woman who participated in the nationalist movement in Casablanca in the 1940s and 1950s, the words with which she prefaced her oral history narrative. And they provide the simplest explanation of my purposes in writing this book: I wanted to let Moroccan women speak for themselves, to let their voices be heard, and to introduce American readers to a particular time in history and a particular group of Muslim women. These women are storytellers, and they lived through stirring times. By participating in the fight against French colonialism, they also challenged and redefined traditional Moroccan ideas about women's roles in society. The women's narratives reconstruct the little-known history of Moroccan feminism and nationalism, and take us into the lives of a remarkable group of Islamic women whose voices have never been heard.

My first sight of Morocco was from a plane, looking down at the brown patches of fields. It was an early morning in January, on the Royal Air Maroc night flight from New York to Casablanca, and the Moroccan passengers broke into applause as the plane set down on the runway. The sky was gray with a slow, steady rain. I fell in and out of sleep sitting in the back of the taxi driving to Rabat, and noticed men walking along the side of the road dressed in heavy brown wool robes with the hoods up, monklike, to protect them from the rain.

Later that day, I went to visit the *medina*[1] of Rabat, stepping out of the modern city of wide boulevards and traffic, into the narrow streets and alleys of the old walled city, where I was pushed and caught up in the crowds of shoppers, looking down to dodge the puddles. I passed clusters of old men sitting and chanting the Koran; a waterseller with his red tasseled hat and his polished brass cups; shops with neatly stacked piles of dates and nuts, figs strung on loops made of palm fronds, sheep's heads spread out and entrails hanging for display, and buckets of olives, richly green and black and reddish. From all sides, I heard the cacophony of Arab popular music, different songs blaring from competing stalls. I walked through the section where shoes are sold, shaded by a roof of woven reeds. Drawn into a little alley by the pungent smells, I found open gunnysacks, filled to the brim with different spices; there were the dried green leaves of henna too, little vials of *khol*, a sooty powder used as eyeliner, and other beauty product—I could only guess what they might be. I came out the other side of the medina into the traffic of the modern city, my senses still alive with a jumble of new sights, sounds, and smells.

On that same day, I walked through downtown Rabat, along the broad central Avenue Mohamed V, with its formal center strip, grass, and severely pruned palm trees. I was struck by the way men and women seemed to occupy separate spaces, without mixing; and by the sharp juxtaposition of traditional and modern styles of dress, especially among the women. I saw older women in old-fashioned *djellabas*,[2] with face veils, walking arm in arm with young women in trim straight skirts (even one in a miniskirt). There were groups of young women walking down the street together, jostling and chatting, some of them wearing jeans and others djellabas. A few young women were covered from head to toe, only their hands showing, and their faces framed tightly in the austere *hijab* worn by Islamic fundamentalists.[3] The sidewalk cafés were populated entirely with men, sitting grouped around tables, but all facing the street to be able to watch the passing crowd. I saw both women and men walking up and down the broad sidewalks in a late afternoon stroll, to see and be seen, but no mixed groups or couples.

This was the opening of a long journey for me, to discover Morocco. I began it in 1990 as the academic director of a semester-abroad program for American college students, and as time went on, I got to know a good many young Moroccan women—professionals and teachers. Sometimes I would visit them at home and meet their mothers, women of my own age (early fifties) or a little older. I discovered that most of these older women had not gone to school, and that many of them were illiterate. Most had been married while they were still in their early teens. I wondered what these mothers and daughters talked about, whether they knew or cared about each other's experience. Was there an oral tradition that was passed down from one generation to another? I began to ask questions about storytelling in families, especially folktales and stories about the past.

At the same time, I started reading, to see what historians had written about the period of the 1930s, '40s, and '50s, the years in which these women were growing up, and soon discovered that women were absent, scarcely mentioned.[4] Virtually nothing has been written on the women's organizations of the political parties, on women's roles in the free school movement and social action, or on women in the armed resistance. Men were the leaders of most resistance cells and organizations, and the roles that were specific to men— planning and directing the action, and using weapons—are viewed as more important than women's roles. What men say is called "oral testimony"; what women say is just "stories."

Yet I had heard stories of women who had participated actively, even heroically, in the national liberation struggle, and I saw all around me the dramatic changes in women's lives from one generation to the next. I suspected there might be a relationship between what women had done in the independence movement and the rapid social change I saw around me. My investigation was shaped by several memorable encounters—what American anthropologist Clifford Geertz describes as the "emblematic" experience of every field anthropologist:

> to come upon individuals in the course of research who seem to have been waiting there, at some unlikely place, for someone like you, bright-eyed, ignorant, obliging, credulous, to happen along, so as to have the chance not just to answer your questions but to instruct you as to which ones to ask: people with a story to tell . . . concerning what it is that they . . . "really," "genuinely," "truly,"—*in fact*—are.[5]

The first woman to stop me, with a story to tell, took me back with her in memory to the time in the 1940s when she was a young wife and mother presiding over a palace in Fez. She remembered every detail of that luxurious life, and brought out photos, one of her in a heavy brocaded *kaftan*,[6] sitting stiffly on a chair placed in the central courtyard of the palace. Other women had radically different memories of Fez in the forties. They spoke of a city buzzing with nationalist talk. They relived the scandal of those early days when they were among the first girls to break out of seclusion and go to school. In Casablanca, other women helped me to imagine the world of the resistance. They remembered growing up poor in the shantytowns, and the excitement of being born again into the family of the resistance, a dramatic life where they outwitted the police, transported arms, and conducted other dangerous missions.

My strategy in structuring the book has been to let the women speak for themselves, presenting two sets of multiple voices at the center of the book—the nationalist women in Part II and the women of the armed resistance in Part III. My own author's voice in these parts is muted and marginalized as commentary.[7] Thus, in the oral history chapters, where the women have the authority, we hear their stories and their views. My observations appear around the margins—in Part I and Part IV and the introductory chapters of Parts II and III—to provide a historical and cultural context for the interviews, and also to speak to broader issues in oral history.

Of course, in focusing on the stories of several women of the national movement and armed resistance, the book leaves out other stories, other views. We don't hear much from men, and we don't hear from the colonizers, the

Moroccans who worked with them, or minority groups such as Moroccan Jews or Algerians living in Morocco. We don't hear anything from rural women—the women of the Rif, the Middle Atlas, or the Ait Baamran in the south—the people that many Moroccans consider the real resistance fighters.[8]

I have tried to write a book that will provide a useful addition to the scholarly literature on Moroccan and women's history, but one that is also accessible to the general reader and not conventionally academic. I have not tried overly hard to maintain a critical distance or scholarly objectivity in relation to the women themselves. The book as a whole is unabashedly celebratory. I like and admire these women, and I wrote to celebrate their extraordinary lives and their contributions to the Moroccan independence movement.

I

Introduction

1

Oral History in Morocco

Anthropologists and Historians in Morocco

Morocco got its independence in 1956; now only people over fifty have an actual memory of the colonial period. Yet in all this time, surprisingly little has been written about Morocco under the protectorate or about the Moroccan nationalist movement in general—only a few political histories and memoirs, and virtually nothing about women's roles and contributions. This may be because Moroccan women's tradition is generally oral rather than written, and most Moroccan historians consider written records to be more reliable and thus more important as source material. A few scholars who have focused on the armed resistance do use oral testimony, but even they don't include women among their informants.[1] Women are recognized neither as important agents of history, nor as reliable reporters and interpreters of history.

In the oral histories that are at the center of this book, Moroccan women speak freely about their personal lives—growing up, going to school, their roles as women, wives, mothers, and especially about their involvement in the resistance against French colonialism in the 1940s and 1950s. However, these histories don't tell us much about French colonialism itself. What emerges instead is a picture of women engaged in what Australian literary critic Michael Hall calls a "double rebellion": rebelling simultaneously against colonialist occupation and oppression and against the restrictive attitudes of traditional society.[2] The women know Moroccan society intimately, and describe it in vivid detail. French colonialism, on the other hand, remains a shadowy enemy, talked about only in the most abstract terms.

My interests were somewhat different from those of most of the anthropologists and historians who have worked in Morocco.[3] On the whole, I found that while historians have minimized the contributions of Moroccan women or left women out entirely, anthropologists who focus on women are not generally concerned with history—reconstructing the specificity of the past and the process of change over time. I was interested in both women and history, and especially in women as agents and interpreters of history. I wanted to find out what happened when Moroccan women took on "men's roles" in the independence movement, as well as to explore the relationship between that chapter in history and roles of women in present-day Morocco. By doing so, I hoped to chart the process of social change not only in its visible, public manifestation but also in less tangible, private ways, in the consciousness of individual women.

Moroccan Women's Oral Traditions

In doing oral history interviews with Moroccan women, I was tapping into a strong oral tradition. These women learned their history first from their mothers or grandmothers—a history rich in myth and meaning, telling of the heroic exploits of the Moroccan men and women who resisted foreign invasions. In the late thirties and early forties when these women were growing up, there were people still alive who had experienced the 1920–26 Rif War against Spanish colonialism led by Abdelkrim El Khatabi, and women especially had created an oral tradition that included not only vivid, detailed descriptions of scenes from the war, but also songs. The women I interviewed were also aware of the larger Islamic tradition, with its numerous accounts of women warriors who played an active part in the armed struggle to establish the faith (*jihad*) that took up so much of early Islamic history.[4] Some of these women actually took up arms on the battlefield, while others urged men on to fight to the end. Later, in Morocco and elsewhere, a conservative Muslim (male) tradition developed, which relegated women to more passive, supporting roles in war, but the fact remains that there were women warriors in early Islamic history, and their lives and deeds were celebrated in biographical works. Ibn Sa'd's *Tabaqat*, a tenth-century biographical work, tells the story of Umm 'Umara, a woman who stayed to defend the Prophet while others fled, even though she herself had been "wounded twelve times at Uhud and her hand was cut off."[5]

Because these women warriors were engaged in jihad, their actions had a religious sanction; Islamic ideology exhorted all Muslims to defend the faith. Similarly, the women from the resistance insisted that everything they did was for their king, their country, and God. It was a jihad that they were fighting, and their exceptional courage was God-given. Indeed the women I interviewed spoke of almost everything in their lives in terms of a larger moral purpose. Every action (sometimes even marriage) was taken in the service of God or nationalism, never just for their own fulfillment or pleasure.

Several women warriors in the Islamic tradition were known for their spirit of defiance. One, named Hind, was not even a Muslim; in fact she was a major enemy of the Prophet.[6] She arranged for Hamza, Mohamed's uncle, to be killed, and then ate his liver raw on the battlefield. After one battle she danced among the bodies of the dead Muslims as she sang: "If you battle us, we will crush you in our arms/ If you retreat, we will let you go/ Farewell to love."[7]

Historians have written copiously about Hind, presenting her in all her complexity—courageous, witty, bloodthirsty.

For a defiant and outrageous heroine in a different vein, there is Sukayna, daughter of the Prophet's grandson, Hussein. She was celebrated for her beauty, intelligence, and wit, married five or six husbands, and refused to pledge obedience (ta'a) to any of them. In all her marriage contracts she specifically stipulated that she would do as she pleased, and that she did not acknowledge her husband's right to practice polygamy. She continued to actively pursue her interests in political affairs and poetry even after marriage, receiving visits from poets and attending meetings of the Qurashi tribal council. She even took one husband to court for violating the monogamy stipulation in the marriage contract.[8]

Storytelling is an important part of Moroccan popular culture; even today, in women's circles, storytelling skills are highly valued. Many of the women I interviewed revealed childhood memories of long, enchanted evenings when all the women and children of the household would gather to hear an older aunt or grandmother tell the tales of the Arabian Nights, stories of Islamic religious figures and saints, and Moroccan folktales.[9] Now, as older women themselves, they have become practiced storytellers; and many of the Moroccan folktales in their repertoire feature a strong, smart heroine who outwits the men in authority to get what she wants—an archetype in marked contrast to the sleeping beauties, Cinderellas, and other more passive heroines of Western folktales.

Life Stories

We all use narrative to construct our sense of ourselves. We find identity and meaning by telling stories about what we have done in our lives, our actions in history.[10] But the specific form that life history narratives take, and their main points of reference, are often culturally determined. For Moroccan women the most significant turning points are times when the family moves, times of famine, times when a girl takes on the brunt of the household work (after her older sister is married, for instance), and most important of all, a girl's marriage and her move from living with her own family to living in her husband's family—under what is often described as the heavy hand of her mother-in-law. The key event is marriage. It represents the transition from being a part of one family to becoming a part of another, the transition from childhood to adult identity.[11]

The women I interviewed diverged significantly from this pattern in telling their life stories. The nationalist women who were among the first Moroccan Muslim girls to go to school recall that experience in great detail and see it as a turning point in their lives. On the other hand, the women who participated in the armed resistance construct a life history that centers on their experience in the resistance. The events that these women stressed were their awakening to consciousness of the struggle against colonialism, the exile of King Mohamed V, entering the "family" of the resistance, and carrying out missions for the resistance that tested their courage and resourcefulness.

Nationalist Women/Women of the Armed Resistance:
Differences and Similarities

The most obvious differences between the nationalist women and the women of the armed resistance were differences of class and education. The experience of growing up in Fez as a daughter of the traditional bourgeoisie was a world apart from the experience of growing up in Casablanca as a daughter of the new proletariat.[12]

The nationalist women were part of a very small Moroccan elite. Not only were they born into the great families of the great bourgeoisie, a class which consisted of only a few hundred families in all of Morocco; but they were also among the very few girls of that generation to have access to education. Education brought these daughters of the bourgeoisie out of seclusion, and thrust them into positions of leadership among women in the nationalist movement. While they were still in their teens, they began to give classes to older women, teaching literacy and nationalist awareness. Starting in the mid-forties, they became leaders of the women's organizations of the political parties, and leaders in education and social action.

The women of the armed resistance were born into poor families, most of them recently migrated from rural areas, members of a growing neoproletariat in Casablanca and other industrial centers. Some of them participated in meetings organized by the Istiqlal (Independence) Party in the forties or joined the first cells of the armed resistance as they were formed starting in Casablanca in 1947. Most did not begin to participate in the armed resistance until after the exile of King Mohamed V in August, 1953.

From 1944, when the Istiqlal Party began a mass mobilization which also targeted women, until late 1955, when King Mohamed V returned from exile, there was a great deal of solidarity between different classes. In this period, the nationalist women and the women of the armed resistance played overlapping roles in the national liberation movement. In the late forties, proletarian women attended secret meetings organized and led by nationalist women, and in the early fifties, nationalist women helped to smuggle arms and hide partisans for the resistance. But after independence, in 1956, the solidarity between the Istiqlal Party and the armed resistance quickly disintegrated. The (male) political leaders from the party joined with King Mohamed V in forming the new government, specifically shutting out leaders of the armed resistance and liberation army. While women of the nationalist movement took on leading roles in education and social service, women of the armed resistance went home and back to their domestic roles. For the next decade, the government and the social service organizations headed by women from the nationalist movement all ignored the women of the armed resistance, while the women themselves were preoccupied with survival.

The difference in class makes a big difference in women's experience, perceptions, and memories. Nationalist women see their lives as a continuous development, their childhood and education preparing them for participation in the national movement, and the national movement in turn preparing them to take on leading roles in social service and education after independence. Women from the armed resistance don't want to talk about their childhoods or the period after independence. They focus almost entirely on what they did in the resistance, framing that narrative in myth and the history of other wars Morocco has fought against foreign invaders.

Gender Ideology: Images and Self-Images

The main thing that women from the two groups had in common was their gender, an important bond given the prevailing Moroccan ideology of separate roles and spaces for men and women. The nationalist women spoke frequently of French opposition to Moroccan women's education (especially Islamic, Arabic-language education) and emancipation. They also spoke of Christians as generally fearing and respecting the power of Islam, and of Islamic learning and faith. But above all was the conviction that educated and politically aware Islamic women were a force to be reckoned with and would pose a serious threat to French colonial rule.

I found no evidence for this idea in French sources, but it was certainly very widespread among Moroccan nationalists, both women and men. It is true that the French were extremely elitist, and this elitism was evident in their views on education. They wanted to limit education for Moroccan Muslims to a small male elite, and for that purpose they established a very limited number of schools, with a curriculum focused on French language and culture.[13] It was the Moroccan king and the nationalists who promoted education for Moroccan Muslim girls, and it was the nationalists who created schools and began to offer education to girls and eventually to different classes of Moroccans.

Moroccan Muslim women did not have much exposure to European culture, or much contact with "Christians" during the period of the protectorate.[14] While some Moroccan Muslim girls from the urban proletariat went out to work in French factories or as domestic servants in European homes, Moroccans and Europeans lived in separate areas of the city, and there was very little mixing. Almost no Moroccan Muslim women spoke French, and almost no Europeans spoke Arabic, so there was little possibility for interaction. Despite this lack of contact, both the bourgeois women in the nationalist movement and the proletarian women in the armed resistance were well aware of the stereotypes that the French had of Moroccan women.[15] French officials "respected" Moroccan women, and normally would not touch them or search them. They thought women incapable of getting involved in politics or in militant action, and the women learned to use the French officials' presumption of their ignorance as a part of their disguise, playing these stereotypes to their advantage.

The women all felt that Moroccan collaborators were more dangerous than the French officials themselves, and of course they were intimately acquainted with the extremely negative stereotypes that Moroccan men had of women, and with the norms of traditional Moroccan society: the seclusion and veiling of women, and the absolute authority of the husband in the patriarchal Moroccan family. Again, they used these stereotypes to their advantage: when a woman insisted that it was *unthinkable* for a man to come into her house while she was there alone without her husband, there was nothing a Moroccan collaborator could do but stay outside.

Gender Roles

By their active participation in the nationalist movement and armed resistance, women from both groups moved beyond traditional gender roles. The nationalist women had already created a revolution and a scandal as the first girls to go to school, especially if they continued in school after they reached the age of puberty. By walking through the streets to get to school, and by attending school together with boys and getting the same education, these women were breaking out of their seclusion, their restriction to the "women's space" inside the house, and moving into the "men's spaces" of the streets and the schools. Then they took on roles that were new for Moroccan women in the women's associations of the political parties, mobilizing and organizing other women, and learning how to make them work together.

Women who joined the armed resistance took on active, militant roles, working together with men. Missions for the resistance not only brought them out of seclusion, but sent them into dangerous situations, traveling long distances by themselves, carrying messages and weapons, even setting bombs, all the while using their wits to escape detection. Several of the women defined these roles as "men's roles" that they were taking on in the resistance. One woman, Fatima Roudania, a resistance fighter in Casablanca, is described as dressing in "men's clothes"—wide-legged golf pants and a man's head covering.

These were dramatic changes in the roles that women played and in the spaces that they occupied. Yet as the women talked, it became clear that the women themselves usually defined even these new roles largely as "women's roles" in the sense that they were different from and complementary to the roles that men played. American scholar Margaret Collins Weitz, in her work on women and the French Resistance, found a similar phenomenon. Women's roles in the resistance were looked on (by men, at least) as an extension of traditional female responsibilities—offering food and shelter to male resistance fighters, typing and coding secret papers (clerical work), and liaison (running errands)—and this led to minimizing women's contribution.[16]

The women's organizations of the political parties were quite independent in organizing their own activities, but followed the political direction of the party executive committee, which was made up of men. Social service organizations were headed and staffed entirely by women, and the women raised money and took care of housing and food for students in the nationalist free schools who needed help. In the oral histories, nationalist women speak with pride of women's accomplishments, emphasizing the activities that were organized and funded entirely by women. In the period before independence, it was still unusual to have meetings or classes where men and women mixed. So women had separate meetings, organizations, and areas of activity, thus reproducing the patterns of traditional society, with separate spaces and different, complementary roles for men and women. Political leadership seemed to have been largely reserved for men.

Women from the armed resistance talked about being inspired by photographs of women carrying guns in Palestine or Algeria, in the 1936-39 Palestinian uprising or the Algerian national liberation struggle against French colonialism.[17] For the first time in their lives they got the idea that Muslim women could play men's roles in the fight against colonialism. But in the Moroccan resistance only men actually used arms. Men also planned and directed resistance operations, and were the heads of most resistance cells and organizations. Transporting arms and messages was something that was usually assigned to women, because the colonial authorities were less likely to search them, and because it was easy for a woman to conceal arms in the voluminous folds of her haik or tucked in under her baby strapped on her back.[18]

Relations between Men and Women

Women from the armed resistance noted a dramatic improvement in their relations with men during the period of the resistance. Not only were women in the secret cells given the same responsibility as men in carrying out missions, but relations between men and women generally became much more relaxed in this period. Whereas before it would have been unthinkable for a young woman to receive men in her home when her husband was not present, during the resistance that happened often, and men in that situation would treat the woman like their sister, or their mother or their daughter.

Many women worked in the same resistance cell as their husbands. In some cases their husbands had brought them into the resistance, but in other cases, men had refused to allow their wives to participate, and the women had challenged their husbands and forced their way into the organization. In either case, there was usually more equality in the relationship during the resistance than before.

It was a great shock to women from the armed resistance to discover after independence that not much had changed in the society at large, especially in regard to the status of women. This harsh reality was brought home to some in a way that struck at the very core of their newfound sense of themselves. These were women who had worked with their husbands during the resistance, and then suddenly, after independence, found themselves repudiated.[19] None of the women I interviewed wanted to talk about that part of their lives, so I will turn here to the words of the fictional character Zahra, the protagonist of Abouzeid's *The Year of the Elephant*. The novel opens shortly after Moroccan independence, as Zahra is returning to her hometown after her husband has repudiated her:

> I come back to my hometown feeling shattered and helpless. . . . He had simply sat down and said, "Your papers will be sent to you along with whatever the law provides." My papers? How worthless a woman is if she can be returned with a paper receipt like some store-bought object! How utterly worthless!
>
> Those few seconds destroyed the whole foundation of my being, annihilated everything I trusted.[20]

Women from the resistance who had lost their husbands through death or divorce were relegated to the marginal social status of women without men, and had to struggle to survive and to support their families. Women who kept their husbands generally found themselves back in traditional domestic roles, secluded and inactive.

Nationalist women owed their emancipation to men, under the leadership of the Moroccan king and men in the nationalist movement. Aicha Terrab, director of the National Union of Moroccan Women in Casablanca, especially stressed the role of the king: "[In Morocco], instead of beginning [women's emancipation] with demonstrations in the streets against the state, we had an emancipation that came from the state itself, from His Majesty Mohamed V himself, who in his person incarnated both temporal and spiritual power."[21]

When these women were young girls growing up in families of the bourgeoisie, their fathers (or sometimes their grandfathers) made the decision to send them to school, and encouraged and supported them as they continued their education. Their husbands and other young nationalist men were also supportive.

They brought the women into the nationalist movement, supported the women's organizations of the political parties, and helped women launch social action projects. The nationalist women did note that there were some diehard Moroccan men who opposed any change in the roles of women, and some parents, fathers and mothers, who opposed sending girls to school; but their own experience was of being encouraged and supported by men. Nationalist women insisted on this, and considered Moroccan women fortunate to have men's support rather than having to fight against them for emancipation. Some contrasted that with Western feminism, where women went out into the streets "without their bras" and shouted and demonstrated in order to gain equal rights and emancipation.

Nationalism and Islam

The women in both groups say that everything they did was done for their King, their country, and their God; it runs through the oral histories like a refrain. Even now these women remain profoundly committed to Islam, to the Moroccan nation, and to the king who is both head of state and "Commander of the Faithful" (*Amir al Mouminine*). In Morocco, it was the Salafiya Islamic reform movement that called for educating upper class women, and it was the nationalist movement that called for mobilizing women and getting them involved in political action. Thus the modern Moroccan women's movement was born out of nationalism and Islam. But finally nationalism and Islam had very mixed messages for women. The Salafiya Islamic reform movement was socially conservative, and the nationalists wanted to preserve a distinctive Moroccan national identity and tradition. Both Islam and nationalism emphasized women's traditional (and subordinate) roles in the family.

Now, forty years after independence, the women who were active in the independence movement have political views that are more or less the same as those of the men in their social milieu. They are still profoundly committed to Islam—as older women they devote more time now to prayer and religious life and most have made the pilgrimage to Mecca at least once—and they are conservative on most social issues. Although many of the women from the armed resistance have suffered personally under the provisions of Moroccan family law, they do not necessarily identify with current feminist demands for changes in the code. After all, it is the oulema and the king, in his role as the nation's religious leader, who control Moroccan family law and the personal status of women, and the women are unlikely to question religious authority.

2

Nationalism and Feminism in Moroccan History

The Roots of Moroccan Nationalism

Nationalism is generally considered a modern development, starting with the emergence of Western Europe's nation states in the sixteenth century, and reaching its height in the nineteenth century, the great age of European industrial development and imperialism. In this definition, nationalism is linked to the rise of a merchant class and capitalist economic system, a centralized, bureaucratic state, a common language, and an educated public. But these definitions and models are drawn from the European experience. To understand Moroccan nationalism, we need to look at the specifics of Moroccan history and experience. In recent years, several Moroccan historians have begun to explore the meaning of "nation" and "nationalism" in the Moroccan context, focusing on Morocco's long history as an Arab, Islamic monarchy, a nation with a distinctive cultural tradition and a system of rule that have endured for more than a thousand years.[1]

The roots of Moroccan nationalism—and of the Moroccan nation—go back to the seventh century, when Arabs started arriving in Morocco. The Arabs not only conquered the country and took political power, but they also converted the local Berber populations to Islam and began a process of Arabization, changing the ethnic makeup of the population, the language, and the culture. Morocco's first national government was the Islamic monarchy founded in 787 AD by Idriss I,[2] who established from the very beginning a monarchy whose political legitimacy was based in blood descent from the Prophet Mohamed.[3] The Moroccan sultan (now king) was, and is, not only the head of state but also the nation's spiritual leader, symbol of the Moroccan nation, the Muslim nation, and the community of believers.[4] This was an enormously powerful symbol. The system of rule has lasted right up to the present day.

Soon after the Arab conquest, the Muslim world of North Africa entered an era of enormous prosperity, based on trans-Saharan trade, gold, and sugar. Morocco came to dominate the great western trans-Saharan trade routes; and the city of Fez became the intellectual and cultural center of the known world.[5] By the twelfth century, Morocco was an imperial power, with an empire that stretched north into Spain, east to Libya, and south below the Sahara. Then, in the fifteenth century, the balance of world power began to shift: the countries north of the Mediterranean were gaining in military and economic strength, while the countries to the south were weakening. In the western Mediterranean, power shifted dramatically from Islamic Morocco to Christian Iberia. The year 1492, known to most Americans as the date that Christopher Columbus set sail for the Indies and discovered America, is known to Moroccans as the date of the fall of Grenada, when the Spanish Inquisition drove all Jews and Muslims from their homes, marking the end of Islamic Spain. Many of the bourgeoisie of Fez, Tangiers, and Tetouan are the descendents of Muslim and Jewish families that fled Spain in 1492.

The other countries of the Middle East and the Maghreb were conquered by the Turks and lived under Ottoman rule for almost three hundred years (about 1550 to 1830), but Morocco remained independent.[6] For almost four hundred years, Morocco successfully resisted not only the Turks, but also the continual attacks and encroachments of European imperialism.[7] Moroccans are proud of this long history of maintaining their country's cultural and territorial integrity in the face of attack. By the nineteenth century, the Moroccan sultans were faced, and often virtually immobilized, by conflicting pressures: European imperialism was eating away at the powers of the sultan and his makhzen government and threatening to conquer Moroccan territory on the one hand; while on the other hand, an increasingly conservative and xenophobic Moroccan public opinion resisted any efforts by the sultan to reform and modernize the country.[8] Finally, Morocco succumbed to vastly superior French forces, and in 1912, a weakened sultan was forced to sign the Treaty of Fez, establishing a French protectorate over the largest part of his kingdom, with a Spanish protectorate in the Sahara and the north of the country.

Of the three countries of the Maghreb, Morocco had the shortest period of colonization (less than fifty years)[9] and for much of that time, the French ruled the country in alliance with traditional political and religious forces.[10] It was Marshall Hubert Lyautey, the first French resident general, who set the tone and policy for the French protectorate in Morocco. He loved the colorful ceremonies and traditions of Morocco, much preferring life in this other world to life in contemporary France, where traditions and the class system were under attack. By leaving the old walled cities untouched and inhabited entirely by Moroccans, and building the villes nouvelles outside the walls, laid out in the French style with broad tree-lined avenues, Lyautey kept traditional Moroccan urban society separate, intact, and almost unchanging. Lyautey was an extreme elitist. Under the French protectorate, government positions and schooling were reserved for only a handful of Moroccans, the sons of the traditional elites. Thus French policies and programs in city planning and education amounted to a kind of apartheid designed to protect Moroccan traditions and to limit social change.[11] In Morocco, French colonization came too late to be effective in modernizing the social and political systems of the country, and may even have interrupted the social and political modernization that was already in progress.[12] The French blocked social change, and at the same time promoted a process of rapid economic change. Their contribution to economic "progress" was to build roads and railroads to open up the country, and to create a capitalist economy based on domestic and foreign trade. They focused on developing commercial agriculture and mineral production in the countryside and a modern industrial and commercial complex in urban areas.[13]

Morocco has occupied the same territory from the beginning of the sixteenth century until the present; this geography has played an important role in Moroccan political, social, and economic history. The Atlas mountains divide the country into two distinct zones. To the north and west of the Atlas lie the great plains, fertile agricultural areas where the Arabs settled, site of the great bourgeois cities of Fez, Rabat, Salé, and Tetouan (centers of the nationalist political movement), and of the new industrial city of Casablanca (birthplace of the armed resistance). This was the *bled al makhzen*, where the sultan and his government ruled directly. The other zone is made up of the Atlas and Rif mountains and the Sahara desert—poor, arid areas inhabited mostly by Berbers. This was the *bled al siba* (areas of dissidence), ruled loosely and indirectly through the *bey'a* (contract of allegiance).[14]

The French, when they came to occupy Morocco, seized upon these dualities and used them for political purposes. The economic motivation for the protectorate was that Morocco had a higher proportion of fertile regions than either Algeria or Tunisia. So the French dubbed these fertile regions, which could be exploited for commercial agriculture, *le Maroc utile* (useful Morocco), and the rest of the country—the mountains, arid lands, and desert—*le Maroc inutile* (useless Morocco). In an effort to divide and rule the Moroccan population, they stressed the Arab–Berber duality, constructing a Manichean world of "good Berbers" and "bad Arabs" (or *sales arabes*—dirty Arabs), and developing policies that favored Berbers over Arabs.

At one point during the protectorate, the French tried to remove Berber areas from the jurisdiction of the sultan's makhzen government; this was the infamous Berber *dahir* (decree) of May 16, 1930. But this effort to divide the Moroccan population had exactly the opposite effect. Arab and Berber populations both rose up to protest the dahir and the French encroachment on the authority of the sultan, recognizing it as an attack on Islam, the very soul of the Moroccan nation. Clearly the French had underestimated the attachment of Berbers to Islam, to Arabic as the language giving access to God, and to the Moroccan sultan who combined both sacred and temporal authority.

The Roots of Moroccan Feminism

There is no unambiguous term for *feminist* in Arabic. *Nisai* has been used to mean feminist, but it can also just mean having to do with women. Even the nationalist women who spoke in French, where there is a clear distinction between *féminin* (female or having to do with women) and *féministe* (feminist), used the more ambiguous and inclusive term women's movement (*mouvement féminin*). It is in this sense that both "Moroccan feminism" and "Moroccan women's movement" are used here, as a general rubric including everything from women in legend and myth, to the active roles that women played in social and economic life throughout Moroccan history, to the emancipation of Moroccan women in the context of the nationalist movement, to the situation of young women in Morocco today.

Every woman I interviewed took pains to point out the contributions that Moroccan women have made throughout history, especially the economic contributions. Moroccan women have always worked. Not only have they always worked, but they work very hard. In rural areas, where the vast majority of the Moroccan population lived during the protectorate, women worked in the fields and took care of domestic animals, as well as doing all the work of the household. Even now, in rural villages, little girls start working—tending livestock, hauling water, washing clothes, running errands—at a very young age, while their brothers play or go to school. Moroccan anthropologist Fatima Hajjarabi has documented the enormous time and backbreaking labor involved in fetching firewood for cooking in the north of Morocco, a task that is performed entirely by women.[15] Fetching water is similarly onerous in some areas of the country, where village women have to walk miles to the nearest well. In cities, much of the most demanding artisanal work is done by women: decorating pottery, knotting carpets by hand, doing intricate embroidery, as well as the work of processing and spinning wool. Even upper class women, secluded in the women's quarters of the great houses, did embroidery and other hand work. And because women were often married to men much older than they, it was not uncommon for a woman to be widowed while she was still quite young, left with eight or nine children to raise and the full responsibility of supporting her family.

As noted in the previous chapter, separation of the sexes was the rule in traditional Moroccan society. While that prevented women from participating in "men's activities," it also provided separate and autonomous spaces for women. Wherever we focus our attention on these women's spaces, we find examples of women's autonomous expression, a sort of underground, "invisible feminism."[16]

Many scholars have recently become interested in the women's *souks* (weekly markets) in the north of Morocco, in the area of Al Hoceima.[17] These souks still exist, although in smaller numbers than before. They are managed and frequented by women only, and strictly forbidden to men. In fact, they are not just forbidden to men, but also to "women with men," that is to say married women; so the souks are restricted to young, unmarried women, divorced women and widows. They serve not only as centers for commercial exchange, but also as meeting places for the exchange of information and gossip, and for important social transactions such as arranging marriages. Moroccan historian Amina Leuh stressed the autonomy that women had in running these souks:

> If there were ever any quarrels or misunderstandings, it would be the job of the president (of the souk) to solve them. If things got worse, then they took the people who had the problem to the police station. But it was strictly forbidden for men to enter these souks. It is said that a man once wanted to penetrate this secret, and so he disguised himself as a woman, wearing a veil. He went to the souk, but he was discovered when he spoke. He was arrested, beaten up by the women, and then taken to the *Qadi* (local official). This is to tell you that women were independent, since they had the choice to go to men's souks, but they would not allow men to enter theirs.[18]

Women in Moroccan History

There have been Moroccan queens, women saints, and women mystics.[19] The famous Islamic Qaraouine university in Fez was built by Fatima Al Fihria, a woman who had emigrated from Al Qaraouine (modern Tunisia). In the Almoravid dynasty (1069–1147), Moroccan women "didn't know the veil" (didn't wear veils) because of Zineb, the wife of King Ibn Tachfine, who played a role in directing the dynasty. At that time, "the education of women was normal and quite widespread, and the princesses set an example for the people in this. The most outstanding woman teacher was Hafsa Rqinya who taught advanced courses to the women in King Al Mansour's palace, and was considered by Ibn Bachkwal as one of the most outstanding teachers of his time. In the family of Ibn Zahr, the well-known philosopher, there were two woman doctors, living in Marrakesh."[20]

The women I interviewed gave numerous examples from history, illustrating the roles that Moroccan women have played in resisting foreign invasion, as spiritual virtuosos, and in government and diplomacy. Oum Keltoum El Khatib, a nationalist woman from Casablanca, told me that in 1578 women cut their hair so that it could be made into rope to pull the boats that Moroccan warriors used to fight off Portuguese invaders. The mother of the Saadian King Adahabi El Mansour (a hero of the Battle of the Three Kings), famous under the name Lalla Aoudad, carried the rocks herself to build a mosque and fountain in Marrakesh, doing penance for having broken her fast during the holy month of Ramadan.

Moroccan writers don't mention what women did in wars against foreign invasion, but there are accounts written by Portuguese and Spanish military officers and journalists which describe the roles of Riffi women (women from the Rif mountains) in the wars against Portuguese and Spanish invasion.[21] Portuguese documents on the occupation of Ceuta, dated August 21, 1415, state that: "Destiny would have it that the first Portuguese martyr, Officer Vasco Ataydi, was killed by a Moroccan woman, who dropped a stone on him from the top of the tower known today as the Moroccan woman's tower (*Torre de la Mora*)."

During the 1909–1912 war against Spanish occupation led by Sidi Mohamed Ameziane, a Spanish journalist who came to Mellila to report on the war wrote in one of his early dispatches: "How can this miserable people move forward or become civilized when women's only functions are to give birth and to do heavy labor . . . ?"[22] Then, just two days later, the same journalist wrote back to his paper: "Something happened today that made me change my mind about Moroccan women. We journalists observed the military operations which took place today in Sidi Hmed Al Haj center, and we saw that it was the women who took care of all the support services at the rear. They assisted the injured, carried them away from the battlefield, and provided the fighters with water and everything." From then on every dispatch from that journalist mentioned the ways in which Moroccan women assisted the men in battle. Later, he published a book, collecting all his correspondence, including some that had been censored at the time. One entry stated: "The defeat that has come upon us today (September 30, 1909) . . . is the result of the decisive role played by Moroccan women."

Spanish sources note that women lit signal fires on the mountain tops to alert the Riffi fighters when Spanish forces had left the city, and that in ploughing season they did all the ploughing so that their men could continue fighting. One eyewitness described how the women of a Riffi village treated a man who refused to participate in the war against the Spanish invaders. They stripped him of his djellaba and turban, and dressed him in a woman's gown and a woman's head scarf, and they took him to the village square and started circling around him, beating on tambourines, singing insulting songs, and spitting on him.[23] In this same village it was women who guarded the house where four Spanish soldiers were detained.

Women participated in active, even armed, resistance against the colonizers from the very beginning of the protectorate, especially Berber women in the Rif mountains, the Middle Atlas, and the Anti-Atlas and Sahara in the south. In 1913, one year after the establishment of the protectorate, the women in Khemisset organized the first known demonstration against the French: It was so large and effective that the French had to resort to the military to bring things back under control.

There is a rich oral tradition, transmitted almost entirely by women, which tells of women's participation in the 1920–26 war against Spanish colonialism in the Rif led by Abdelkrim El Khattabi.[24] Even the songs they sang are passed down. Oum Keltoum El Khatib learned women's songs of the Rif war from her grandmother, and Amina Leuh learned the history and songs from her mother. The women of the Rif brought weapons to the guerrilla fighters, made bombs, cut telephone lines, carried messages, and set traps for the enemy. They took care of the wounded and provided fuel, water, and food for the fighters. Women incited the men to fight, and old women carried food and water to the battlefield from the nearest village.

In the center of Morocco, in the Middle Atlas mountains, women were active in an armed resistance that lasted for twenty-six years, from the establishment of the protectorate in 1912 until the rebellion was finally put down in 1938. Here, according to oral tradition, women followed the male fighters into battle, loaded their guns, and even carried guns themselves to take their turn fighting when the battle got really intense. They urged on the fighters with ululations (youyou's), and carried bags of henna in order to throw the henna on any man who tried to run away from the fight. In that way he would be recognized and shamed afterwards. Among the women who fought in the Middle Atlas, there was Itto, the daughter of Mouha U Hamou Zayani, who fought the French for eleven years, and then died as a martyr next to her father. "All of his sons had deserted the battlefield, according to his orders, except for his daughter Itto who stayed and died with him."[25]

What is striking in this brief summary of Moroccan women's roles in myth and history is the extent to which it provides direct precedents for women's activities in the nationalist movement and armed resistance. Throughout Moroccan history there have been exceptional learned women who were active in teaching (both religious and secular education) and in giving political advice. And rural women, especially Berbers in the Rif, the Middle Atlas, and the Sahara, have been actively involved in all the wars against foreign invasions—the jihads, beginning in the fifteenth century, which became a dominant theme in nineteenth and twentieth century Moroccan history. Like the women warriors of early Islamic tradition, Moroccan women supported (male) guerrilla fighters, urged their men on to battle, shamed those who tried to retreat, and took up arms themselves when necessary.

While female heros appear throughout Moroccan history, their exceptional contributions in work and war do not seem to have brought about any changes in the status of Moroccan women generally.[26] In Europe at the beginning of the nineteenth century, the industrial revolution was under way, opening an era of dynamic growth and change, and European women started down a road that would lead them toward equal rights and emancipation. At the same time, across the Mediterranean, Morocco and the other countries of the

Maghreb lay dormant.[27] In Morocco in the 1930s, when most of the nationalist women were growing up, women of the urban bourgeoisie were still living as they had for centuries, subject to polygamy, seclusion, and the veil. Women's roles in the home, at the center of the family, had come to assume a symbolic importance. Women were the guardians of Moroccan tradition, and the family was the basic cell of Moroccan Muslim society: Nationalist leader Allal El Fassi called it the "mother of all social institutions."[28]

Women and the Nationalist Movement

Following the defeat of Abdelkrim in the Rif War in 1926, there was a shift from armed resistance based in rural areas to political resistance based in the cities. The Moroccan nationalist movement arose initially out of a concern among a few individuals in the cultural and intellectual elite that the values of Moroccan Islamic culture and society were being subverted by France.[29] It was in this context that the young Moroccan nationalists turned their attention to the status of women.[30]

At first, in the early 1930s, the debate on women's emancipation was dominated by young Moroccan men educated in France, who took Europe as their point of reference and model. The battle with the French protectorate was joined after the French issued the Berber dahir in May, 1930, a decree establishing separate political and legal systems for Arab and Berber areas. Moroccans protested against the dahir, calling it a direct attack on Moroccan cultural and spiritual unity, and a group of young French-educated Moroccans responded to the challenge of the dahir by launching their own proposal for comprehensive reform. Their *Plan des Réformes* called on the French residency to honor the terms of the 1912 Treaty of Fez and to strictly implement its provisions. Taking France itself as their model, the Moroccans demanded democratic freedoms, reform of the legal system, improvement of the condition of Moroccan peasants and artisans, abolition of the Berber policy, and reform of education. The last two demands brought up questions about the legal rights and education of women, and this in turn led to a much broader debate. In the early 1930s, articles on the situation of Moroccan women began to appear in the French-language reformist Moroccan press published in Morocco and in Paris. An article signed "A.M.," which appeared in 1933, illustrates the modernist approach of the French-educated nationalist men:[31]

> Compared to the situation of her sisters in Europe, the position of the Moroccan woman is really lamentable. . . . While Moroccan men who are in contact with foreign culture move ahead, make progress, and get with the rhythm of the times, Moroccan women live stuck in a medieval routine. . . . If Islam gave women rights, we men have usurped those rights, and we

have turned women from free people into slaves. . . . [The Moroccan woman] can neither read nor write, stays emprisoned in her house. . . . [Let's] give them a good education. . . . Let's not free them in the manner of the Turks, as this means seems too radical, but little by little.

The author objects to the speed with which Attaturk freed women in Turkey, but he doesn't object to the final result, and, like Attaturk, he takes Europe as his reference and model. The status of Moroccan women—their seclusion and lack of education—had become an embarassment to French-educated Moroccan men who wanted to show that they were civilized and modern by getting rid of everything that was backwards in the old society. Thus they imagined a "new woman" who was presentable in colonial society, yet whose primary role was still in the home.[32]

In 1937, the French launched a large-scale repression of the nationalist movement, sending many of its leaders into prison or exile. It became clear that the French colonial authorities were not interested in real reform, and the leadership of the developing Moroccan nationalist movement shifted from the French-educated modernists to a group of young graduates of the Qaraouine university in Fez. At this point, "reform was thrust into the background as the nationalists became preoccupied with party organization, mass support and independence."[33]

The new nationalist leadership based its ideology of social reform, and especially its ideas about women, not on European models but rather on the Salafiya Islamic reform movement, which came to them through Syria and Egypt. As it was this ideology and reform program that most directly affected the lives of the nationalist women whose oral histories appear in this book, we will take a little time here to discuss its origins and its manifestations in Morocco.[34]

The Salafiya movement originated in the nineteenth century in Iran, Syria, and Egypt, in a period of history when the Ottoman Empire had just collapsed, leaving a weakened Islamic world to face the encroachments of European colonial power. Intellectuals in the affected countries came to the conclusion that the crisis in Muslim society was essentially moral and religious, and therefore could best be solved by moral and religious reform. The Salafiya is not so much a doctrine as a point of departure and a method of analysis. It starts from a conviction that Islam and the Koran provide guidance for all times and places. If the Muslim world is stagnant, it is because Muslim populations have either neglected or misinterpreted Islam. What is needed is *ijtihad*, an established method of going back to sources in order to reinterpret the general principles of Islam in the light of the current situation.

Following this process of reasoning, Moroccan neo-Salafiya theorists concluded that the neglect or misinterpretation of Islam were both due to ignorance (*jehaliya*), and that this ignorance began in the family. Therefore, in order to rebuild Muslim society, the first step was to fight against false traditions and ignorance within the family. And one of the most effective ways to do this was through women. The nationalist reformers thought in terms of city life and the bourgeois family. Thus, a large part of the social reform movement was directed against superstition—the lively religious life centered around saints tombs (*zaouiya*)—and against extravagant spending during celebrations. Women were at the center of these "false traditions": they were heavily involved as participants in zaouiya, and they were the ones who organized and controlled the spending for marriages and other family celebrations. The nationalists saw the education of women as one of the most effective means of fighting ignorance in the family. This is why they took up the cause of girls' education, and why they created their own free schools where instruction for girls (and boys) would focus on the Arabic language, the Koran, and nationalism.

It is important to note the conception of the family that was at the core of neo-Salafiya thought. The Islamic reformers didn't promote the education of women or defend the rights of women under Islamic law primarily in order to let women develop as human beings, but rather to buttress the Muslim family, and through the family, to reinforce social cohesion against the menace of colonialism. The family, the Moroccan nation, and the Muslim nation were all key and interrelated concepts, and women were important because of their traditional roles at the heart of the family. Thus the reforms sought to *strengthen* the basic structures of the old society, especially the bourgeois family, not to *change* them. This was a distinctly conservative bias.

3

Colonialism, Conflict, and Independence

Oppressed by Colonialism

Nationalist women talk of the many ways in which they resisted the restrictions of traditional social codes, and women of the neoproletariat talk of struggling against the oppression of poverty. But women from both groups refer to the time in which they grew up as the time of "colonialism," and blame this colonialism for all the hardships, inequities, and lack of opportunity in Morocco under the protectorate. They speak of being smothered, with "no liberty, no human rights," feeling that while they lived in their country, they didn't profit from its wealth. They complained that the French had not delivered on their promises of schools and hospitals.[1] On a very personal level, one woman said she still hates the names Fatna and Ahmed, and would never consider giving those names to any of her children, because the French used to call all Moroccan women Fatna and all men Ahmed—summoning them by: "my Fatna" and "my Ahmed"—just as they used the familiar *tu* form in addressing all Moroccans, to express their contempt.[2]

The Moroccan women I interviewed spoke in general terms about the oppression of colonialism; but it was Moroccan men, who went out of the house more and thus had more interaction with Europeans, who described to me the details, the little things that added up to an atmosphere in which Moroccans felt like second-class citizens in their own country.

Driss Benjelloun, the scion of a well-known Fassi family living in the Mnebhi Palace in Fez, had a passion for the movies when he was a young man. He complained that if there were a line of Moroccans waiting to get into the cinema and a French person came along, the French person automatically went to the head of the line and got in first. Resistance leader Thami Naamane, who at that time was a bookseller in Casablanca, said:

> To begin with, it was forbidden to live in the areas where there were French living, forbidden to work with them. There were movie theaters that were forbidden to Moroccans, with the excuse that the Moroccan was not well dressed, that his shoes were not polished, or that he wasn't

wearing a tie. The bus, the train—we had to stand in line and there was always a struggle. The daughters of the French said that they wouldn't stand in line with Arabs. "Let them have a train that is just for the Arabs and one that's just for us." As for the long-distance bus, Moroccans were forbidden to get inside the bus; they had to get on top. . . . One day, I wanted to talk with the bus driver—because they were all French—and when I told him that I was traveling to a certain place, he shoved me and shut the door in my face, telling me: "Go to your sultan, and get him to give you a bus!" He said it exactly like that!

Moroccans had no rights in the courts, or in the administration. . . . If it were a question of a foreigner—an Algerian, a Tunisian, or a Frenchman—they had rights. But a Moroccan—no rights at all! They had absolutely no rights. If you went to the police or to the administration of the courts, they did whatever they wanted. What's more, as soon as a Moroccan came in the door, the policeman would begin to slap him and kick him. It was because of that, that all the Moroccans began to be afraid, and no longer even thought of their rights, in order to avoid going to the administration. . . .

All of that was among the reasons that pushed the people to go ahead and do something about this colonialism, because it was too much. Because if the colonialism had not been so harsh with the people, France might never have left."[3]

Women Come Out into the Streets

These were the sorts of daily acts of humiliation and repression that began to build resentment against the French, especially in Casablanca, where there was the largest European settlement. The French also began to launch major attacks on the nationalist movement in various cities, starting in the late 1930s. From then on, the confrontation between the French and Moroccan urban populations escalated in intensity and violence. Each wave of repression launched a new, more militant stage of the nationalist movement; and each expansion of the nationalist movement brought about a new, more violent wave of repression. Women were increasingly involved in these incidents, as observers, participants, and victims.

It was in January of 1944, following the presentation of the Independence Manifesto and formation of the Istiqlal Party, that large numbers of urban women began to be directly involved with the nationalist movement. At the end of January, the French closed off the old city of Fez. An eyewitness, Mohammed Tazi, described to me what happened:[4]

The city of Fez was shut off by the French—no water, no meat—the gates were all closed. For fifteen days, Fez was "independent" [i.e. thrown back on its own resources, under siege]. Everyone shared what they had. Then the French came, with the Senegalese [black African troops], and they pacified the city, street by street.[5]

Women on their roof terraces cried out their youyous. And the youyous of Fassi women, they were not found anywhere else. Like, I don't know how to describe it: you, you, you, you, you . . . [with rising intonation], gradually mounting up . . . and then fading away at the end. . . .[6]

And there were some women who took the big basalt rocks that were on all the roof terraces to use in spreading out the wash to dry. When things were freshly out of the wash, the women would stretch them out under four or five big stones. So these were a weapon against the soldiers down below, a weapon in the hands of women. Later, the soldiers got authorization to fire on women on their terraces, not just firing at random, but well-aimed bullets.

In Casablanca, in 1947, there was the "slaughter of Casa." The level of violence had escalated severely; and once again, the French brought out the Senegalese. Thami Naamane, the Casablanca bookseller cited above, was an eyewitness:

They brought out the Senegalese to attack women and children, even to kill them. There were a great number of them who were killed. I was there at that battle, and I was there when they gathered up the intestines and legs and took them down to the cemetery to bury them. It was very dangerous. And when people saw that, they preferred even death to staying alive.[7]

It was after this that Thami Naamane and a few others in Casablanca began to prepare the armed resistance. They had come to the conclusion that political meetings and talk were not enough: it would take armed force to stand up to colonialism.

We were thinking of a well-organized resistance throughout Morocco. We thought it should not come out of the [Istiqlal] party, because the party had political considerations, and the party people were afraid. They would not be able to take part in things that demanded force. . . . So we started a resistance movement, but in a small circle, and we began making contacts. We began first with five people,[8] and we created an organization that was built on the idea that "whoever contacts someone does not know the others". . . . We made a contact for Casa, for Rabat, and for Marrekesh. Those were the first contacts. . . .

Meanwhile, ever since 1944, the Istiqlal Party had been mobilizing the Moroccan masses in support of the party and the demand for independence. In Casablanca, the party was especially concerned with getting the support of workers and the trade union movement. Benacer Harakat, who was secretary general of the Istiqlal Party in Casablanca at the time, described the period leading up to the next great confrontation with the French: the general strike of December 8, 1952.

> In the mid-forties, we asked members of the Party to become members of unions. . . . Moroccan workers began more and more to belong to the French union [there was no Moroccan trade union organization until 1955], in spite of laws which threatened people with punishment and prison.

> The strike came about in circumstances where enthusiasm ran so high that people were asking themselves, "How long do we have to wait?" The people were driven by a desire to liberate the country on the one hand, and by their aspirations for a better life on the other hand. The other aggravation that should be mentioned is the arrival of [General Juin, French resident general from May, 1947 to September, 1951] and his policies of repression, and the pressure he put on the citizens, the nationalists and the Palace. . . . So this was the climate that preceded the strike.

> The assassination [by the French] of Ferhat Hachad [the Tunisian trade union leader], came about in this atmosphere of tension. On the 6th of December, the orders of the Party came through to Casablanca, and then to all the sections at El Jadida, Marrakesh and Safi . . . to order a general strike on the 8th of December. . . . The climate was so favorable that we were able to mobilize tens of thousands of citizens in a few hours. This was what enabled us to execute the orders of the Party.[9]

Abdelkrim Ghallab, another Istiqlal Party leader, explained further:

> The assassination of Ferhat Hachad was a good opportunity. Actually, there was solidarity between Morocco and Tunisia, but not to the extent that it would have involved us in the great adventure that brought about the massacre of December eighth. The Party seized the opportunity only to show the whole world that the Moroccan people refused the policies of Juin and then of Guillaume [the resident general who succeeded Juin], and that the Moroccan people had decided to demand its independence.[10]

By this time women workers were playing an important role in union demonstrations and strikes. In August of 1952, textile workers in Rabat, more than half of whom were women, stayed on strike for a full month, demanding improved working conditions and the right to form a union. In Casablanca, women participated in great numbers in the general strike and large-scale demonstrations that took place on December 8, 1952, and several were killed in the ensuing repression.[11]

The first uprisings broke out in the biggest of the Casablanca shantytowns, the *Carrières centrales*, on December 7. A crowd that the local press later estimated at five thousand surged into a few shops that had stayed open (in defiance of the strike order) and into a police station. The next day the uprisings continued, and then the French troops opened fire. Some demonstrators carrying the Moroccan national flag and Istiqlal Party signs tried to enter the European quarters, and were driven back under police fire. The police surrounded the main labor union office where a group of Moroccan union leaders were meeting peacefully, and proceeded to arrest them, delivering them to a virtual lynching at the hands of excited, angry Europeans. Through the night of December 8 there were bloody confrontations between the French police and the thousands of unarmed demonstrators. The dead and the wounded were too numerous to count. Families spent the night burying their dead or hiding their bodies. In the Carrières centrales, where it had all begun, the police repression was so violent that it amounted to a massacre.

Later, it was found that four Europeans died in the confrontation, one of them a former member of the administration who had fired twice into the crowd with a revolver. There was some dispute about the number of Moroccans who were killed; certainly it was more than a hundred.[12] Boniface, the French police chief who was in charge of the Casablanca region, used the uprisings as an excuse to conduct a violent repression of trade union members and the general population—the massacre of the Carrières centrales—followed by a "surgical operation" to arrest or eliminate Istiqlal Party members and communists throughout the country.

Less than eight months later, on August 20, 1953, on the eve of the *Aid Kabir*,[13] the most important holiday in the Muslim year, the French sent the Moroccan King Mohamed V into exile. For days there had been rumors that the king would be exiled, and when it happened the country exploded. Men and women took to the streets spontaneously in mass demonstrations in cities all over Morocco. Women who had never before gone out of their houses came out to join these demonstrations; some women, looking up from their rooftop terraces, saw the face of their beloved Mohamed V in the moon. At the same time, an organized armed resistance went into action, targeting Moroccans who were collaborating with the French. This urban armed resistance lasted until the king's return.

Independence and After

On November 16, 1955, King Mohamed V returned to Morocco. By sending him into exile, the French had made him into a martyr; when he came back, he was the hero and symbol of the Moroccan nation, the king who would go down in Moroccan history as "the liberator." Everywhere the king went, crowds of Moroccans came out to greet him. Along all the roads leading to Rabat, there was a steady stream of trucks flying Moroccan flags, red with green stars, from the cab or the hood, the back of the truck crowded with veiled women or with men in brown djellabas and brown or blue turbans. Standing in the back of the truck, swaying, packed together, all along the roads they shouted, chanting: "Mo-ha-med Ben Yous-sef"[14] over and over, without even stopping for breath. It was said that these people came from Taza or from as far east as Guercif, that some even came all the way up from the Spanish Sahara. Everywhere the crowds were cheering, delirious with joy to see their sultan returned to them. Women were especially visible, leaving their villages, coming out of their houses, veiled and unveiled, asserting themselves, claiming their space in the cities, proud of their role in bringing back the king. The women set up a call and response, just as the women of the Rif sang back and forth across the mountains during the war of Abdelkrim. One group of women in the crowd would sing out, "With bombs and revolvers . . ." another group would answer, repeating: "With bombs and revolvers . . .", and all would join together for the final cry, "We have won back our king!" Others in the crowd shouted, "Long live the king!" and "Long live independence!"

A few days later, on the 21st of November, the Istiqlal Party held a congress that proclaimed the equality of women. Large numbers of women took part, all of them without veils and many dressed in European dress. Zhor Lazraq, a nationalist woman in Fez who was then just twenty-one years old, impressed everyone with her skill as a debater and her fiery speeches in defense of women's rights. On March 2, 1956, Morocco got its independence, and everything seemed possible.

And then what? For the women of the nationalist movement, the struggle continued; only the enemy had changed. Although they had won the fight against colonialism, they were just beginning an even bigger struggle: the fight against underdevelopment. The nationalist women continued their work of broadening access to education, raising money to provide scholarships for children whose families couldn't afford to send them to school. They also began "the struggle against illiteracy," with courses for older women; and they organized courses to raise women's awareness of the country's situation and needs. Nationalist women were designated by King Mohamed V to work with his daughters the princesses in the newly created National Alliance for Social Welfare (*Entraide Nationale*), and in the Moroccan Red Crescent Society. All of

3.1

Meeting to prepare Moroccan delegation to 1957 Congress of Arab Women in Damascus. Second from left, Zhor Lazraq; center, Princess Lalla Aicha; second from right, Amina Leuh; far right, Fatima Hassar.

Source: Amina Leuh.

the women stayed involved in social welfare or education, focusing on various causes such as the protection of the Moroccan family and children or promoting the Arabic language. Several got their first international exposure shortly after independence; there was a delegation of Moroccan youth to the first international youth festival, held in Moscow, and a delegation of Moroccan women (led by the Princess Lalla Aicha) to the first congress of Arab women, held in Damascus.

Amina Leuh, who was a member of the delegation to the Arab women's congress in Damascus, told a story to illustrate King Mohamed V's continuing involvement in women's issues.

Before our departure for Syria, we were sitting in the royal cabinet discussing matters concerning the conference, when His Majesty King Mohamed V came in. He started asking about the conference and what was going to be said. At that time, [Istiqlal Party leader] Mehdi Ben Barka was there, and he asked him who was going to Syria, and who were the people accompanying Lalla Aicha. Then he asked him about the princess's speech, and told him to read it. He was reading it, and then he reached a sentence that said that 'The Moroccan woman has asked for the right to vote, and we have agreed to give her that right, to vote and to run for election.' At that sentence, he stopped him, and asked: 'Could you tell me when the Moroccan woman asked for the right to vote?' Then he added, 'She never did. She always had the right to vote; she never needed to ask for it.' I remember his words as though it were yesterday. This is only to show that he followed every single step, and was involved in everything. He then insisted that the sentence should be changed.[15]

Women's Personal Status: The Moudouana

While women had equal rights as citizens of the new Moroccan nation, their status within the family was defined by Islamic law. Istiqlal Party leader Allal El Fassi was appointed by the king to head up a committee to draft a new family law code (moudouana) shortly after independence.[16] Allal El Fassi was the main theorist of the Istiqlal Party, and is generally considered to represent the enlightened wing of the Moroccan neo-Salafiya reform movement. Some women told me they thought that El Fassi would have preferred a more progressive family law, but that he was outvoted by the other more conservative members of the committee.

While the new law incorporated some reforms of existing law and practice that benefited women, such as raising the minimum age for marriage and prohibiting forced marriages, it kept most of the provisions of the old Moroccan family law, largely based on the *shari'a* and the Malekite rite, which are the most conservative interpretations of the text of the Koran. The moudouana applied only to Moroccan Muslims; Jews had their personal status regulated by Moroccan Jewish law.

In Moroccan family law, women are put in a position of inferiority, subject to men in the family. A Moroccan woman, no matter how old she is, cannot contract her own marriage; she is obliged to be represented by a male guardian (*wali*). This can be any male who has reached the age of puberty—it can even be her son in the case of the remarriage of a widow or divorced woman. The institution of the wali does not exist in the Koran; it comes from tradition rather than from religious law. Indeed Allal El Fassi defended this provision of the moudouana against some legal scholars who wanted to abolish the institution of the wali, by deferring to the claims of "Moroccan public opinion" and "customs of modesty and respect":

If a woman who had attained her majority were to personally contract marriage without any guardian or authorization, it would be, in the eyes of Moroccan public opinion, a transgression of Islamic morality, difficult to justify because of the customs of modesty and respect. The criteria by which we distinguish between [moral] depravity and the form of marriage reside in this tradition of paternal guardianship. If we have taken away the right the father used to have of forcing his daughter to marry; [this is all the more reason that] we should maintain the moral character [of his guardianship].[17]

The moudouana also retains the Moroccan man's right to divorce by repudiation. The wife, on the other hand, cannot initiate divorce except in a few narrowly defined cases, such as when the husband fails to provide any maintenance, or abandons the family and cannot be located for more than a year, or is discovered to have some terrible vice. The only other way a wife can get a divorce is by paying her husband to repudiate her. In practice, most wives can't afford to buy their way out, so their only recourse is to incite their husbands to repudiate them three times, at which point the divorce becomes final. A man is allowed to have as many as four wives in Islamic law, with the stipulation that he must treat them all equally.

The moudouana states that the wife's responsibilities to her husband are these: "to be faithful; to obey [according to social conventions]; to nurse children born of the marriage if possible; to take care of the house and manage the household; and to show deference to the husband's father, mother and near relatives."[18] She has the right to "such upkeep as is provided for by law, such as food, clothing, medical care and housing; equality of treatment in relation to the other wives in the case of polygamy; the authorization to visit her parents and to have them visit her, within customary limits; and complete liberty to administer and dispose of her property without any control from her husband, the husband having no control over the property of his wife."[19]

This last is often cited by defenders of Islamic family law as a provision that gives women more economic independence and power than most secular, Western family law codes. It is true that legally the Moroccan woman is entirely independent in everything that concerns her property—she can sell it, invest it, or even designate another person outside of her family to take care of it. In theory, if a wife works, this is also the case with her salary. The husband continues to be responsible for providing for the upkeep of his wife and the household, while the wife can spend her money as she pleases. In practice, of course, wives who work usually contribute their salaries to general household expenses.

In the case of divorce or widowhood, the mother cannot exercise legal guardianship over her children; that is an exclusively male prerogative. In the question of inheritance, the moudouana strictly follows the Koranic prescriptions: women inherit only half as much as men. Thus in a situation where a man and a woman have the same relationship to the deceased, as in the case of a son and daughter inheriting from their father, the daughter will only get half as much as her brother. A wife cannot engage in any activity or work outside the home except with the authorization of her husband,[20] and a Moroccan woman needs authorization from her father, her husband, or a male guardian in order to get a passport and to travel abroad.

No women were involved in drafting the moudouana, and there was no public comment on it after it was issued. Nationalist women do not seem to have taken up this question of the personal status of women as one that concerned them. And indeed, it probably did not concern these women directly. They all had fathers and husbands who were supportive; thus, they were unlikely to suffer under the moudouana's provisions regarding divorce, polygamy, or inheritance rights.

After Independence: Women of the Resistance

Moroccans in the independence movement spoke of an extraordinary solidarity between men and women, and among Moroccans of different classes and regions. When Mohamed V returned, he was cheered by his people as the leader and symbol of a unified, independent Morocco. They called him "the liberator," and they were proud that it was the Moroccan people—especially the armed resistance—who "with bombs and revolvers" had "won back their king." Everyone had high hopes for the future in an independent Morocco. But this national solidarity and unity of purpose quickly disintegrated. For many of the women who participated in the armed resistance (who had hoped that after independence their lives would somehow be different and better than before) the optimism gave way to disappointment, anger, and finally, resignation.

For many Moroccans, the decade after independence was a murky, ambiguous period, when rival factions of the resistance and the nationalist movement fought among each other and attempted to settle accounts. It was in this period that Touria Chaouia, the first woman pilot, died, apparently assassinated by the "Black Hand" resistance group. Nationalist leader Abdelaziz Ben Driss was apparently killed by Istiqlal Party members shortly after independence.[21] In June of 1956, Liberation Army leader Abbèss Messadi was killed in the Rif mountains. There was some evidence that Mehdi Ben Barka, then secretary general of the Istiqlal Party, was implicated in his death.

Ben Barka and some other young Turks broke with the Istiqlal Party in 1959 in order to form a new party, the *Union nationale des forces populaires* (UNFP), which came to represent the major hope of progressive forces in the period after independence. Ben Barka himself was a charismatic leader who believed in both socialist reform and the monarchy, a leading figure not just in Morocco but in the international Marxist movement. When he came back to Morocco from Paris in 1962, crowds cheered him wherever he went. In May of 1963, he was elected from Rabat to the national constituent assembly, winning 90 percent of the vote. Then on October 29, 1965, Ben Barka "disappeared" under mysterious circumstances while on a visit to France. More than thirty years later, his family is still trying to get a full accounting of what happened and to discover who was responsible for his abduction and death. There are rumors that the Israeli Mossad and the American CIA may have been involved.[22]

On February 26, 1961, Mohamed V died, suddenly and unexpectedly, following a minor operation. The whole country was plunged into mourning, the people shocked and grieving. They had lost their beloved king, the king they had welcomed back from exile only five years earlier, the one who would always be remembered as "the liberator" of the Moroccan nation and people. On March 2, 1961, his eldest son, Hassan, became king.

Leaders of the armed resistance and the political leaders of the Left were pursued and arrested in 1960, when Hassan was the crown prince, and again in 1963, when he had succeeded his father as King Hassan II. While UNFP leaders were accused of plotting against the government and against the monarchy, "Moroccan public opinion believed strongly that there was a conspiracy against the UNFP by Colonel Oufkir [Head of Security Forces] and the President of the Royal Guard, Colonel Madbouh."[23]

Colonel (later General) Oufkir was a product of the French colonial system, trained as one of the elite officer corps of the French colonial army. Right after independence, he became head of security; in 1964 he was named minister of the interior; and in 1971 he became minister of defense. For the first fifteen years of Morocco's independence(1956–1971), Oufkir carried out a systematic and brutal repression of leaders of the armed resistance and liberation army, as well as of the political forces of the Left. Moroccans still speak bitterly about Oufkir as the strongman who carried out these repressions, but some foreign analysts have suggested that Oufkir was only executing policies, strategy, and directives that came straight from the Palace.[24]

The monarchy and the Istiqlal Party were the two main political forces in Morocco after independence, while the liberation army in the Rif was a significant military force. Party leaders wanted a constitutional monarch with diminished powers, and their own Istiqlal Party in control; but the nationalists had helped to create a powerful, living symbol in Mohamed V, and he was determined to maintain the power of the monarchy. As soon as he returned to Morocco, Mohamed V began to eat away at the political hegemony of the Istiqlal Party. He turned to traditional allies, enlisting the support of the great *pashas* and *caids* so as to neutralize the Istiqlal as a political force.[25]

The leaders of the armed resistance and the liberation army were also a force to be reckoned with. Many of the leaders of the liberation army in the Rif were determined to continue fighting until Algeria got its independence from France, and some had gone on to form a liberation army of the south to reconquer the Sahara, which was still under Spanish control. In May, 1956, just two months after independence, Mohamed V created the *Forces armées royales* (FAR), an army directly under the control of the Palace, and named his son Hassan as commander-in-chief. Within two years, a process of "*farisation, fonctionnarisation et assassinat*" (integration into the FAR or the government bureaucracy, and assassination)[26] had eliminated the liberation army and the armed resistance as independent forces, and French and Spanish military forces that were still in Morocco were called in to wipe out the liberation army of the south.[27] Finally, in the early 1960s, the police, under Colonel Oufkir, went after the leadership of the UNFP.

The women I interviewed from the armed resistance were not directly implicated in these events; they were not considered important enough.[28] On the whole they didn't even talk explicitly about this national political situation. Nonetheless, it was within this context that their own lives unfolded.

Veterans of the resistance and liberation army were invited to apply for a carte de résistant, and women as well as men did this, beginning in 1959.[29] But then the government gave out sixty thousand cards (apparently some cards were bought and sold) so that getting a card ceased to mean much, and brought little in the way of recognition or benefits. The only women who got some real benefits from the new government were the widows of martyrs. For example, the widow of Allal Ben Abdellah (who was martyred when he tried to assassinate the French-imposed Sultan Ben Arafa in 1954) said, "When the king Mohamed V returned, I went with the wives of the martyrs to receive him at the airport. Abdellah went back to school, and Allal went to the martyrs' children's school in the Mohamedia neighborhood. Then he went to the school of tourism, and then to Sweden. Now he is a steward and we are all in good health."[30]

For most women from the armed resistance, life changed sharply after independence. Some women went back to their former routines; others, whose husbands were leaders in the resistance and liberation army, spent years in hiding or in exile with their husbands and children. The decade after independence was an especially difficult time for these women. The women all insisted that they had worked and fought and suffered in the armed resistance for "God, King, and Country" and that their only purpose was to bring about the return of Mohamed V and Moroccan independence. Nonetheless, there were other hopes and expectations, however tentative or inchoate, and most of the women were disappointed. Many had hoped that independence would bring a better life for them and their families, and that they would somehow be recognized and rewarded for the extraordinary contributions they had made in the struggle for national liberation.

3.2

Rabat resistance fighter Halima Ben Moussa (1993).

Credit: Ann Jones.

Halima Ben Moussa was forty years old when independence came. She and her husband had participated in the armed resistance in Rabat, and her husband had spent long stretches of time in an underground prison and was even condemned to death. He survived, but when he emerged from prison he was aged, sick, and mentally deranged.

Because he had gone crazy, he left his children and went back to his home region. . . . I had to make my son leave school in the fifth year of primary school, so that he could work as a mechanic to earn money to buy food for his brothers and sisters.

My husband said that once the king had returned, good things would come. And yet when our country got its independence, it was other people who benefited. *Ouallah* [oath], my girl! That angers us to death!

3.3

Halima Ben Moussa (1965).

Photo from dossier at High Commission for Veterans of the Resistance and Liberation Army.

We were in the first rank of the fighters in the resistance, and now we're among the last to be considered. No! We should get what we are entitled to! My husband was condemned to death, and all they gave him was an *agrément* for a twelve-ton truck![31] Is he a child?! That woman there, that Ghalia Moujahide, got a truck *agrément* too. Well, she's just a woman!! They're making her equal to someone who was condemned to death, and buried underground. Is that right? That's all we're asking for—our rights!"[32]

As this demonstrates, there was no feeling of solidarity among women as women. On the contrary, women felt that they should be compensated for their husband's resistance activities, especially those whose husbands had died, and some resented it if a woman got as much or more just for "women's" activities.

Most women applied for their carte de résistant in 1959 and got the card in the mid-sixties. Then, in 1973, the High Commission for Veterans of the Resistance and Liberation Army was established, and all sixty thousand dossiers were reviewed, in an effort to weed out those people who had not really participated. The criteria were quite explicit for deciding which events could be considered as evidence of participation in the armed resistance: The event had to have taken place between 1953 and 1956, it had to have involved arms, the participant had to have acted as a member of an "official" resistance organization, and the cell and organization leaders both had to corroborate the testimony given in the dossier. In this second round, status as a veteran of the resistance had become more valuable to women (and men), not only as validation of what they had done, but also to be able to apply for some economic benefits such as a pension, housing, a taxi or truck *agrément*, or help in getting a job or starting a small business. The women (and men) from the armed resistance all had their dossiers reviewed starting in the mid-seventies. In this process, some of them had to argue their case all over again and provide additional information, supporting documents, and testimony from the heads of their resistance cells and organizations. Women faced special problems in getting recognition for their participation. Most of them worked directly under their husbands and other close male relatives, who were thus the only people who knew firsthand what the women had done. But their testimony was suspect precisely because they were relatives. The burden of proof was heavier on a woman, to convince the Commission that she herself had carried out resistance operations, as there was always the suspicion that she knew the details of operations because her husband had been involved.

For many women, like Halima Ben Moussa who was just cited, the distinction between what they did on their own and what they did with and for their husband is arbitrary and doesn't make sense. Of course they were supporting their husbands; that's what they thought they were *supposed* to do. Does that make their courage or their suffering any less? Even some of the women who were successful in getting the second card feel bitter about their treatment at the hands of the Commission, and complain that they have not received the benefits that are their due. Some women who were unsuccessful in getting their second card are really angry. One woman complained that she still gets notices from the commission addressed to her husband, who is dead, and yet she herself has gotten nothing, neither her new card nor the benefits that she deserves.

Many of the resistance leaders had hoped that Moroccan independence would lead to a redistribution of wealth and power—real economic, political, and social reform. Some women too had that vision, and some were involved with the UNFP, the main party of the Left, starting in the late fifties. As the party never came to power, it never had a chance to implement its program of economic and social reform, a program that might have included reform of the moudouana and defense of women's rights. With Ben Barka's death in 1965, the Left lost its most important leader and spokesperson, and its influence in national politics declined.

A few of the women who participated in the armed resistance had hoped that after independence Moroccan women as a group would take on a larger public role and begin to make their voices heard in the political arena. Khaddouj Zerktouni, the sister of martyr Mohamed Zerktouni and herself a member of the resistance in Casablanca, reflected on why women from the armed resistance didn't participate in public life after independence:

I think that if the resistance had lasted longer women would have registered a different level of participation. They would have played a more tangible and effective role.[33] After independence, Moroccan women haven't taken on the same sorts of responsibilities as before. If, after the period of colonization, Morocco had taken the direction of organizing women and improving their political awareness—the sort of thing that had started during the [French] occupation—then women would have reached a better and more important level [of participation]. The proof [that women are capable] is that women were in the front line [of the resistance], sometimes enduring hardships and accomplishing feats that surpassed those of men, at a time when they were threatened by arrest, torture and death. During the [colonial] occupation there were also women who assumed responsibilities in the Istiqlal Party, for example, and that proves that women did participate in political life, and were aware in that field in spite of the danger.[34]

Conclusion

In general women were notably absent from participation in public life in the decade after independence, especially in the political arena.[35] The social service associations that were formed by leading nationalist women did not have the combative, political dimension of the old party women's associations, and their goal was to provide services to poor women rather than to mobilize them. The government itself had similar goals in creating the National Union of Moroccan Women[36] and other associations, employment centers, women's clubs, and associations of family planning. These centers offered social services to women and served as places to promote the government and its ideology concerning women.[37]

Former members of the armed resistance and other working-class women were preoccupied with survival, and there was no political force willing to speak for them or to defend their interests. The political parties of the Left which emerged in the period after independence[38] neglected women's issues almost entirely, fearing that these issues could prove divisive in a period in which the parties' main preoccupation was to gain power.[39] There was no discussion of the relationship between the emancipation of women and larger social change; and there were no women in the leadership of the parties who might have raised these issues.

Here we come to the end of the first thirty years of the modern Moroccan women's movement, a feminist movement rooted in Moroccan nationalism. After the mid-1960s, the leadership of the women's movement passed out of the hands of the older generation of women who had participated in the independence movement, as younger generations took the lead.

II

Nationalist Women

4

Fez and the Nationalist Women

> Mystery and labyrinth. Complex streets. Anonymous walls. Secret luxury. Secrecy of these houses without windows on the streets.
>
> —Anais Nin, *The Diary of Anais Nin: 1934–1939*

The Great Bourgeoisie of Fez

The old city of Fez (*Fès El Bali*) is remarkably unchanged from when Anais Nin visited in 1936. The complex streets, the houses that are uniformly plain from the outside, the high anonymous walls without windows on the streets— all are still there. But while the great houses are still there in all their secret luxury, the families that used to live in them have gone, most of them moved to Casablanca. Some of the houses have been turned into restaurants; others are used as carpet emporia. Most of them are still owned by the same families, deeded to the fourth generation, but they sit empty, slowly deteriorating, with only a caretaker in residence.

It was in these great houses that many of the nationalist women were born and grew up in the 1930s and 1940s, and it was these great Fassi families that produced many of the country's professors, lawyers, and intellectuals, as well as high officials of the Moroccan administration, and that controlled much of the wealth coming from the traditional commercial and agricultural sectors of the economy. From the very beginning of the protectorate, they were more or less active supporters of the nationalist movement.[1]

Women in the Bourgeoisie: Growing Up

The bourgeois family was patriarchal and polygamous. Polygamy was a luxury, a sign of wealth, as was the seclusion of women. Each house (palace, really) sheltered several families: the head of the family with his wife or wives, his concubines, his unmarried daughters, his sons with their wives and children, the servants, the slaves, and some other indigent members of the family. This, of

4.1

Interior courtyard of the Mekouar house in Fez.
(Author and Mohamed Mekouar in background).

Credit: Anne White.

course, was the great bourgeoisie. In such a household, the women and children lived in a world apart, separate from the outside world and from the world of men.

In this sort of bourgeois family, little girls usually received their first education from women in the family and other women in the household, nurses—often slaves—especially. (Slave women were brought as concubines from Senegal and the Sudan, where Fez merchants did a lot of trading, and although slavery was outlawed in the first part of the century, it did not begin to disappear until after 1922, when the French issued an administrative order giving slaves the right to sue their abductors and owners in court.)[2] At the age of about seven or eight, if there was noone in the house who could teach her embroidery, a girl might go out to study embroidery and other artisanal work with a *ma'allma* (a woman who taught girls artisanal skills in her home) or to study the Koran with a *fqiha*. As children, boys and girls both participated in the communal life of the women's quarters. A little girl would mix freely with her male cousins and brothers in the house, and a little boy would be taken along to the women's *hammam* (Turkish bath).[3]

As soon as a girl reached puberty, at age twelve or thirteen, she would stop going out of the house. It wasn't necessary that she should actually have reached puberty. It was enough that someone (a man either in or outside of the family), catching a glimpse of her on the street, would notice that she was growing up and make just one comment to that effect to her father or grand-father. This would bring about an abrupt change in a young girl's life, a very severely enforced seclusion. At this point, a young girl would stay home and begin to prepare a trousseau for her marriage, which would occur while she was still quite young. Marriages were usually arranged by the two families, without consulting the girl or boy involved.

A marriage between two families of the great bourgeoisie was an elaborate and expensive affair. There was a substantial bride-price to be paid by the family of the groom, which was usually matched by the father of the bride and used to purchase all that was necessary for the new household.[4] There was also the cost of the marriage itself, a ceremony that lasted seven days and demanded orchestras, food, drink, and lodging for the large company of family and other guests, and at least five or six different outfits for the bride to wear during the wedding celebration, each in a different style, very elaborate and expensive, and each worn with different necklaces, diadems, and other jewels.

After marriage, a young woman would go out from her own family to live with her in-laws. The basic conditions of her life did not change; they were just transferred to a new setting. In her new home, the young bride was relieved of most domestic and child-rearing work by the other women, servants, and slaves. Most of her time was spent in sewing and embroidery, and other activities with the women and children within the household. The women of the great bourgeoisie left the house as seldom as possible, only to go to the hammam, family celebrations, visits to their parents, and visits to tombs of the saints. When they went out, they were covered from head to toe, wearing a haik or djellaba and veil, and often escorted by a male member of the family.

Images and Self-Images

French observers of Moroccan society were appalled by the situation of Moroccan women. Excerpts from one rather curious compilation of citations from French writers, a mix of scholarly observations and superficial impressions, will serve to give a sample of French images of Moroccan women around 1926, when the book was published:[5]

> It is a well-established fact that the Moroccan woman, whether urban or rural, occupies a position of inferiority. In the cities, it seems that Islam is the main cause of this low status, but in the least Arabized parts of the country you also often hear ideas expressed about women that are equally deprecating and brutal, and that don't have any roots in religion.

They painted a particularly negative picture of women of the great bourgeoisie:

> What dominates in them, taking account of everything, is their nervousness, and this is certainly the effect of being secluded. They have a "bad character", and "do nothing but feel sorry for themselves, and complain about their situation". They develop "strange caprices, wild joys, and heavy sorrows". "They are extremely tyrannical, especially as soon as they get old.

Of course none of these French writers actually had any contact with women of the great bourgeoisie. One does acknowledge that "those rare writers who have been able to see harems up close, are careful to correct these negative impressions, saying that alongside the cruelties, the nervousness and the moral degradation, they also noticed the women's charming gestures and smiles, their spirited repartee, and their quick wit." The very few Moroccan men who were willing to share their ideas on this subject were intent on minimizing the differences between the situation of their women and French women. They maintained that "with the exception of a small minority, women in Moroccan cities enjoy almost complete freedom, and in any case their situation is infinitely happier than people generally suppose."[6]

Women were not necessarily stifled or unhappy in this life; some of them look back with nostalgia on those days filled with luxury and beauty and fun. In fact women sometimes resisted their husbands' efforts to make them come out of seclusion. Moroccan historian Amina Leuh told me of a man from Tetouan who spent some time in Egypt, where women were more emancipated, and when he returned to Tetouan, wanted his wife to go out of the house without wearing her djellaba. When she refused, he divorced her and married a new wife on the condition that she be willing to go out without a djellaba. Everyone in Tetouan was talking about this event in the 1930s.[7] French sociologist Yvette Katan, in a 1955 study of Oujda, found similar examples: a doctor's wife who was horrified when her husband wanted her to go out and visit his colleagues' families; a woman who accompanied her husband to France where she was free to go out as she pleased, but who stayed locked up in her apartment just as though she were still in seclusion in Oujda. In Morocco, the only women who went out alone in the streets were women who worked as servants in European homes, women from the country, and prostitutes. Most bourgeois women would be afraid of degrading themselves if they acted in the same way, going out in the streets.[8]

Women in seclusion were not entirely unaware of what was going on in the outside world, especially in the Arab world, which reached even illiterate women through the "Voice of the Arabs" and other broadcasts of Radio Cairo. There were more than a hundred thousand transistor radios in Morocco, and the "Voice of the Arabs" played a major role in sensitizing the Moroccan population to the evils of colonialism and in rallying their support for the nationalist cause. What's more, women were quite familiar with the lives of Arab heroines, including several Egyptian and Lebanese feminists of the nineteenth and twentieth centuries, such as Huda Sha'raoui, an Egyptian feminist, born in 1879, who successfully fought the British occupation of Egypt and fought her own way out of seclusion.[9] But Moroccan women themselves did not have access to education until about a generation later, so Morocco would not have its own (written) feminist voice until Malika El Fassi wrote her first article calling for girls' education in 1935.

Girls' Education

There was a good deal of discussion of women's issues in the Moroccan nationalist press in the late thirties and early forties, but it was a feminist discourse largely generated by men.[10] The one woman who wrote in the papers at the time and contributed to the debate on girls' education was Malika El Fassi, born into one of the great intellectual families of the Fez bourgeoisie, and educated at home starting in the late twenties. She began writing in the mid-1930s, in the Arabic-language press published in Morocco. The mere fact that a woman was writing in the papers, expressing her views in public, created a sensation at the time and provided a strong role model for young women.

Malika El Fassi took up the cause of girls' education as the first priority for Moroccan women. Her articles are mainly addressed to men, to persuade fathers of the necessity of sending their daughters to school, because in the 1930s there were practically no Moroccan women who could read, and it was still the men in the family who made decisions on whether to send girls to school. Malika El Fassi understood that it was access to education that would emancipate Moroccan women.

Starting as early as 1920, the nationalist bourgeoisie had begun to create its own "free schools" as an alternative to the protectorate's French-language school system. As the schools charged tuition, it was largely children from well-off families who went to free schools at the beginning; but little by little the intellectual middle class also began to enroll their sons and daughters, and eventually education became a major factor in breaking down class barriers. Nationalist women organized and raised money to house and feed students from out of town and to pay students' tuition when they couldn't afford it. Girls began going to the free schools in the late 1930s. They studied together with boys and got the same general education: religious studies, Arabic language (grammar and composition), history, geography, and arithmetic. Generally these schools led to the primary school certificate. Most of the women who participated in the nationalist political movement were educated in these schools, and it was also there that the first female school teachers were trained.

Although more and more girls started primary school, very few of them got to the level of the fifth year, and the age of twelve, when they could sit for the exam for the primary school certificate. As soon as girls got to the age of twelve or thirteen, their parents would keep them home, as it was hshouma (shameful) for a girl to go out of the house once she reached the age of puberty. Between 1943 and 1953 only fifty-two Moroccan girls got their primary school certificate; the nationalist women in these oral histories were among that small pioneer group of girls, the first to complete primary school. Once the movement for girls' education had started, it quickly gained speed. In 1953, there were 150 Moroccan girls who got their primary school certificate, and four who got their baccalaureate;[11] and in 1957 the first women graduated from the Qaraouine university.

Access to school meant everything to this generation of Moroccan women. For daughters of the bourgeoisie it meant the end to their seclusion. Nationalist women who were among the first Moroccan girls to go to school still remember the details of that experience. Women who couldn't go to school still regret the missed opportunity. And many women told of starting school, and then being abruptly pulled out once they reached the age of twelve or thirteen. Madame Naamane, the wife of Casablanca resistance leader Thami Naamane, talked about her own experience:

4.2

Girls going to school in Tetouan in the early 1940s.

Source: Amina Leuh.

I remember that in 1946 [an Italian] doctor came to us at home for someone from our family who was sick. We were playing in front of him, my sister, who was younger, and me. He turned to my grandfather and asked him, "Those girls there, don't they go to school? Why not? It's a shame; you shouldn't keep them from going to school!" He influenced my grandfather. The next day, my grandfather looked for a place where we could go to study. I was nine years old; no, maybe older; maybe eleven years old. It was already too late for the beginning of the school year. . . . The school director told him that there were no longer any places left at all. But still they made two tables for us, which my grandfather paid for, not my father, because it was the grandfather who was in charge. . . . We entered in the middle of the school year.

I was very intelligent. It's too bad; it would have been better if I hadn't received all that intelligence. . . . I spent three months in one grade and then they moved me into another after passing an exam, because I did very well . . . In short, I went through five grades in two years. When I finished those two years, my grandfather wanted to move me to another school, because I had finished the first one. Only there was this Moulay Ali, may God pardon us and pardon him, who told my grandfather, "Does that girl still go out at her age?" I was thirteen years old. So my grandfather said, "Stay at home! You've finished with school; you have no more reason to go out." . . . I was devastated—and from the age of thirteen I was a prisoner in the house. No more going out to the hammam or to visit family. I was not allowed even to go to the hammam! I couldn't go to visit family, not even for festivals or on any other occasions.[12]

The Princess Lalla Aicha, Symbol of Women's Emancipation

It was men—fathers and sometimes grandfathers—who made decisions in the family, and who had to be persuaded to send their daughters to school. Thus it gave great impetus to the movement for girls' education when King Mohamed V set an example by educating his own daughters. Aicha Terrab, who now directs the Casablanca office of the National Union of Moroccan Women, went to school at the palace, studying together with the king's eldest daughter, the Princess Lalla Aicha. She described their schooling as "very traditional and very modern at the same time":

[The late king Mohamed V] had visions for his country that were so farsighted. . . . Already in that era (in the late thirties) the princesses went out in dresses, and they practiced all the sports . . . all sports, including riding, swimming, tennis, everything . . . and they studied dance, and the piano. And at the same time, they began every morning with the Koran. At six in the morning they began with reading the Koran and prayer, so that they would stay connected to their traditions. And all through the day we had an education that was bi-lingual, perfectly bi-lingual, in Arabic and French. And there was also English, and we did some Latin. Really, there was a sort of union between the East and the West that was fabulous! And we were inspired by the (Salafiya) Islamic reform movement that was born in the Middle East.[13]

When the Princess Lalla Aicha got her primary school certificate in 1943, she became a potent symbol of the renaissance of the Moroccan woman. Also in 1943, the king himself took a public position in support of the education of girls by promising to personally supervise the selection of male teachers of Arabic for the public, French girls' schools until the time when female teachers of Arabic were trained. Soon after that, as Aicha Terrab recalled,

[The king] sent his eldest daughter, the Princess Lalla Aicha, all across Morocco. She went to the principal cities of Morocco, where she encouraged people to send girls to school, telling them why it was useful for girls to be educated. Her point of departure, and her main principle, was an Islamic principle of the equality of men and women—equality in instruction, in human dignity, in everything that is essential for human beings. She put her finger on the essential point that in front of God, men and women were human beings, in the full sense of being human, and that both men and women had a right to everything that was important. . . . The Princess had an absolutely extraordinary eloquence. [What she said] was revolutionary in relation to the attitudes that prevailed at that time; but it was not [revolutionary] in relation to religion, because she based her ideas on religion. . . . And everywhere she went, she was accompanied by a very famous theologian, in order to solidly reinforce her words and actions, and to keep her out of the reach of critics. His name was Mohamed Belarbi Alaoui; later he was also Minister of Justice, but it was in his capacity as a theologian that he appeared with the princess. . . . When she gave her speech, the theologian would stand up and say, "Here is what the Koran says, and here is the life of the Prophet", and give examples [to support what she said in her speech].

When he was a young man in Fez, Dr. Mohamed Tazi attended some of the meetings where the princess spoke. He stressed the significance of her role:

There was the emancipating action—and that is an action that cannot be ignored by history—the emancipating action of the Princess Lalla Aicha.

It was a driving element in the action—no, not the political action, but in the action of emancipation. That is to say, it was the first time, in the history of Islam, either in the East or in the West, that a great woman from a great imperial family *dared* to tear off her veil in public; to encourage others in the audience, which was made up of women and professors and all that, to do the same thing! . . .

The Princess Lalla Aicha was gifted with an extraordinary dynamism—especially considering how young she was—a dynamism that was amazing! She stood up to the administration of the protectorate in Fez in order to create a free school. It was a professor who had been my professor, director of a private school, who had bought a big house in the medina near Bab Boujeloud which he wanted to convert into a free school. The French didn't agree with that. They didn't want a free school right in the medina at the entrance to Boujeloud, and especially not the way he wanted to build it, in a really Moroccan style, with arcades and everything. And so they were at loggerheads. Then he had the idea of going to the Princess Lalla Aicha, who signed her own name as co-owner of the property. And so with that they were able to do it, and to found the school; it still exists. . . .[14]

The Princess Lalla Aicha became a symbol, a heroine for Moroccan women, especially the younger generation. On April 11, 1947, in the international city of Tangiers, where King Mohamed V, in his speech, broke definitively with the French protectorate in order to align himself with the Moroccan nationalists, the Princess Lalla Aicha also gave a speech. She was only about sixteen years old at the time, and as she stood outside in the Tangiers city square, on a platform with a lectern and microphones in front of her, unveiled, she was an electrifying presence. The square was packed with the thousands of women who had come from Tangiers, Tetouan, and the surrounding area. Young women and old women, veiled and unveiled—all had come to see and hear the princess. The king, her father, watched the event from the terrace of a house overlooking the square. She delivered her speech in three languages— Arabic, French and English—and she spoke about the need for girls to go to school and for women to take their places as full participants in the Moroccan nation. The princess said that the Moroccan nation was at a crossroads, at the beginning of a renaissance; she drew on models from Moroccan history and especially from the experience of Egypt.[15] The speech ended with a triumphant cry: "Long live the King of Morocco, long live the Moroccan nation, and long live the renaissance!"

I asked Malika El Fassi about the role of the princess and the impact of her speech.

4.3

The Princess Lalla Aicha addressing the crowd in Tangiers (1947).

Source: Amina Leuh.

Yes, Lalla Aicha was a kind of symbol; she played a big role. And the speech that she gave was unbelievable! First, she had a voice that was really warm. (When Malika El Fassi said this, her own voice became low and warm and thrilling, so that you could imagine the princess speaking.) And then the ideas in the speech—of course it was written with the help of the nationalists and His Majesty Mohamed V—the ideas were revolutionary. She said that it would be impossible to have real independence for Morocco as long as half of the population didn't participate, and that it was necessary for women to be educated. Because Lalla Aicha was a leader for the women's movement.[16]

It was this visit of the princess to Tangiers that mobilized women in Tetouan and led to the creation of a women's association of the Reform Party. Amina Leuh, who was active in girls' education in Tetouan, went to Tangiers to hear the princess and returned to Tetouan "a different person. No more doubts, no fear."

Women's Organizations of the Political Parties

While a small group of girls from bourgeois nationalist families were going through school, Moroccan women of all classes and in all regions were taking part in the growing nationalist political struggle. Malika El Fassi was the only woman among the group of nationalists who drafted and signed the Independence Manifesto which was sent to the king and the French resident general on January 11, 1944. But after this first manifesto, great numbers of women signed petitions for independence, which they sent to the governors of the provinces. Women also participated in the demonstrations that took place after the demand for independence, especially in Fez, and the nationalist political parties began to see the importance of mobilizing women.

Starting in the middle of the 1940s, three women's organizations were instituted in association with the major political parties: These were the *Akhawat assafa* (Sisters of Purity), the *Union des femmes du Maroc* (Moroccan Women's Union), and the women's association of the Istiqlal Party.[17]

The Akhawat Assafa was one of the first Moroccan women's organizations instituted by a political party, formed under the aegis of the *Parti démocratique et d'indépendance* (PDI) or *Shoura*, which became the second force—the first force being the Istiqlal Party—in the nationalist movement based in Fez. At the first congress of the Akhawat Assafa, held on May 23, 1947 in Fez, the main goals of the association were summarized by its president, as follows: (1) To fight ignorance and illiteracy among Moroccan women; (2) to fight false traditions and extravagant spending at family celebrations; (3) to give material and moral support to indigent women who wanted an education; and (4) to exchange useful information in order to benefit from one another's experience. In this way, the president explained, "the Moroccan woman would emerge from the shadows and move towards knowledge and progress." Twenty-nine people participated in that first meeting, and the resolutions were adopted and read in Moroccan Arabic.[18]

Zahra Skalli, a member of the Akawat Assafa, described cutting back on expenditures for marriage celebrations in her own family:

> I remember as a young girl those old traditions: the kaftan of *khrib* (very expensive embroidered kaftan), the bride with all those *ngafat* (plural of *negafa*, the woman who dresses the bride), and all that stuff. This is what the PDI woman wanted to fight.

> My mother, may God rest her soul, was one of the women who appreciated these changes and welcomed the new attitudes. So my sister Meriam got married in this very simplified fashion, without all those heavy jewels and pearls. My sister Halima also married in this style, and I myself also got married that way. In these new-style weddings there was just one kaftan of *ntaa* (a simpler kaftan), and I also had a diadem and a white dress (rather than the five or six different outfits that were traditional). There was only one *negafa*, because we had another woman, the *galassa*,[19] a woman hired to take care of the room where the bride gets changed, and the first person to testify that the bride is a virgin. So in this way the wedding party was just a simple, ordinary event, without so much showing off and exhibitionism. Because poor people do get affected when they see the amazing extravagance of traditional weddings.[20]

The second congress of the Sisters of Purity, held in Fez on December 12, 1947, passed additional resolutions calling on the women in the national and regional bureaus to finance the education of children from poor families and to establish workshops to train women in sewing. For the first time, this congress also broached questions of women's legal rights and personal status, resolving to "examine the rights of Moroccan women in Islamic law, and the problems of polygamy and divorce."[21]

The Moroccan Women's Union was instituted by the Communist Party in 1944, to get Moroccan women involved in social action to mitigate the hardships brought about by World War II. But the Union's leadership was predominantly French and Jewish, and they never joined up with the Moroccan independence movement.[22] Therefore, the union lost credibility among Moroccan women and eventually disintegrated.

The Istiqlal Party created its women's association in 1946, presided over by the ubiquitous Malika El Fassi. In creating the women's association, the party showed that it recognized the connection between the nationalist movement and the women's movement. The association had three main objectives: to draw women into the struggle for national independence, to organize efforts to help those in need, and to open up secondary and higher education to girls. Many of the oral histories describe women's meetings organized by the Istiqlal women's association in the late forties and early fifties. These served to disseminate the party's principles and its views on particular issues, and to mobilize women in support of the nationalist cause. The party could not have done this without the women's association, as it would not have been possible in that era to hold meetings with men and women together. Ftoma Skalli, who was involved in Istiqlal Party women's activities in Fez in the forties, describes the dual purpose of women's meetings: to explain the party's position on current issues, and to bridge the gap between social classes.

> Of course I was in Hajja Mekouar's meetings.[23] These were gatherings of twenty, thirty or forty women. We were of the Istiqlal Party, but articles and pamphlets were the men's job. They would give us [material on] an issue, and we would read it to the women.
>
> At our gatherings, we would have very rich women, and we would seat them next to poor women. And we used to tell them that if they didn't like it they'd better not show up the next time. [That way] I used to teach them equality. I had the husbands and sons of some of these rich women come to my house to thank me for the change in their lives. They said that they had been getting close to divorce because their wives were so concerned with showing off, and with gold and diamonds. I myself don't like to show off; I would rather do something useful that would allow me to show my face honorably to God.[24]

The women's association also organized a wide range of social service activities: They supported political prisoners and their families with food, clothes, and money; and they provided poor girls (and boys) with clothes, school materials, and room and board so that they could attend the nationalist free schools. In return, these girls taught literacy classes for older women.

In direct action to improve the status of women, the first priority of the women's association was to open up secondary schools for girls, and then, in 1949, to open a women's section of the Qaraouine university in Fez. The idea that women should be able to study at the Qaraouine was something that Malika El Fassi had dreamed of many years earlier, when she was a little girl. When she asked the king for his advice and support, he said that it would only be possible if the women themselves took care of everything. So they did. Abdelsalam Kabbej, a nationalist and the father of a girl who was one of the first Qaraouine students, rented a house for the women's section, and the women themselves did the rest, selling their bracelets and belts made of gold to raise the money to pay the professors and all the other expenses.

In the last period before independence, beginning in 1949, *Risalat-al-Maghrib* (Letter from Morocco) started a new section, entitled "Your turn, Madam."[25] This section was designed to be read by women, and even solicited contributions from educated women who could write. The section was edited by a man, signed "Tahar," who in the preface to the first issue reassured male readers that "our objective is only social reform, and our goal is to help the ladies of the house to accomplish their family duties."[26] The education of girls was no longer a subject in the paper, since it had become a reality. Now, the subject was how to guide these educated young women so that they would respect the Islamic traditions that defined their social roles. One writer advised that "women should participate in the progress of the country . . . in accomplishing their social role as mother and wife and in fighting against superstitions and false traditions."[27] However, as young women of the Istiqlal began to participate more and more in this section, and in another which opened in May of 1950 in the Istiqlal Party paper *Al-Alam*, they began to change the subject, to ask for the first time about problems that had to do with their status as women: polygamy, repudiation, early marriage, the veil, and so on. When an article appeared saying that the phenomena of women unveiling and mixing with men in public places were at the root of a decline in Islamic values,[28] these young women were quick to respond with articles: "Islam didn't make women into slaves"; "The veil of ignorance must fall"; "Other Muslim countries have done this before us"; and finally, "What are these gentlemen afraid of?"[29]

Unfortunately, this debate in the nationalist press was cut short in 1952, when the women's page was replaced by a workers page. Although the workers' page included some articles on women workers, the emphasis was on their role as workers.

The traditional bourgeois and artisan classes of Fez had provided the leadership and set the tone of the nationalist movement through most of the forties, but by the early fifties most of the original bourgeois leaders of the Istiqlal were in prison or in exile, except for a few who were leading an international diplomatic campaign to get foreign and United Nations support for Moroccan independence. A whole new leadership began to emerge in the Istiqlal and other political parties—a leadership group made up of young militant nationalists of working class origins.

Nationalist women also took on new roles. Oum Keltoum El Khatib, whose husband went to prison in December of 1952, got a passport so that she could travel to the international city of Tangiers or to the Spanish zone in the north. Like many other nationalist women at the time, she began to go out alone, leaving her house at two o'clock in the morning to catch the bus to Kenitra in order to visit her husband and other nationalists in prison, to bring in food and clothes, and to transmit messages. All of this, of course, would have been extraordinary behavior for a young woman under ordinary circumstances. Khadija Bennouna, a nationalist woman who lived in Tangiers in that period, began to go out at night to help smuggle arms.

Nationalist Women: The Oral Histories

In addition to the seven women whose oral histories appear in the book, I interviewed another seven women who could be considered in the same category: women from the traditional bourgeoisie with significant involvement in the nationalist movement. The women included here were selected because of their importance in the Moroccan nationalist movement and women's movement, and because they grew up in several different Moroccan cities and were active in various fields of work.

Malika El Fassi, the "mother" of the group, came from the El Fassi family, the leading family of the bourgeois intelligentsia of Fez. Allal El Fassi, the leader of the Istiqlal Party, was her cousin, and she married another cousin, Mohamed El Fassi, who was rector of the Qaraouine university in the 1940s, and Minister of Education after independence. Zhor Lazraq and Fatima Benslimane (Hassar)[30] are the next generation. Zhor Lazraq grew up in Fez;[31] and Fatima Hassar is from a prominent Fassi family although she herself grew up in El Jadida. Oum Keltoum El Khatib is from a Fassi family of skilled craftsmen, the class that set the tone of the nationalist movement through the forties. Khadija Bennouna and Amina Leuh come from leading families in Tetouan, the center of traditional culture in the northern part of Morocco. Rqia Lamrania is a *sherifa* and related to the Alaouite royal family.[32]

These women were born into nationalist families. Their fathers and uncles were the founders and leaders of the Moroccan nationalist movement, which was just gathering strength in the early 1930s, when most of these women were born.[33] In their oral histories, the women make a point of this. This was also the reason that these few girls were able to go to school: Their fathers and grandfathers were nationalists, and had been influenced by the nationalist movement's call for girls' education, and by the example set by King Mohamed V.[34]

It would be impossible to overestimate the importance that schooling had in these women's lives. In the oral histories, the women all start talking about their own lives by describing their first exposure to education. Zhor Lazraq started Koranic school when she was about three years old in a school that was normally reserved for boys. Amina Leuh's family, in the north of Morocco, actually moved from Al Hoceima to Tetouan in order for her to go to school. After she had reached the level of the primary school certificate, her father wanted her to continue her education, and even thought of sending her to live with an English lady in Tangiers for that purpose—an idea that was vetoed by the rest of the family as too extreme. All of the oral histories recount in some detail this experience of being the first girl to enter a regular Koranic school, the first girl to get a primary school certificate, the first to enter secondary school, the first to get a baccalaureate and to go on to higher education, and even the experience of being one of the first group of women to go to the Qaraouine university in Fez.

Many of the narratives also mention the critical influence of strong women in the family—mothers and grandmothers who believed that girls and boys should have the same education and the same rights, who set an example, and who provided the first lessons in Moroccan history and nationalism. When they speak of coming from a nationalist family, they are talking primarily about men in the family who are in the nationalist movement. But when they speak of other people in the family who influenced them, they often refer to women. Fatima Hassar spoke several times of her grandmother, an extraordinary woman who believed that girls should have the same rights and the same education as boys.

Most of the women in these oral histories did their primary and secondary school studies in the nationalist free schools, where the curriculum was Arabic and Islamic, and also strongly nationalist. Whereas the (male) leadership of the nationalist movement was about evenly divided between those who had studied in France (and in French schools in Morocco) and those who had an Arabic, Islamic education, the nationalist women were almost all educated in Koranic schools and (Arabic, Islamic) nationalist free schools. Thus, these girls grew up and were educated to feel a particular responsibility to safeguard the threatened national identity (Morocco as an Arab, Islamic monarchy) against French, or Spanish, cultural assimilation.

Fatima Benslimane (Hassar), the one woman in the oral histories who was educated in French schools, in El Jadida, saw this as a way to fight French colonialism from the inside. As the only Moroccan and the only Arab in her class at school, she felt a particular burden to get good grades, to speak up, and to excel.

These women started working in the nationalist movement at a very young age, teaching literacy classes for older women and speaking to gatherings of women to raise their level of political awareness and to mobilize them to participation in the struggle against colonialism. Oum Keltoum El Khatib talks about directing meetings to raise women's political awareness when she was only twelve years old, and Fatima Benslimane was also no more than twelve or thirteen when she began to give literacy courses to older women.

In school and later in life, there was a heavy burden on these women to excel in everything they did, in order to prove by their own example that Moroccan women were capable. They were working against strong stereotypes and prejudices about women in traditional Moroccan society. Malika El Fassi describes how her efforts to open up access to education for girls were resisted at every turn. When Zhor Lazraq talks about graduating from the Qaraouine university at the head of her group of women and men in 1957, she emphasizes the importance of her achievement in giving significance to Moroccan women among Islamic peoples and in opening a path for women in a realm of education formerly reserved for men. Amina Leuh describes "arming (herself) for the battle" as she took on the position of principal of the Tetouan No. 1 Girls School, knowing that she had to be absolutely brilliant in her teaching and absolutely irreproachable in her behavior, to provide a model.

It was these young nationalist women who took the leadership in the women's associations formed by the political parties starting in the mid-forties, raised money for nationalist causes, and worked in education and social services. This gave them valuable experience in organizing, teaching, and mobilizing women of different ages and social classes, and it provided the parties with an enormously powerful tool for raising money and for mobilizing women to support the nationalist cause.

In the early 1950s, when almost all of the nationalist leaders were in prison or in exile, it was the nationalist women who provided the leadership and mobilized other women to keep things going. In Salé, women not only kept the free school going even though its director and some professors were arrested, but they also took care of all the people in prison and their families, and even started something new: organizing the first vacation colony for boys and girls together.

After independence, the nationalist women remained engaged, most of them turning their energies to education and social services. They have actively defended and promoted the right (and responsibility) of women to participate in all aspects of the country's development, as Moroccan citizens, equal with men. On the other hand, these women have not gotten involved in promoting women's rights in the family, in Islamic family law. While they have not been very visible in Moroccan politics, they have remained active raising money for political causes in the Islamic world, helping the Algerian national liberation movement until Algerian independence in 1962, and, most recently, raising money to help Iraq after the devastation caused by the American invasion in Operation Desert Storm. Some of them are concerned that the young generation of Moroccan women today have lost their strong sense of responsibility and of patriotism. They fear that these younger women take for granted the access to education and other opportunities that their generation fought so hard to attain.

The women all spoke in classical Arabic or French (Fatima Hassar and Malika El Fassi), rather than the Moroccan Arabic used by former members of the armed resistance. They avoided talking about their own accomplishments or speaking in the first person. This gives some of the narratives a rather formal and impersonal quality. When they do bring up events in their personal lives, such as marriage and the birth of children, it is in the context of themes of nationalism and self-sacrifice. With a few exceptions, these are heroic narratives, with "no contradictions, no mistakes, and no moments of human frailty."[35]

The oral histories all cover a great sweep of history. Each woman's particular life experience is set in the context of contemporary events in Morocco and the Arab world, which are seen as episodes in the larger struggle of the Arab Muslim world against colonialism. The women see their lives as continuous, all of a piece, and portray their lives and their life's work as exemplary, demonstrating the capacity of the Moroccan woman and her active role in liberating and building the Moroccan nation. The various themes are orchestrated in a continuous narrative, fully shaped, articulate, with lots of analysis and commentary.

5

Malika El Fassi:
Foremother of the Modern Women's Movement

When I began asking about women in the nationalist movement, the one name that I heard over and over again was that of Malika El Fassi. It would be no exaggeration to say that Malika El Fassi all by herself constituted the first generation of the modern Moroccan women's movement, providing a model and mentor for the generations that followed. What made her unique for her time was that she was able to get an education, in the late 1920s and early 1930s, when no other Moroccan Muslim girls had that opportunity. Perhaps as a result of that early experience, the one cause which she has promoted from beginning to end is the cause of women's education.

She was born into the El Fassi family in Fez, the leading family of the traditional bourgeois intelligentsia. In her own immediate family, she was the only girl. It is easy to imagine how exciting it was for her as a young girl to grow up in Fez in the twenties and thirties, right at the heart of the developing Moroccan nationalist movement, in the midst of a lively household of brothers and cousins, discussing and debating the issues of the day. In an interview with Latifa Jbabdi for the feminist paper 8 mars, *Malika El Fassi talks about her education, her writing, and her participation in the nationalist political movement.*[1]

Education was one of the factors that pushed Moroccan women to join the political action and the national [independence] struggle. However, in the twenties women didn't have access to education. That it was possible for me was mere chance. My father, may God rest his soul, took me to a *fqiha*'s house, from 1928 to 1930. After that he opened a real school for me at home, where I was taught by all the greatest teachers, such as Mr. Abdeslam Serghine, Fqih Quri, Mr. Abdelrahman Bassoum, Mr. Mohamed Benchikh, and Bourqadi. Starting in 1935–36, I began to join the debates of my brothers and cousins about national issues. And I started wondering why girls and women, generally speaking, didn't enter these debates, in spite of their energies and their opinions on the subject. So why were they absent? That was the question that troubled me, and in 1935, in *Al Maghrib* magazine, which was published by Mr. Salah

Missa, I wrote an article to demand the education of girls. It was the first article
written by a woman. A series of articles followed, and someone in the magazine
signed them: "A Young Girl." Then I started to sign, "The City Researcher."
What is exquisite, is that a number of readers wrote to the magazine asking
whether the writer of those articles was a woman or a man.

*If we read the articles that Malika El Fassi wrote in 1935 now, they seem
rather restrained and conservative. But it is important to consider the time in
which these articles were written, and the prevailing views on women and
education. In the mid-thirties, girls were still struggling to get access to primary
school education; it was revolutionary to suggest that they should go on as far
as the level of secondary school. What made this especially significant was that
it crossed that critical boundary of the age of puberty, the age at which girls
were traditionally confined to the house in strict seclusion. To suggest that girls
should continue in school to the level of secondary school was to suggest that
girls who had already reached puberty would be out walking through the streets
on their way to school and would study in school together with boys. In
Morocco in 1935, this was a shocking suggestion.*

*Malika El Fassi's views evolved with the times. By the mid-forties she
began pushing to open up secondary education to girls, and even higher
education. In 1949, she was instrumental in opening a women's section of the
Qaraouine. Her view that a woman's primary role was at the center of the
family, especially her role in educating future generations, was the prevailing
view of the neo-Salafiya reformers in the nationalist movement—a view still held
by most nationalist women a generation later.*

Here are some excerpts from her first article, published in Al Maghrib
magazine in March 1935, entitled "About Girls' Education."

Those who have studied the conditions of civilized nations, either in
ancient times or in our own time, discover women's wisdom and values. They
realize that human society urgently needs women's contributions, and that
women are one of the pillars of the renaissance, a firm foundation and a great
majority of the nation, because they are the first teachers of our youth. It is
women who assume the heavy responsibilities of molding our youth. This youth
will become the men of tomorrow, the leaders who will run the country. How
will it grow up? And what will become of it? Will our young men be cowards,
participating in false traditions and corrupt practices, who will cause the nation
to become decadent and to disintegrate? Or will they be virtuous, proud, and self
confident? If we want the latter to be the case, then what is necessary is girls'
education.

I am not one of those who say that girls must attain high degrees; I tend
rather to favor a high school education that includes every subject, and that
makes a girl able to read and write and take care of the house, and to live with
her husband and socialize the children. That is enough for her, and it is what

5.1

Malika El Fassi (1992).

Source: Editions le fennec.

suits our environment. She can graduate at age fifteen or sixteen with a good education, and afterwards, if she wishes to increase her knowledge, she can read important books, papers, and scientific magazines, because these are the best route to an education. There is no doubt that when she reaches this recommended level she will be competent and have enough knowledge to create the renaissance that we expect from Moroccan youth. That is what Moroccan girls aspire to and anticipate day and night. I wish that their hopes might be fulfilled.

In the October, 1935 issue of the same magazine (Al Maghrib), she joins the debate that is going on—a debate that her articles helped to provoke— between those who advocate girls' education and others who are afraid that education will corrupt young girls with Western values and religions.

I was sad to read an article in *Al Maghrib* magazine with faulty ideas which called women's progress "Western," and claimed that it would only lead women to separate from their religion and to lose their values. . . . I didn't think that such ideas could be published [anymore], ideas that set back girls' progress, and postpone their education. . . . I was afraid of the influence that such an article might have; I, who cling to our language and religion and to those of our traditions that do not harm Islam or Moroccan civilization. I wanted to answer that article, but for various reasons I restrained myself. But now I think that I must write a word on the subject.

It is no secret that the Moroccan woman's life is stillness and languor. Why not, since she only leaves her mother to go to the handicraft mistress's house. And when she finishes there with skill in some craft, she becomes a prisoner in the house. All she knows of the secrets of life is what her grandmother and some old women tell her, such as stories about *djinn* [wicked spirits, imps] and the *baraka* [blessing, holiness] of saints: Sidi so-and-so, he who swears by him becomes blind; Sidi so-and-so, he who spends time in his shrine will be healthy, rich and vigorous . . . and so forth and so forth.

Is it fair that the young Moroccan girl remains the way she has always been, in an era of science and knowledge? Is it good that she stays the way she was, when her sisters in the Middle East have already gained a significant amount of knowledge? Is it good for her to stay the way she was, when a number of the most talented Moroccan youth have scattered to Eastern and Western countries to get knowledge and high culture; when the Qaraouine university is wide open and training students every year; when schools are full of boys; when the Middle East is sending us torrents of books, and papers and magazines, written by the region's best scholars; when knowledge is rapidly spreading throughout Morocco? Yet the young Moroccan girl knows nothing of all this, and gains nothing from it. How can educated youth accept her as a wife and be comfortable with her, and give her the reins in socializing their children, when the youth have dealt with knowledge and formulated ideas, and gained enough learning to make them despise an ignorant woman?

This situation may lead to disaster: either marrying a foreign woman—and we have seen the signs of that, and the Middle Easterners have known its calamities and write about it[2]—or it may lead to celibacy, which is a second calamity that destroys even civilized nations, let alone underdeveloped countries. It is possible to avoid these two calamities, since there is a way out: Giving girls a good education that will raise their level of culture and lead to the happiness of both man and wife.

But will this education be primary, or secondary, or superior? I think that what is appropriate for girls is secondary education, because the primary level alone will be incomplete. . . . As for superior education, it is usually used to obtain a career, and careers are men's duty because of the life responsibilities that are imposed on them. . . . We know the social harm caused by women's work from Westerners' experience and from Middle Easterners who have imitated them. For when a woman works outside of the house, she who is responsible for the housework and the socialization and welfare of the children, it does nothing but take men's work and tear apart the family bonds because of the clashes that it causes.

The word equality, which is thundering now in the West and the Middle East, is nothing but a fraud. I don't understand woman's imitation of man, by working and taking on rights that are not hers, thus neglecting her human responsibility and all the burdens related to it. Is earning money man's only virtue? Are there not other social virtues equally or more important than earning money? Isn't the socialization of children and the managing of the house a great and gracious accomplishment? . . . Men and women were created to cooperate, to confront the difficulties of life together. Man works hard outside the home and woman inside, and it is through this association and cooperation that they reach equality, not in doing the same work.

While she was writing this series of articles on girls' education, Malika El Fassi was also joining in debates on politics. In 1937, she joined the national party. She discusses this, and the events leading up to the 1944 Independence Manifesto in the interview with Latifa Jbabdi of 8 mars.[3]

I used to join my brothers, cousins, grandfather and family friends in their debates and I was roused by the nationalist spirit. I joined the national movement in 1937 [after the national action block *kutla* became the national party]. I used to participate in the debates about national issues, about how to ignite the national awareness, and about the ugliness of colonialism. At the same time I continued to write articles for the papers that were published by Said Hajji, and then by Zhiri after Hajji passed away.

At that stage there was no scheme to spread awareness among women. Women were absent. Therefore my work was only with men.[4] During that period, the group of nationalists worked on spreading national awareness, and they contacted King Mohamed V. A large number of them used to visit him to

5.2

Malika El Fassi with children (1943). Rear left to right: Abdelwahed, Hassan.
Front left to right: Roqia, Amina.

Source: Roqia El Fassi.

exchange ideas and advice. Also [during that period] branches of the organization were established in many towns.

My husband was then teaching the Crown Prince. He had been doing that since 1942. Then we moved to Fez, where Mohamed V had appointed him as director of the Qaraouine university, in order to reform it, and I went with him. He used to go to Rabat every week to meet the rest of the nationalist group members who were constantly in touch with Mohamed V.

After long debates, it was decided to form a select group of nationalists who would be ready for any sacrifice and prepared to keep a secret. I was the only woman in the group. Its activity was specifically political, to work for political reform and independence, no matter what sort of sacrifices that would entail. The national party was limited to a very small group of nationalists, so [in the early 1940s] it was decided to found the Istiqlal [independence] Party, with a new goal: the demand for independence and the broadening of the party's [base of support].

I worked in the secretariat then, and among the most important articles I wrote then was one I entitled, "The renaissance of the Moroccan woman," written on the occasion of Princess Lalla Aicha's graduation from primary school. The truth is that the first group of girls had graduated from primary school in 1942. This created huge possibilities for work among women. And looking at local and international developments in the early forties, we started thinking about going beyond the stage of presenting demands for reform to the authorities, [a tactic] which usually led to arrests. We decided to create a popular mass party and to politicize a broad spectrum of citizens, and to present the demand for independence.

I participated alongside the brothers in taking this decision, and indeed I was the only woman then. But my status as a woman didn't present any obstacle in my work with them. They considered me as their sister, and I still consider them as brothers. I used to visit them and receive them at my place whether my husband was present or not. They didn't look on me as a woman, and I didn't look on them as men, but rather as brothers in the full sense of the word, because nationalism had linked us together.

We were expecting things to turn ugly [after we presented the Independence Manifesto on January 11, 1944]; that they would undoubtedly answer this demand with repression and arrests. That's why we thought about the necessity for organization. Each responsible group in every town started thinking about how to confront the repression and how to resist the colonialist tyranny and arrests. They planned how to organize demonstrations; and decided who was going to start things off, and who was going to take care of the pamphlets and writing, and first aid [for the wounded], and carrying off the dead. So work committees were formed to take care of these different responsibilities.[5] The names of these committee members were top secret, and they had to stay in their homes.

There were no women in the organization at that stage, because it was not yet opened up to the people at large, and it didn't yet give much importance to action among women. And yet the fact that women were not party members did not mean that they were completely absent from the field. For instance, a great number of women gathered in Fez (I mention Fez because that was where I lived and experienced events after 1942) to declare their solidarity with the demand for independence. They were led by the wife of Mr. Ahmed Mekouar, may God rest his soul. She, with two or three other women, collected women's signatures. The women who could write signed their names, and those who couldn't write put some kind of mark. So a great number of women supported the manifesto. Afterwards, these petitions were delivered to the *pasha* of the town or to the governor.

Women showed their solidarity with the manifesto by their boldness and courage during the events that followed January 11. Because the colonial authorities, of course, had turned down our demand, and had hit our brothers in Rabat [where Al Yazidi, Balafrej and others were arrested]. Demonstrations broke out everywhere in Morocco. Since I was in Fez, I will talk about the events that took place there. Demonstrations flared up all over town. My husband was the director of the Qaraouine university, and the colonialists believed that he was responsible for the introduction of nationalism into this institution. Si Mohammed El Fassi [my husband] was therefore the first person that had to be removed, and he was arrested with some other brothers, and a number of demonstrations blazed.

A number of people were killed, and there was a woman from the Rif among those martyrs. Her name was Hasna or Yamna—I'm not sure. The colonialist authorities had set barbed wire all around the Qaraouine mosque; and the demonstrators were trying to enter the Qaraouine to read the *llatif* [prayer for the dead]. This woman had torn away the barbed wire to let the demonstrators into the mosque, and was standing at the entrance of the mosque, shouting and invoking the name of the Prophet, when they shot her down. She was the first woman martyr to fall on that front.

Women participated strongly in these demonstrations. They yelled nationalist slogans supporting independence and shouted out youyous. They dropped flower pots from their roof terraces, and poured boiling water and oil on the soldiers. [A woman named] Manqada, for instance, was killed when she was dropping things on the soldiers from her terrace. Women's participation in these demonstrations was spontaneous; the nationalists didn't have to mobilize them. Nationalism had penetrated every Moroccan home, and the people went out into the streets spontaneously. What is even more wonderful is the national solidarity which was evident in women's opening their doors to the demonstrators. You could enter any house as if it were your own. Women brought out sheets to bandage wounds, and they cured the injured; they even tore up clothes for that purpose. Besides, citizens opened up wheat storage rooms to each other, because the colonialists had imposed a food blockade on the Fez medina. They had cut electricity. Also martyrs were buried without the colonialist authority knowing where their tombs were.[6] The demonstrations lasted a long time. A number of nationalists died, others were arrested, and the rest continued the direction of the movement.

I met with Malika El Fassi in her home, an expansive villa in the Souissi section of Rabat. When we finally got together it was after a number of failed attempts: her husband had died only a few months earlier, and then, just before we were supposed to meet, the mother of King Hassan II (the wife of King Mohamed V) died. She was still quite shaken by these events when I met her and was dressed in white, in mourning for her husband.[7] Soon after I arrived, her two daughters came to join us for the interview. She spoke in French, and while she clearly had not spoken French for some time, nevertheless she spoke eloquently.

I didn't want to go back over ground that she had already covered in the 8 mars *interview and elsewhere, so I asked her especially about her father, who was so remarkable for his time in setting up a school for his daughter at home, and about the sequence of events that led to the opening of a women's section of the Qaraouine university.*

My father *was* remarkable, and I studied with all the best professors. I remember once in that period I was working at my desk, studying my lessons, when one of my aunts came over to me. She didn't approve of girls studying or getting an education, and so she was always criticizing me for reading books. She said,"What do you think you are going to do with all that? Why are you doing all that studying? I suppose you think you're going to go to the Qaraouine [university]!!" And from that moment—I was about nine years old—I had that idea, the idea: Why shouldn't girls be able to study at the Qaraouine? And I think it was that, from my aunt, that pushed me to open up education for girls, and to open up a women's section of the Qaraouine.

In 1935, I launched my first call for girls' education. Then in 1937 and 1938, I continued to write for various magazines. There was one that was called "The Letter from Morocco" [*Risalat-al-Maghrib*]. There were several magazines and newspapers at that time. As for me, I always wrote to promote girls' education. Girls began to go to school, up to 1943, when the Princess Lalla Aicha got her primary school certificate. At that point, I wrote an article with the title "The renaissance of the Moroccan woman." That was the title, and it was a true title, because after that parents began to send their daughters to school, and then His Majesty the King Mohamed V also took an interest in Moroccan girls and their education. That was the call I launched, and in the article, after discussion and after saying what had happened, I made the achievement of the Princess Lalla Aicha an example, an emblem, a symbol of the renaissance of the Moroccan woman.

Here are excerpts from her article, "The renaissance of the Moroccan woman," which was published on August 31, 1943 in Risalat-al-Maghrib:

I am filled with delight and enthusiasm when I contemplate the girls graduating from the Babjdid School in Fez, taking away their primary school certificates. . . . The education of girls has now achieved excellent results, now that many girls have obtained their primary school certificates, among them our eldest princess Lalla Aicha who was awarded two primary school certificates, one Moroccan and one French. The Princess's certificate has given new life to our hopes for girls' education, now that girls have started down this path and their efforts have already begun to bear fruit. Nevertheless, we assert that girls who have gotten their certificate this year should not cut short their education, should not lay it aside or forget the knowledge that they have gained and the efforts that they have made by shutting themselves up in the house. Because girls will never progress in their knowledge if they just stay at home reading books and trying to educate themselves. They say that we get knowledge from the mouths of men, and it is true that a girl who only has a primary school certificate cannot yet appreciate the pleasures of studying, or her own interest [in further education]. Learning needs to be nurtured, and [the mind] expanded by directed lessons which explain and expose the ideas which underlie knowledge. . . .

Therefore men are called upon to instruct the women of tomorrow, but they should take care not to act in ways that might provoke those who are the enemies of all progress.[8] Because morality is acquired in man by means of learning and knowledge, the respected professor who takes on the duty [of instructing girls] cannot conceive of the female student in front of him other than as his own daughter or one of his sisters, the same feeling that is evident when the student in front of him is a boy. The young girl will acquire virtue once she knows herself and recognizes her value in life, and realizes the duties that she has in life. This is a goal that cannot be attained without real learning. Oh brothers! The future of our girls is in your hands from now on. Take good care of them, and carry out the duties which are demanded of you by reason and by the law of Islam. . . . [His Majesty] has insisted several times on the necessity of teaching girls, and has given specific advice reflecting on the best and most effective methods [of education] in order for girls to be able to plumb their share of knowledge. . . . Here I want to emphasize [His Majesty's] words [of advice in a speech which He gave recently at the Qaraouine university]:

Another area which interests us strongly is that of the instruction and education of our girls, in order that they can grow up and develop their capacities, following the right path, in order to carry out their duties towards their husbands, their children, and their household. The only correct road to the acquisition of knowledge is through the institution of a program which conforms to the directives of religion. . . .

Girls should follow these directions, as should we all. This will guarantee the welfare and happiness [of our young women]. Because no real life is possible without knowledge, and no nation can progress as long as half of its people are ignorant. [Signed, "The City Researcher"]

So there, that was how it was. After that, that was in 1943, of course, there was the incident of the Istiqlal Party [demand for independence] in 1944. The Moroccan woman was involved in that, demanding Moroccan independence. Yes, yes, naturally there were also women who were interested in the question of independence, nationalist women. By 1944 and 1945, the [first girls to enter school] were young women of seventeen or eighteen. They were already well educated [by that time]. By that time we had already begun to hear the sounds of—to feel the presence of—the Moroccan woman. . . .

By 1947 there were girls who had gotten to the end of primary school; they had reached the level of the primary school certificate, and they had reached the level where they were ready to enter secondary and higher education. But there wasn't any school [open to girls] for secondary level studies. The French, for example, had only created primary schools [for girls]. And for the girls who had been taught in the Moroccan system, who had learned Arabic and whose professors were Arab—because the free schools were above all interested in Arabic education—once they got to a certain level they were stopped: There was a wall in front of them.

At that moment, in 1947, I was a member of the committee, the executive committee of the party. . . . I saw a wall in front of us, which kept us from moving forward. So I looked for a way to create a serious movement among the Moroccan women who were tied to the Istiqlal Party. [I wanted to create a group of] women, with the help of some men as well, to seriously study the question of women—the education and status of women. This was in order to educate women and to prepare them for the moment when there would be a serious resistance, when the real resistance to liberate the country would break out. So that was the women's movement. This movement that was created was parallel to the [party's movement for men], and there were also men involved, those who wanted to encourage and push women.

We were talking about finding a way to open . . . to solve this question. And it was then that it occurred to me that we should open a women's branch of the Qaraouine university. Here, the idea that I had as a young girl; I had kept that idea with me all those years, and now was the time to put it into effect. My husband was the rector of the Qaraouine, and I told him that I wanted to launch this idea, for the party and for myself. He said to me, "Go ahead! As for me, I'm ready to help you." Like that. We got together some meetings with groups of women and with groups of men. How were we going to do this? People said we should demand that secondary schools be opened to Moroccan girls, that is to say the schools that gave a Franco-Moroccan education, and that girls should be able to follow all the branches of study, just like men. And then we also wanted to create—because there was another system of [Arabic] education that led to the Qaraouine—we wanted to make a special section of the Qaraouine for women. [The Qaraouine] was located in Fez, and of course I was in Fez. We formed some committees; we prepared our demands [to open the Franco-Moroccan secondary schools to girls and to create a women's section of the Qaraouine] and everything. And then we formed a delegation of young women who went to present the demands to His Majesty Mohamed V and also to the [French] resident general.

This was to demand that secondary education be opened to girls; we demanded all that. But it was really . . . They got really angry and refused, saying: "Oh the Moroccan woman is a disaster!" And you know, when women enter into something, they don't play around. Women are capable of doing anything. You know it; you're a woman too; you know women. When women want to do something, they're serious; they move straight ahead without any zigzags. What they say about women is not true.[9] Because when women want to do something they are honest and straightforward, and they are capable of doing what they set out to do.

Well, these girls, who were fifteen or seventeen years old, came before His Majesty [to present the demand], like that. Afterwards there were some things that were unclear. You see, I had some relations with His Majesty Mohamed V, naturally. And then we decided to do . . . But for secondary school, it was the French schools. The French just gave us the authorization; we were the ones who paid the professors, out of our own budget. We gave them the names of the professors and everything. But then it was . . . finally they agreed. The French opened up a classroom or two, and gave us a professor or two, for example one professor for *6ième*[10], one for *5ième*—it was using the French system.

There was still the question of the Qaraouine. That, [the French] didn't want to accept. Afterwards, I went to see His Majesty by myself. I asked him, "How can we do this?" He said, he told me, "If you can pay . . ." Because normally it was the Ministry of Islamic Affairs that paid the professors, but [the French] didn't want to give the authorization for that. He told me, "If you can pay the professors, and you can rent a house, for example, and you do all that, then after a certain time they will be forced to accept [the women's branch]." As for me, I told him, "I accept [that challenge]! I'm going to do it."

I gathered women together—naturally it wasn't the girls, it was women—and I said, "Here's the question. If you are prepared to pay the professors, then we will have a women's branch of the Qaraouine." Right then, in those few minutes, we started up a movement. The women said, "This is for our daughters!" and,"That will really bring about progress for women!" Well, naturally, there was also a gentleman, the father of a daughter, who agreed to rent the house [for the women's section] himself. It was Mr. Abdelsalaam Kabbej, the father of Ftoma Kabbej, who was one of the first women to get a diploma from the Qaraouine. So he rented the house, with money from his own pocket. He also hired women to take care of the house, for example a woman to clean and one to watch over the place. And we, the women, what did we do? Women began to give money, to give jewelry. For example they would give bracelets and other jewelry made of gold. Then they sold the gold; either the women sold the jewelry themselves [and gave us the money] or we collected the jewelry. And it all went towards paying the professors. It was professors from the Qaraouine. They agreed to teach the women, and we didn't pay them a lot, but they agreed to teach. There were about a hundred young women. And after that, they followed all the subject areas of the Qaraouine, right up until they graduated with a diploma.

And that was it for the Qaraouine. Other young women followed a modern curriculum, and they studied all the subject areas leading to the baccalaureate and the B.A. Afterwards, little by little, there were all the secondary schools, everywhere: in Rabat, in Casablanca, in Marrakech, and so on. And the Qaraouine remained the Qaraouine. There were women who got diplomas from the Qaraouine who are now professors, women in various professional positions. And it was from there that it all started. It all started with a little girl who had an idea. But as I told you, when women want something, they have to push for it, to push hard until the door is opened. So that is the question of the Qaraouine.

Yes, Tazi was a student,[11] and then his wife was also a student. They know what I went through in the struggle to create the women's section of the Qaraouine. Because he too was young; he saw the efforts that I was making, and then he admired the women who gave their jewelry and their money. There were members of the *ulama* and professors who really admired what the women were doing. Because for them too, they were helped. Because it's also a question of money; and for them, they made an effort by agreeing to go teach at the women's section—it was a little distance to go—but they also got some money. Because you know, even now, professors don't make a lot of money. So they did two things: to contribute, they sacrificed a bit, but they also profited for the sake of their country and for their own sake. Yes, you know, we did this for years and years. And it wasn't just one professor, there were a hundred, and there were years when everyone was saying they couldn't do this or that. But the young women were really serious in their courses, and they did well in the exams . . . everything, just like the men. And there you have it, that's it.

Yes, that's right, there was also the fight against illiteracy [*maharabet oumia*]. But I can't keep talking about myself, saying "I, I, I" all the time! Around 1942 or 1943, the party—the nationalists—created literacy courses. Well, I played a big role in this; I did the inspection. Yes, the women, the

5.3

Malika El Fassi (1952).

Source: Roqia El Fassi.

women's movement everywhere—Rabat, Fez, Marrakech—decided to adopt
poor children and to send them to school. It was the women who paid. They
gave their gold belts and their necklaces and everything, and we sold these

things, and there were hundreds and hundreds of girls and boys who were illiterate and learned to read and to write. And there were people who continued their studies right up to the baccalaureate—and this was all before independence. All the nationalist free schools gave courses for poor children.

A few years later I met Malika El Fassi again, together with her daughter Roqia.[12] *Our conversation ranged over many subjects, including the leading roles that she had played in the Istiqlal Party and her relationship with King Mohamed V.*

I saw His Majesty Mohamed V on the eve of his exile, at four in the afternoon; I was among a handful of people who saw Him. And he said to me: "If I go away [into exile], I don't want the Moroccan people to stay quiet. I want them to continue the struggle." I said to him: "Your Majesty, I give you my word. Throughout the country, from north to south, until there are no more Moroccans left alive, we will carry on the struggle until you return!" And when he got off the plane, when he returned, I was there; and the first thing he said to me was "Well, here I am!" And I answered: "Your Majesty, here I am!" [In other words, we have both kept our promises.]

I was able to play a great role because at that time I still wore a veil. I did this on purpose in order to move about without being noticed. I went to see the King dressed in a veil and djellaba, so they took me for just an ordinary woman, just a "Fatna." In 1953 [after the exile of the King] I was the one responsible for directing the [Istiqlal] Party, for directing the action. The day that Mohamed V came back, I took off my veil, and all the other women did the same. I said, "Now women have played their role; now it is time to take off the veil."

Yes, the women who participated in the armed resistance are like the others [who participated], like the men. There are some women who have gotten a card. And then there are others who participated in the resistance, like me, for example. I'm on the committee for the resistance, but I don't need to get a card. For people who don't have much in the way of resources, under the reigns of both His Majesty Mohamed V and Hassan II, these people have asked for something to help them. And there are others. . . . But you know there is always this question, for women . . . That's another subject, because women distanced themselves a little. . . . But in fact, those women who were honest and capable . . . For example, there were women who were killed, who were witnesses . . . because they were there, among the men. They played a big role in the resistance. It's not just one or two, but lots of women. There were some who threw hand grenades and bombs. They played a *great* role. The Moroccan woman played a very big role. And all the men recognized the contribution of women. In all the parties, they have always kept their eye on women who were respectable.

My children were raised to be equal, the girls and the boys. One is an architect, one a professor of literature, one an engineer. I always did my best to treat the girls like the boys, without any distinction between them.

6

Zhor Lazraq: Fez, the Next Generation

Zhor Lazraq was born in Fez in 1934, part of the generation that followed in the footsteps of Malika El Fassi. Her family was not wealthy, but they were staunch nationalists, and her father was determined that she should be able to go to school. She got her primary school certificate from one of the nationalist free schools in 1947, and in 1957 was one of the first group of women to graduate from the Qaraouine. Just after independence, a Moroccan delegation was sent to participate in the first international Arab women's conference held in Damascus, Syria. The Princess Lalla Aicha, eldest daughter of King Mohamed V, was the leader of the delegation, and Fatima Hassar, Amina Leuh, and Zhor Lazraq were all members. Zhor Lazraq was in her early twenties at the time, the others just a few years older; they are all photographed dressed in simple skirts and blouses. I asked Amina Leuh why they all wore European dress at a time when Morocco had just gotten free of European domination, and she said no, I had it wrong. It wasn't European dress, it was modern, *emancipated dress. No modern young Moroccan woman in that era would have appeared at an international conference wearing a djellaba. Young women had torn off their veils and put away their traditional dress, just as they had torn away the veils of ignorance and seclusion.*

Of all the young Moroccan women of this new generation, Zhor Lazraq was the most talked about. Women referred to her as Zhor Zarka, feminizing her family name to symbolize her role as a leader in the women's movement. One woman remembers today, "We were always discussing among ourselves, saying Zhor Zarka did this, said this . . ."[1] She passed the Qaraouine university exam at the head of her class; she was known for her fiery debating style and her fierce defense of Moroccan nationalism, Arabic language and culture, Islamic religious principles, and women's rights; she worked tirelessly to improve the status of women, students, and youth. In everything that she did, she was the first and the best, setting an example for other Moroccan women.

In 1963, Zhor Lazraq founded the Association for the Protection of the Moroccan Family, and when I met her, in the spring of 1992, she was still active as director of the association. She was also a researcher at the Institut universitaire de la recherche scientifique *and a member of the Istiqlal Party women's*

6.1

Zhor Lazraq.

Source: Zhor Lazraq.

6.2

Moroccan delegation to 1957 Arab Women's Congress in Damascus.
Left to right: Zhor Lazraq, Fatima Hassar, unidentified woman, Amina Leuh,
unidentified woman, Princess Lalla Aicha.

Source: Amina Leuh.

association. I had heard that she was quite sick, so I was not surprised when I called to ask for an interview to hear that she might not be able to see me. But a few days later she called back, inviting me to come to the Association for the Protection of the Moroccan Family center to attend a Chebana, a women's party traditionally held in the month of Chban, the month that precedes Ramadan, the Muslim month of fasting. I had some difficulty in finding the center, which was located in a working class district of Rabat, but still arrived just about on time, which for such a party is much too early. Hardly anyone was there, and the band was just warming up. I got a tour of the center: a library, classrooms for women's literacy classes, and some areas for children's classes and play areas.

Gradually things got going, more people arrived, there was food and drink and music and dancing, and then Zhor Lazraq herself arrived. She was a small woman, wearing a djellaba and a scarf tied under her chin. Soft-spoken, with a gentle expression on her face, she nevertheless gave an impression of great strength and intensity. At the Chebana party, she moved around the room, the center of attention, with just the right words, a smile, a joke for each person

*there—women of different ages and social classes and even children—quietly
making everyone feel at home; making the party work without any visible effort.*

*A few weeks later I recorded an oral history interview with Zhor Lazraq.
She wanted to go through with it even though she was still very ill and it was an
effort for her to speak. We met in a classroom at the same center in which the
party had been held. Much of the time, Zhor Lazraq spoke more as an observer
and historian than as a participant; even more than other women of the
nationalist movement, she was reluctant to talk about herself. This gives the oral
history a somewhat formal and didactic quality.*

*Zhor Lazraq's views on women seem to have been greatly shaped by the
neo-Salafist thought of Allal El Fassi. Like him she sees the family as the basis
of society and civilization, and sees women primarily in their role as mothers. In
her own life, she has tried to balance family and public responsibilities, to set an
example for other women, and "to do what it was her duty to do."[2] This was a
generation of women whose lives were transformed by access to education, and
a generation who took on adult responsibilities early in life. They had no real
childhood, no time for carefree play. Since 1962, she has devoted her energies
to humanitarian work, which seems to be where her real passion lies.*

*I have kept the interview in the sequence in which it occurred, to reflect
Zhor Lazraq's sense of the flow and meaning of her life story. In 1993, about a
year and a half after this interview, Zhor Lazraq died. I hope that she would be
pleased with this book and with what I have done with the material of the
interview, and that it will be read as a memorial to the life and work of a
remarkable woman.*

In truth, throughout history, the Moroccan woman has been known for
the way in which she has struggled alongside the Moroccan man, both in the
political system and the economic system. Because the Moroccan woman has
never been a woman who didn't work. In cities she worked in industry and
commerce, and in the country she worked in agriculture and trade. And when
colonialism arrived—because Morocco was colonized by France, Spain and a
group of other countries—after the protectorate treaty was signed in 1912,
French armies began to invade each Moroccan city. And each time that they
tried to invade, there were strikes by the inhabitants, and then massacres,
until finally the inhabitants of the city were defeated, because the French
army had great military strength, and had soldiers from Africa, from France,
and others. . . .

Women were there in the cities; I lived through that during my childhood
in Fez. The role that Fez played in the fight against colonialism was very
important, and the colonialists really tortured the people of Fez because of the
role that the city played on the national scene. Because Fez is the city where the
Qaraouine university is located . . . and Islamic scholars and students came to
the Qaraouine from all regions of Morocco.

The women of Fez also played a role in fighting against the colonialists. . . . When the soldiers went through the streets, for example, women in the City of Fez had little windows, which were made so that the woman could see what was going on in the street while no one could see her. Thanks to these windows, the women could throw stones down on the French soldiers and pour boiling water on their heads. . . . And all the rooftop terraces in Fez were full of smooth stones which were used to pin down clothes to dry. So instead of using them to pin down clothes, they used them as weapons to fight the enemy. . . .

The colonialists tried by every means to achieve two things: (1) first, to divide the Moroccans, and (2) to wipe out Moroccan religious spirit and the Arabic language. In that way they tried to make Morocco lose its principles, so that it could be exploited by the colonialist, who took money, phosphates, and so on. They took everything. Of course they built some parts of the railroad, but that was for their own needs, to transport phosphates from one place to another. They also built roads to transport their products to the coasts. And they took all the fertile land. In Morocco, they stifled freedom of thought, even though that freedom existed in their own countries. Their aim was not to bring modernization to Moroccans, but rather to bring the wealth of Morocco to France or to Spain.

So, given these conditions, Moroccan families lived in this atmosphere. Children, when they were born, were born into this atmosphere. We felt that we lived in our country but we didn't profit from its wealth. We lived in our country, but there were no schools, no hospitals, nothing of what had been promised by the protectorate. While Moroccans couldn't find work, the French could, and the Spanish too, and they were put in charge. They earned four or five times what a Moroccan could earn. And it was in this atmosphere that I was born.

So I was born in 1934. . . . By 1937, the problem was that all the greatest nationalist leaders of that era in Morocco were exiled. For instance Allal El Fassi was exiled to Gabon. At that time I was a very young girl, about three years old, but in spite of that I still remember that I heard about Allal El Fassi and the word Gabon. And I understood that it was not an atmosphere or climate for playing, but rather a time for serious things and hard work. I realized that we were threatened and that the situation in Morocco was not normal. This was especially true for me, because the family in which I was educated and grew up was above all else a nationalist family, both my immediate family and the extended family of my uncles, aunts, and so on. They were all members of the nationalist movement. Most of the Moroccan people at this time were members of the nationalist movement, even without a membership card. Because whenever any young person from the nationalist movement would go through the *souk* [market] and say "Close up your shops," all the shops would be closed, in the wink of an eye.

I was born in 1934, so I entered the Koranic school while I was still very young. I started Koranic school when I was maybe three years old. And one of the things that made me unique, or different from other women, was that . . . In Morocco, girls went to the *dar l'fqiha* [house of the *fqiha*], where a woman taught the Koran and held classes for children at her home. And for boys, there was the *msid* Koranic school, and that Koranic school was reserved for boys. But my father, may God rest his soul, noticed that the apprenticeship in the Koran at the boys' Koranic school was better than that at the dar l'fqiha. Because at the dar l'fqiha the fqiha moved around a lot to see what was going on in the kitchen, whether the lunch was finished cooking or not. When her husband came, she had to be ready to welcome him. At the Koranic school, in contrast, once the fqih came in, he didn't leave the school until he left for his lunch, and the lunch was all ready prepared for him at his house. You understand?

So my father asked the fqih, who lived in the same street that I lived in, to take me into his Koranic school. This fqih came from the *Bani-oueryaghn* clan in the mountains, a family who are famous throughout Morocco because of the quality of the apprenticeship in the Koran that they provide. Members of this clan came to Fez to teach the Koran. This fqih didn't need a copy of the Koran when he taught. Each student would begin a verse and he would complete it [from memory]. It was unbelievable how good he was. He set as a condition for my father that he would bring *his* daughter, who at that time wasn't studying either at home or with him at the school, and said that she would sit with me in the place that was reserved for the fqih, a platform a little higher than the floor. I sat down on the platform, and his daughter also sat there, while the boys sat on the floor below the platform. There were just the two of us, the only girls. She only came so that I could go to study there. My father didn't want me to be the only girl among all those boys. He asked the fqih to drop me off at my house each time that he had to leave the school to do an errand, and then to come back and pick me up when he returned. These were the conditions that my father set.

I stayed at the Koranic school and I read sixty chapters of the Koran, and afterwards another thirty chapters. At that time the Istiqlal Party had created private schools [the free schools] that were for both boys and girls. This was among the fundamental goals of the party that were very important for the Moroccan woman. The first work that the Istiqlal Party did, in addition to political work, for women, was to open the door to women's education. That was very important.

So I went to this [free] school, and I spent one and a half years there. Since I had been to the Koranic school I already knew how to read and write, and my father taught me mathematics and other subjects at home. So when I went to the primary school, I spent three months in one grade and then they gave me a special exam and I was promoted to the next grade, and so on. And that was why I only stayed in that school for a year and a half. And besides that, Brahim El Kettani taught me extra classes in addition to the school classes. Since we were the first group with him at the school, and we were the first group that would graduate with the primary school diploma, he was preparing us specially in order that his school would have the highest scores on the exams. So after the other students finished school at five o'clock in the afternoon we stayed with him, and he taught us history and the rules of grammar, and all the other subjects. And we stayed until there was no more sunlight; once it was dark he sent us home. Every day. And in that way we studied more than three hours every day. And we had to learn what he gave us specially, and we had to recite it. We didn't have any time for playing; the time was meant for serious things.

There were very few girls, but there were a lot of boys. So when I got my primary school diploma it was a big event that a group of girls got their diplomas from primary school. It was something of enormous value, because it was the first time in modern history that it happened. . . .

In 1944 there was a very interesting event, while I was still at the Koranic school. The [French] attacked the nationalists and put them in prison, which pushed the nationalists to call a general strike. I was still in Koranic school, and one of the young men—I didn't know him, because I was still very young—said to the fqih, "Send the children home right away!" In just a few seconds the woman who helped my family at home came to the school. She took me on her back and carried me, and she rushed out, running home. At that moment, all the streets were full of soldiers, and there were soldiers and barbed wire on the rooftop terraces. All traffic was stopped. And we were forbidden to go out on the terraces, because there were soldiers keeping a close watch on how the people of Fez reacted. I remember this event in the year of 1944 very well, because they cut off the running water for the houses. And we were very young, and because I was very young, it was the first time that I had taken a pail to go out and get water from the fountain. And when the soldiers saw that I was just a little girl they didn't pay any attention to me.

There were French soldiers, and Africans, Senegalese. They took people who didn't know Arabic so that they wouldn't have any contacts with the citizens. . . . And at that moment, in the early 1940s, we hoped that after the end of the World War we would get our independence. Because Morocco fought at the side of France, and was able to liberate France, which had been colonized by Germany. But when France refused to start down the road of liberating Morocco, relations between Morocco and France were spoiled. And the upshot came when the Istiqlal Party presented a manifesto demanding democracy. Every since 1944 we have demanded democracy. . . .

During these events women had several roles. They took care of feeding and clothing prisoners, and they took care of the families when the head of the family was in prison. Women gave their money and their clothes to help families when the person who took care of the family was dead or imprisoned, and also to help the prisoners themselves. They worked to get money for schools, for education. Because one of the problems that was widespread was the problem of ignorance, and that demanded education, instruction.

They went about helping schools through the intermediary of the Party. The Party would open a school, and there would be a number of young people who would enter of their own accord for classes, and some other young people would sometimes need money to live on. So they collected money from these women and spent it on what was needed for the schools. And it was women who did these things, through the intermediary of the Istiqlal Party.

I got my primary school diploma in 1946 in July, when I was about eleven and a half years old. Around that time Allal El Fassi returned to Fez from his exile [in Gabon]. And Professor Brahim El Kettani sent for me and asked me to come to his place, and when I got to his place we went together to the house of Haj Ahmed Mekouar, where Allal El Fassi was staying. There I swore allegiance to God and to the nation. And the person in whose hands I swore was Allal El Fassi! Then, when I was still a child! And afterwards Professor Si Abdelaziz Ben Driss took me to his place.

Abdelaziz Ben Driss was among the first young people who had proposed the nationalist movement and who founded the nationalist political movement. He was among the greatest of the political leaders, and he was one of those whose actions matched his words. He did everything that he said he would do. He spoke Arabic and also some Berber languages, and he was able to speak with authority on everything concerning politics and religion. In order for the Istiqlal Party to eliminate this force, after independence, they killed him at Tahnout. . . . In truth he was among the great leaders who spoke for Morocco and for all humanity. He was a serious man, patient, and modest. He lived with ordinary people, and sat on the ground with them. Wherever he was, whether he ate a lot or very little, it didn't make much difference to him. What was important to him was to do what it was his duty to do.

It was thanks to Sidi Abdelaziz Ben Driss, may God rest his soul, that I learned how to create the first stages of a secret women's organization, and how to make women work together. He urged me to ensure that women were active in all areas in order to seize our independence and to liberate Moroccan society. I took charge of lots of women's groups. There were the groups that I formed, and there were other groups made up of certain women who trained other women in their neighborhood, and the groups even included women who were uneducated. They too helped and participated, and played a strong role in forming new groups of women, because they had contacts. They brought together groups of women, and asked me to come to explain to them either a tract that the party had sent us or other subjects that we knew, in order to enrich their own knowledge. And in that way we prepared women, whether in the political arena or in letting them know their rights and responsibilities, so that they would become conscious of what the Moroccan woman should do, and the roles that women should play politically and socially. We wanted each woman to know that she was a citizen, that she should not feel that a man was either better than her or worse than her. That is, there is good and bad among men, and good and bad among women. And what was needed was that everyone should do what she had to do.

At that time there was a problem in the Middle East. The problem was that Palestine had its land taken by Israel—the division of Palestine in 1948.[3] . . . And the Moroccan people are strongly attached to their religion, and as the mosque of Jerusalem is one of the three mosques, it is important that it not fall into the hands of colonialism. . . . So for Moroccans it is impossible to ignore the condition of the mosque or of Jerusalem. It is impossible for them to keep quiet and not come to the rescue when they see an act of aggression against a people. Because human rights is not an empty word or a political slogan for us. . . . Moroccans are a people who know human rights in their purest sense, and know that they must be put into practice. The Moroccan people are a Muslim people . . . and Muslims do not allow anyone to do harm to others, or to kill others, or to take someone else's money. People have to get along with their neighbors, with the weak and the poor. . . . So it is not possible to accept the creation of a nation based on one religion. I am free to be a Muslim or a Jew or a Christian, but I am Moroccan. And the Palestinian people in their entirety are Palestinian, but there are some who are Muslim, and some who are Christian, and some who are Jewish. So it doesn't make sense to drive out the Christians and Muslims. . . .

So the Istiqlal Party started sending material aid to the Palestinian people. And the Moroccan woman gave everything she had—money, rings, bracelets, earrings, lots of money—and gave it to the Palestinian people. . . . Moroccan women in 1948 gave a great deal for the liberation of Jerusalem, and this demonstrated the contributions of the Moroccan woman, and gave her a very important political status. . . .

The world situation now requires women to multiply their efforts in humanitarian work. Because I think that women have a big role to play, and it is important that they do it. Women's role is in the education of future genera-tions—the education of women and of men; the education of children to promote humanitarian values, human rights, justice, equality, and the common good. That is a principal role for women. And if they are convinced of this, women can impart these values in the milk as they nurse their children, and in educating them. Maybe they won't succeed 100 percent of the time, because we don't ever succeed 100 percent in educating our children, and that is natural because of freedom of thought and individual personality and many other factors. But we could succeed with a good percentage, so that children would learn these humanitarian principles, allowing for everyone's personality. That is the role of women, what women must do, and what they must think about. And if they do this, by my way of thinking, they will really be good citizens. Because women, whether in Morocco or elsewhere, and I am just taking Morocco as an example, live under a double oppression—the oppression of men by the society and the oppression of women by men. Women live under these two oppressions, whereas men only live under one.

There are lots of rights that women don't have. . . . The majority [of Moroccans] can't find a good hospital, can't find a good school, can't find a good place to live, and those are the necessities for people. They can't find good training or instruction. And we know the problem of unemployment in Morocco, unemployment for young people and for [university] graduates. These things affect both men and women, both women as citizens and men as citizens experience these injustices. Women live in bad housing along with men. All of that should be reviewed so that there is some equilibrium between all citizens. Between all citizens together, without making a distinction on the basis of sex, both men and women. But there is a second injustice that women are subject to which men are not often subject to. That is that women are denied, by certain men, certain rights. For instance, in Morocco, up until the present day, there have been no women in parliament.[4] Up until now women have not been allowed to give their advice on subjects that come before the parliament.

Women lack nothing! Moroccan women now are like Moroccan men in training, gifts and intelligence. . . . So if they are looking for thirty ministers, males, we could easily find thirty female ministers. In Morocco such women exist. For a start they could at least take twenty male ministers and ten female. In my opinion, women should be ministers and men . . . No! I personally don't want to do that. But what I want to say is that women know as much about problems as men do, even more. For that reason, women should help in resolving problems and in giving good advice to the society in which we live. Because no society can look for solutions from a different society. Each society has its own bases, its own capacities, and that is where we should begin. It is not possible to import the sort of solutions that might not suit us. They might even do us harm.

Moroccan women made many sacrifices during the nationalist struggle. They too were arrested; they too were martyrs during the demonstrations. They distributed arms; they distributed tracts. They opened up their houses for the guerrilla fighters and hid them; they hid them in their clothes chests. And then [when the French came], the woman would stand up and say, "There is noone here with me!" with courage, without being afraid. And that is very important. When there was a guerrilla fighter hiding in a woman's house, she would remain calm and courageous, and defend him, and he would get away because she would save him. There were several examples of this.

The Moroccan woman made a lot of important sacrifices. She sacrificed her husband, her children, and also herself, her money, her tranquility. And we know that she stopped using products made by the colonialists. And that, it was the Moroccan woman who did that. She was the one who decided to wear clothes that were made by Moroccan men or Moroccan women. Me too, when I was small, I wore a wool dress, because wool was the only material we produced in Morocco. At that time there were no factories for making clothes. What we had were the *derraza* [the craftspeople who worked with wool], so they made us wool cloth, and we used it for kaftans or dresses. In my family we stopped using glasses for drinking tea. We no longer bought any glasses, and we began to drink tea in cups that were made by Moroccan potters. No more tobacco. Noone smoked anymore, because we did not produce tobacco.

The Moroccan woman played a very important role in all this. We stopped having celebrations. We no longer celebrated marriages the way we do now, because the atmosphere was not right for celebration. So the celebrations were very simple. There was no *neggafa* [the woman who dresses the bride], no pearls, nothing at all. The woman got married and went to her husband's home; her mother and father and the mother and father of the husband, the family and friends ate and drank something, and that was it; they were married. That was in order not to spend too much money. And who was it who was convinced to do it this way? It was the Moroccan woman. Otherwise, if she had not been convinced, she would have forced her husband [to have a big celebration], and we all know what an influence a woman has over a man, especially in the first days [of marriage]! So the Moroccan woman did all that.

I personally participated in a demonstration when they took away Mohamed V [when the French exiled the King on August 20, 1953]. I headed up the demonstration in Fez. Everyone came out into the streets with me, especially women, and so it was a very big demonstration. I ran around to collect signatures on a manifesto protesting against everything that France had done to exile Mohamed V. And at the time that I was going all over the place with this petition with my friends, there were soldiers and barbed wire everywhere. We were dressed in djellabas, and pretended that we had gone out of our houses and needed to get back home, and so the soldiers let us by. In fact we had another purpose, which was not to go back home, but rather to circulate the petition. In that way we got lots of signatures in the city of Fez.

We also held meetings in the mosques. For example, women used to get together in the Moulay Idriss mosque in Fez. The colonialists were forbidden to go into the Moulay Idriss mosque, so we took full advantage of that. We got the women together and we told them everything we had to tell them, and then the women transmitted that information. Even men attended these meetings, and those that were there transmitted the information to those who were not.

I myself distributed notices threatening traitors who were collaborating with the colonialists. I would go right up to the house and put down the notice, and then leave. I put myself in danger. I distributed tracts and transmitted whatever information the party wanted me to transmit. I traveled by bus to go into distant regions such as Immouzen and others, where I transmitted whatever there was to transmit and then returned, even though this put me into danger.

There were lots of things we did for the liberation of our country. For example, I was a member of the Association for Algeria, and we held seminars and meetings for the defense of our sister country Algeria. We felt there would be no independence for Morocco unless there were also independence for Algeria, because Algeria is the heart of the Arab Maghreb, and if the heart is sick the rest of the body is sick. Unfortunately our Algerian brothers forgot all of that and created problems for us, problems which we are still facing right up to the present![5] But Moroccans are generous, and we reacted the way we were taught to react.

The Moroccan woman opened a door that had not yet been opened in the Islamic world. We entered the Qaraouine university, because one of the Istiqlal Party's main aims concerning women was that they should learn and educate themselves, which was what would permit women to liberate themselves. In my opinion that is the right point of view. Because what is necessary for any people is to have knowledge and education. And when I say knowledge I mean it in the broadest sense, whether it be technological training or other sorts of knowledge. Knowledge is a totality, and without knowledge you cannot contribute. It was this that I believe the party understood, and that was why the party was concerned with the instruction of girls as one of its primary concerns. And it was because of this that we were able to go to the Qaraouine university.

I was among the first group of girls that got to the Qaraouine university. Of course the French colonialists were opposed to our being able to study at the university, and they didn't recognize what we were doing at all for four years while we were studying. We didn't know what the future had in store for us, but we studied in secret. The party rented us a house, and we studied in the rooms of this house and on the terrace. We sat on the floor because there weren't any tables or chairs, and the professors from the Qaraouine who came to teach us were paid very little; some even came for free. We went on like that for four years, until finally the colonialists had to recognize us.

Our group was the first to get a degree. It was in 1957. That meant that the Moroccan woman had earned the highest degree that was given by the Qaraouine university. This was the first group of women in the Islamic world to have this diploma, the first from a specialized Islamic university. We girls studied separately from the boys at the Qaraouine university, but we took the exam together, and the exam results came out together. Luckily I passed the exam at the head of my group of women and men in 1957. That had a good repercussion, not for me personally, as I don't consider myself personally worth anything in relation to the people, but for the Moroccan woman, because it gave significance to the Moroccan woman among Islamic peoples, and opened a path for women in a realm of instruction that formerly had been reserved for men.

Of course we organized literacy programs for women, because the problem of illiteracy is greater among women than among men because of the ways in which women are marginalized and kept apart. That is always the case, and that is why we fight illiteracy more among women than among men, so that Moroccan women will have a certain equality with men. . . .

As you know, I came up through all the stages and all the institutes of the Istiqlal Party, including the central committee and the national committee. The Istiqlal Party was the first political party in Morocco in which women could get to a high level politically. Of course I have worked in all the national committees. I was also responsible for, and the only woman on the administrative committee that governed the operations of Fez and its region in the nineteen fifties. That was a very important position, because the administrative committee dealt with issues concerning students, youth, women, and so on. I became a member of the committee because I was convinced that women should fight and take part and be visible. Whenever a woman can do something and doesn't do it she deprives other women of an example. She should serve as a model for other women. . . . It was in that way that our education at the Qaraouine influenced my thought, so that I tried to find a means to balance my work as head of a family, wife, and mother with my work as a citizen belonging to a cadre that is the Istiqlal Party. . . .

The Moroccan woman, thanks to her religious spirit and her sense of responsibility, has always played a primary role in the education of her children and in society. In a general sense, the Moroccan woman has never been inactive. . . . Women always have done sewing and other crafts inside their houses, and they had girls who came to learn this work, such as embroidery, sewing, carpet-making, and the sewing of leather. Take me, for example. I went to school for just half a day, where I read, learned, and wrote on my slate. The other half of the day my parents put me to work learning artisanal skills. It was not in order to have a trade, but rather so that I would know how to make something. Also, you never know what will happen in life, so they directed me and prepared me in these two areas. As a result of this, I know how to do most kinds of artisanal work.

Of course now the Moroccan woman has made a lot of progress. Now she has become a schoolteacher or professor in primary and secondary schools and in universities, and also in other institutions of higher education. Instead of teaching girls at home, now she has factories. Instead of doing business at home she does it in boutiques, and she does different kinds of work. In truth, the woman of 1940 and the woman of 1990 in Morocco are two entirely different women. There is a big difference in terms of upbringing, of education, of the doors that women have opened for themselves, and the doors through which they have entered full of strength and courage. . . .

What interests us, in summing up, is what the Moroccan woman did during colonialism, generally, and during the fight for independence, especially during the forties and the fifties, which were the most difficult years. . . . The Moroccan woman was up to the task. She was a warrior, a nationalist, and she made all kinds of sacrifices. . . . And now, thanks be to God, she is following her road. All that we can say is that the Moroccan woman needs to resist, and to search out the path that is the right one for her, and that will lead her to the things that she wishes for.

7

Rqia Lamrania and Fatima Benslimane Hassar: The Free School Movement in Salé

The city of Salé, situated just across the river from the capital city of Rabat, was an important center of the nationalist movement, and Rqia Lamrania and Fatima Hassar were two of the most prominent women in the movement. First I went to see Aboubakr El Kadiri, a well-known Istiqlal Party leader who founded several nationalist free schools in Salé starting in the thirties, to get his perceptions on the roles of nationalist women in Salé:

"[Before 1944], we had already prepared a few nationalist women; among them Rqia Lamrania and another woman who has died, may God rest her soul. She was a real leader; her name was Batoul Sbihia. And there was also professor Fatima Hassar, maybe you know her. She was still very young when she came to my school; she wasn't married yet. She worked with me at the school; she helped me, and there were some other women too. We got these women together in a group, formed an association, which you might say had three responsibilities, if not more. The first responsibility was a responsibility in national politics. What that meant was that they got women together in meetings to raise their political consciousness. We couldn't begin a renaissance until the spirit was ready. So that was the first important phase for women. The second thing that they began to do was relief work and providing assistance for poor women, for pregnant women when they gave birth, and particularly for those who were poor and lived in the shantytowns, to help them. We created an association that we called the Crescent Association, and that was its role. Lalla Rqia [Lamrania] was the one in charge. The third thing that was very important that women did—very very important—was to help poor students so that they would be able to go to school. Here we began by looking for a house to rent . . . to house those who came from outside of Salé, especially those poor students who had nothing, to provide housing, food, and drink so that they could come and study with us at the school. What the women did was to take care of these children: They paid their expenses; they organized celebrations for them [on religious holidays]. The role the women played was enormous."[1]

7.1

Rqia Lamrania (1995).

Credit: Anne White.

Rqia Lamrania and Fatima Hassar were the only two of the nationalist women whose names were mentioned by women from the armed resistance. While in general, these women didn't have much contact with the nationalist women, several of them remember meetings in Fatima Hassar's house in Salé, a house that served as a refuge and stop on a sort of underground railroad for smuggling people and weapons for the resistance from Tetouan in the north to Casablanca and further south.

Rqia Lamrania

Rqia Lamrania is of approximately the same generation as Malika El Fassi. She is a sherifa, a member of the hereditary aristocracy of direct descendents of the Prophet Mohamed; and her mother was the granddaughter of the Sultan Moulay Slimane, of the Alaouite dynasty, so they are also related to the royal family—King Mohamed V and the present King Hassan II. She is still active in the field of social services,[2] *and, like many women of her class and generation, her life seems to be increasingly centered on family and religion. Since 1961, the year that Mohamed V died, she has made the pilgrimage to Mecca twenty-two times!*

I met with Lalla Rqia at her home, a luxurious villa in the Souisi district of Rabat. An exuberant woman in her early eighties, dressed in a bright yellow kaftan and head covering, she greeted us warmly. Her son, a caid in the Takkadoum section of Rabat, was also there when we arrived. Before he left to go to a meeting, there was joking conversation about Lalla Rqia's age, and about finding her another husband.[3] *She was funny, even bawdy, and there was obvious affection in the bantering relationship between her and her son. Her son suggested that his mother's charm and spontaneity may be partly due to the fact that she hadn't had an education: Maybe if she had gone to school she would have lost some of that.*

As the oral history interview went on, we discovered that another of her sons, who was living in England, had just died eight months earlier. Lalla Rqia was feeling the effects of that, and came back to the subject of her son's death at various times in her narrative.

7.2

Rqia Lamrania with her son, Moulay Abdellah (left) and author.

Credit: Anne White.

I got married—eight years of marriage during which I had lots of children. That one there [her son the caid], my God left him with me. He was the one who was in the resistance, and they were going to sentence him to death. I will tell you his story—it is that one there, Moulay Abdellah the caid.

Almighty God, we worked and we won; we didn't fail. Whereas if someone works and loses, that's much worse. Almighty God gave us the faith that pushed us to [do what we did]. And afterwards, once we had thrown ourselves into the struggle, *hamdoullah* [thanks be to God], God helped us to win. We came through, and our children also came through. They are nationalists and faithful to the cause. That's the main thing. It isn't enough if you yourself have faith, you are true to the cause, and a nationalist, if you then raise children who are against their country and their nation.

[Referring to her son the caid] It's that one there that his father left me with when he was just four years old. The older one, who was five [when his father died], is a professor of education; he taught the Crown Prince in primary school. The oldest is Moulay Ahmed. That one was born in [the month of] *Rajab* and this one in [the month of] *Chaban*. There's only a year between them. When we got independence, they knocked themselves out proposing [government] positions to him. But he told them, "No". He didn't want anything but sport; so in the beginning he was at [the Ministry of] Youth and Sports. And now, it has already been thirteen years that he is [caid] at Takaddoum . . . *Eiwa!* [an interjection] It is for that that he has the blessings of God—for me, and that he doesn't go far away from me. Eiwa! It is for God. And now: Where should I begin?

My father died and left me as a little girl of seven, may God rest his soul. I was born in Meknes. My mother had a brother in Salé; he was born at the moment when the French came in. He was arrested working with ammunition. That was my uncle, the brother of my mother. My own father died when I was seven years old, and then at the end of the year that my father died, my uncle died. I was eight years old. I told you he worked with ammunition. He grew up in Salé, and he never married. He was sick, and sent away for the *aadouls* [Islamic judges], so that his brothers and his sisters would inherit from him, as he was a bachelor. Among them was my mother. They sent her the authority [to travel] so that she could be present to receive her [share of the] inheritance. It was this inheritance that launched me—me and my brothers. She took along my older brother, who was seventeen, to go to the reading of the will. And after that the family stayed united. My mother came, and they were going to separate from them, and she was about to go away, when they told her: "We won't hear of your doing that! We won't stay without the *shorfas.*[5] Now that Alaoui [her uncle] is dead, you're the one who will take his place with us. Go get your children and stay here [in Salé] with us." And that's what happened. So I grew up in Salé. I didn't go to school. In that era, you know, there weren't a lot of schools.

After that, marriage came at the age of eighteen. I got married here in Rabat, and I have two brothers who were also married in Rabat. And as I told you, for eight years I made a whole heap of children. And God brought death—their father got sick. At that time there was fever, typhoid fever, and there wasn't that medicine yet. He was at the age . . . He died when he was about thirty-one years old. And, as I said, he left me with—Moulay Ahmed was five years old, Moulay Abdellah four years old, and Moulay Slimane who just died recently, as I told you, eight months ago. And it was he that I told you about; it was that one there who was left with me by his father when he was three years old. And you tell me how they all managed to study! . . . And you know what those times were like! We struggled. At that time, they studied, and *hamdoullah* they wanted me to marry them when they were still young. So they were married.

Eiwa, Lalla. We've gotten to the nationalist movement. The nationalist movement started in 1935, after the Berber *dahir*. In that era it was rare that a woman would go out. If women got together it was just getting together, up until, hamdoullah, we were injected with a shot of loyalty and nationalism, and the women's movement. We kept going in that area of work. We held meetings; we trained women, right up to 1944. . . . Me, I held meetings at my place, three to four meetings a day in all the neighborhoods, and two days a week. As I told you, it was spirit that kept you going.

When the year 1944 came, the party brought us together, and said, "You know, [after the Independence Manifesto is issued in January of] 1944, the mosques should be filled with the *llatif*." At that time men still didn't get together much with women. They said, "You, you will take care of the women, and get them together in the mosques, and we will take care of the men, so that at that hour the All-Powerful [God] will help us to reclaim our country!" We kept going in this work; we would knock on the door of this lady, and tell her that on Friday . . . and so on. . . . We began to form groups of women, until by January, 1944 there were several groups. We came out from the mosques shouting, "Llatif!" The women came out from the biggest mosque in Salé, from the biggest mosque. We put the men in front, and we came behind! Eiwa!

We got to Bab El Khbbaz [the gate of the baker]. You know Bab El Khbbaz? It was there that the bullets started. It was there that they began, those who fell, who were broken, wounded, dead. Me, as I told you, [I was kept going by] faith. Not a single woman lost her nerve, or said, "[I can't stand it]; I'm going to go back home." In fact the women encouraged each other: the woman who went out to take part said to the woman who didn't go out of her house that if she stayed at home it would be everyone's loss. They said, "Let's go out and get some instruction! We don't know anything yet, and our children are not educated; they're still small. [As for us, even if] we're not educated, we should at least be educated in spirit! God all-powerful gave strength to Islam!"

After [the events of] 1944, people were in prison. The party got us together and we asked what we should do next. The party told us, "You've got to take care of the people in prison and of the families of the people who are dead. For those that are in prison, food needs to get through to them, and for those who are dead, their children, if they are young, should continue to study. . . ." And so we went into the prisons to bring something to eat to those who didn't have anything. Anyone who already had something wouldn't accept anything more. It was he who helped the others, and what's more he said, "Whatever I have, I am ready to share it, for [the love of] God." Hamdoullah, we succeeded in this phase.

Then they said, "What shall we do now? We'll begin to educate girls! What God required of man, God also required of woman, and it doesn't make sense to let people remain ignorant. Now your political work is to figure out how to attract girls so that they want to study." Eiwa! We started to sit down with women, telling them that girls should study, and that they were going to be educated, *hamdoullah*, and that we would win back our country, and that it would be those girls who would fill the positions, etc. . . . And at that time there were some among the women who said that they were ready [to have their daughters educated]; some who said they would see what their husbands had to say; and some who, when they came back, would say to you, "As for us, Lalla, God has created woman for the house, to make children and to bring them up." But we prevailed. It's not that we didn't prevail. We began to teach girls.

I took care of the school fees. To a loyalist we would say, "You don't have to give the money to us. You can pay the school directly for her education. And if, *hamdoullah*, you're able to, in the summer you can buy her some sandals and in the winter some shoes. And you can buy her a coverall [to put over her clothes for school]." But they told us, "No! *Hamdoullah*, we have complete confidence in you." They gave us that *baraka*, [normally "blessing," but here it means money] and out of it we paid for school for them, we dressed them, some sandals for that one, some shoes for that one, for that one. . . .

Eiwa! We had this great ambition, whether it be at work or . . . We asked our lord, Mohamed V, may God rest his soul, to talk with the Minister of Religious Properties and Islamic Affairs about a piece of land . . . It was in Salé, in the place where the ovens are. There were people living in that area down there whose children spent the whole day playing in the dirt and under the sun, and were in the hospitals all the time. We held a meeting, and we decided to begin with these people. The Minister of Islamic Affairs gave us this piece of land. Again there were loyalists who contributed: those who paid for the cement, those who gave money for iron, those who paid the workers at the end of the day. Because in Salé there were sons of [the great] families who didn't need anything; they were very well off, you understand, those from the great houses. You would have to say that the all-powerful [God] helped us a lot. We began with that piece of land.

Dr. Kabbaj came, the medical doctor. Our neighbor came to tell us, "If you want, we'll give you one day a week to see the doctor." One day a week! And what if noone is sick [on that day]! We told him, "No. Whenever anyone gets sick, we will bring him to you. We will give a paper from the association either to his parents, if they are willing, or to him himself, and someone will come to take care of him. But to give us one day! You will be sitting there, and what if noone gets sick?!" And that was how it was, and that is what happened.

After, we held meetings with the party, and the executive committee met with us to give us the party line which we would follow. Hamdoullah, all these things succeeded. Hamdoullah, girls began to study. Girls, hamdoullah, began to develop themselves. In private schools, only primary schools existed; there were no secondary schools. After the primary school level, there was no private school with a secondary school level. So Sidi Aboubakr El Kadiri opened up a secondary school. We got together, and we said, "Here is the school, and we are giving it for God. You, you gave your feet and your tongues for God, and we are giving the school. Now the school has opened. Whoever has a student and can pay for him to attend, welcome. And if he has nothing, the school is open to him anyway." We began it. Who did we begin with? With Mounir Doukkali, who was Minister of Youth and Sports. It was with him that we began. I won't bother mentioning all of the children of people in high positions [who enrolled at the school].

The party was happy, hamdoullah, and the women's movement, which had been asleep—when it was *hshouma* [shameful] to go out and also hshouma to be seen by a man—all of that changed. When groups held meetings, they gave us tracts to educate women in nationalism, and to get them to work [for the cause]. And, blessings of God, the girls that we had taught came and gave these instructions to the women. We got groups together. For example, me, today I would hold a meeting; let's say today twenty would come at three in the afternoon, and twenty would come at five, and twenty at six, like that. With the enthusiasm that everyone had, you couldn't even find a moment to scratch your head anymore. And hamdoullah, we succeeded in our work. The party said, "Now the women's movement has a voice, and the movement has succeeded in what it has done."

It was at that moment that we named ourselves to offices—like, for example, Mme. Hassar the president and me her assistant. We had some women; there are those who are dead; there are only two left now. . . . That's enough. With time, and existence, we have begun to get old.

Afterwards, we went on to the school, the private secondary school. [Students] came to us from Sidi Kacem, among them Mounir Doukkali from Sidi Kacem, and two other students who came with him. I was the one in charge of registering the children at the school. I went to the school and I was seated, and they were seated like that [gesturing to where they would be seated across the room], and they went in to register at Sidi Aboubakr's, and then they came

out and [one] said, "Now one door is open, but there are still two [left]." [The
other] told him, "May God take care of that." I said to them, "Oh, my children.
Me, I am the mother of both girl and boy students. If you have a problem and
you want to tell me about it, I will solve it if I can. If I can't . . ." He told me,
"Oh, Lalla, the problem that we have is a big one." I told him, "If it is a big
problem, God will make it small." And he, may God bless him and keep his
soul, he said to me, "Lalla, we are poor. We don't have any money to spend. We
went to Sidi Aboubakr and registered ourselves, me and this gentleman
[someone who is now in a high position; it's not worth mentioning his name],
and that one there who is a *Slaoui* [someone from Salé]. He was the one who
was our friend, and brought us to the school to register us. But where will we eat
and drink and sleep? There is nothing!" I told them, "Tomorrow at five o'clock
in the afternoon, wait for me here, God willing. If I come and I have solved one
of your problems, I will come and I will call you out of the class."

I went to see Mme. [Fatima] Hassar. She lived right next to the school,
and she gave courses at the school without being paid, and her husband, the
pharmacist Si Larbi Hassar, also gave courses down there. I went to see her, and
greeted her, "*Salaamalikum.*" I told her, "Look; this is how it is." At that
moment, she called her Dada:[6] "Yasmine!" She asked her, "The room that you
have down there; what's in it?" She answered, "There are some boxes belonging
to Sidi Larbi, some medicine from the pharmacy." She told her, "Call M'Barek,
and get him to take these boxes upstairs, and take two beds down to the room.
And it is you, Dada, who will take care of everything. Me, I don't know them.
You will make up two pots, one full of coffee and one of milk, and everything
else that we have for breakfast. You're in charge of preparing it for them. Leave
them alone in the mornings; let them get up by themselves. Don't get up with
them. Show them the refrigerator so that they can take everything that they need.
They should have their breakfast and leave. And for lunch, if I have guests, I
will take their portion and put it aside for them. And if, on the other hand, I am
invited out for lunch, it's the same thing."

The next day, I met them at five in the afternoon. I told them, "There, sirs,
I found you a little bit of a solution!" One of them laughed. [He later became a
lawyer.] He asked me, "Oh, Lalla Sharifa, how did you manage to divide them
up, when they were problems that didn't divide up?" I told him, "But I have a
condition for you." He asked me, "What is the condition?" I told him, "This
house where I will take you is an honorable house, and educated people . . . and
you too will be educated. But what I ask of you is that you should never show
any bad side. Never talk to the girls at school, or ask a boy to study with you at
the house, or anything else like that. The house is a place that is entrusted to you
two, nothing more!" They told me, "Lalla, since you have opened this door for
us, the worst thing that could happen would be for you to see us do something
bad." "Then let's go! Get going!"

I took them; "Welcome, and so on . . ." I told them that the house was theirs, as though they were at their own home, and that I was like their mother. "And here is your Dada Yasmine, if you need anything at all, dishes, or anything at all. You'll take care of breakfast yourselves, and lunch. . . ." Eiwa, may God increase his grace, that very day, before nightfall, they came to spend the night in the house.

That day, may God give us his grace, was a Monday. On Thursday, we had a meeting, every Thursday. We said that the first thing to bring up at the meeting was this important question of the students. I told them, "Now there are just two students, and tomorrow there will be ten, and afterwards twenty, and we could get to hundreds of students." Because Sidi Aboubakr's school was the first private [secondary] school opened in Morocco. Neither Rabat, nor Fez, nor Meknes had a private secondary school. Before the end of the year, we had 78 students . . . [and we went on] up until we had 282 students.

God is witness, on the day of the feast, we left our own children at home. And we went, each of us, one would prepare *ghaif*, another a table of *b'gher*, another fried *crèpes*.[7] Each woman made something, and then we went to spend the day of the feast with the students, and even to eat breakfast [with them] in the morning. We spread out the carpets in the middle of the house, and sent for some mattresses to be brought and put them down in the middle of the house, and we sat down there with [the students]. And me, I prepared the tea. The students were really happy. Sidi Aboubakr El Kadiri came down after the prayer [at the mosque] and stopped by there, and congratulated us. He told us, "Bravo and congratulations for having left your own children to come and be with those who are separated from their parents!" We took the place of their parents.

Eiwa! Hamdoullah! Everything went well. The [Istiqlal] Party was happy with everything we did. They began to give us tracts [to read] to groups [of women]. We would organize meetings of the association; we had become official [party] members. Eiwa! In any case, we did those things.

Now I had a house in Rabat—I still have it; it is our grandparents' house—and whenever I left [the house, to go back to Salé], we lifted up the mattresses and put them against the walls, and we put the pillows on top of them, and we covered them up with sheets. Because then when I came back, we cleaned the floors before putting everything back in place. On that particular day, I had brought the slave with me, and this slave I had was a little inclined to gossip. Eiwa! I told her, "Yasmine! You tidy up the room downstairs, and I'll go upstairs to dust off the pillows and the sheets." Now the room upstairs has a door which opens onto the terrace. I spread out the carpet and I was beginning to dust the cushions, when a revolver fell out. I took it, and I found five bullets. And then I found some other revolvers. That's it; good! I put everything back in the cushions the way I had found it. I covered everything with the sheets. But I have three sons. Who will I tell this to? And what if the one I tell it to didn't know anything about it? All right. I went downstairs. I told her, "Yasmine!" She said, "Yes, Lalla?" I told her, "That's enough for us. We'll just fix up the rooms downstairs, and we'll leave those upstairs for tomorrow or the day after." She said to me, "We still have the afternoon." I told her, "No. That's enough [for today]."

[I went] directly to the prefecture. . . . At six in the evening, I was standing there at the entrance, and there [my son Moulay Abdellah] was coming out. "Lalla, what did you come here for?" I told him, "Oh, my son, I was just dropped off here by the bus." He asked me, "Where were you?" I told him, "I was in Rabat." "Where did you go [in Rabat]?" I told him, "My son, we went to fix up the house there. It's not good for it to stay with all that dust." He said to me, "Ah? Where? How did you fix it up?" I told him, "Well, I just cleaned it up. You take out the mattresses and put them in the sun, you dust them off, and also the cushions, and then there's the cleaning . . ." He asked me, "Did you clean up the upstairs?" I asked him, "Do you have something upstairs? Well, that's the reason that I came here. Now, that's it!" I told him, "Now, my son, that's it. I didn't know if they belonged to your brother Moulay Slimane or your brother Moulay Ahmed. That's why. Now it's O.K., done. And me, now I have the great joy to know that, hamdoullah, I have brought into the world a son who will defend his country. It isn't that I have educated him, and it's not the spirit of nationalism or the spirit of Islam; it is a gift from God." Eiwa! He began to embrace me, and took me in his arms, and we went up to the house by automobile. Goodbye, goodbye . . . I don't know you, and you don't know me, and the prayer be on the Prophet!

Me, I took care of the wives of the resistance fighters. The day when Mohamed V, may God rest his soul, returned [from exile], the party made up a logo which contained some hands drawn in red with chains on them. And we carried [that banner]—the wife of Filali on one side, and me on the other, and the wives of the resistance fighters marched with us. At the entrance to the palace, Mohamed V went in, riding in a convertible. . . .

Eiwa! We continued our work. When Mohamed V came back, we constituted ourselves officially as the Red Crescent unit of Salé, and we got authorization to work the way we wanted to. We didn't have to work secretly anymore. . . . Let's get back to those students, who didn't have anywhere to eat or drink. We got together with people from the party who were from the grass roots. We told them that these children needed somewhere to eat and to drink. Sidi Aboubakr El Kadiri told them, "At the end of the month, the association of orphanages [is meeting, and will elect its officers]. When we have the voting, we will elect Lalla Rqia. If she is elected to [be president of] the association of the orphanages, these children will begin to have a place where they can eat, whereas if someone else is elected, they won't allow these children to eat and drink there." So in fact, your little mother [I] was elected president. There were

7.3

Women greeting King Mohamed V on his return from exile in 1955.
Left to right: Khaddouj M'stsa (wife of Omar Sbihi), Seida Touria (wife of Assafi),
King Mohamed V, Rqia Lamrania, Saadia El Kadiri, Rqia Znebria.

Source: Rqia Lamrania.

some loyalists among us, some nationalists among them, including a certain Sidi
Mohamed Beggali. When the French knocked on his door during the night, they
wrapped him in a black burnous and took him away. He disappeared for one
year, being tortured [by the French]. So I told them, "No!" [Beggali] was going
to be my assistant, but I told them, "No, Sidi Mohamed [Beggali] should be the
president."

And the women that I had organized in meetings came to say that they
were ready to put their shoulders to the wheel. We always brought the old
women, those who didn't have a child or a husband, who were widows, and we
took them to the orphanage. These women went to wash and rinse themselves
off, to comb their hair—in short, they made themselves at home. We went there
with a platter of cakes, and we sat down with them to keep them company at the
orphanage.

Now we have the family welfare association. The president is Madame
Ghallab. I work with her now; me, I'm the assistant to the treasurer. I told them,

"I'm no longer capable of working; let me be." But she told me, "No, you . . ." I told them, "I'll rob the treasury, and then I'll leave!" We also have girls who didn't succeed at their studies, so we created centers to teach embroidery and sewing. And when they succeed, they leave with a diploma, and we tell the authorities to help, and most of them have opened up places for these girls. . . .

Even now, hamdoullah, you can't say that there is noone who will succeed us. That is to say, those [women] who will succeed us have already been to school; they are educated. But I understand them; they have a lot of responsibility. Now, every woman who is educated works. And besides her work, it's also up to her to take the children to school; at noon, it is she who has to go and get them. She's the one who has to do the marketing. The man doesn't know how to do anything anymore. We have no idea what he does anymore! He should tell us what work is left for him to do!

Now sometimes I feel tired. My son comes and tells me, "Lalla, I see that you are tired." I tell him, "I didn't sleep well; that's all." And me, I pray to God that my legs continue to hold me up. But to go to bed and miss a meeting or something like that?! [Not a chance!] We're still at it.

We went to see Mohamed V the morning of the festival, may God rest his soul, and he said to the ministers who were standing there, he said to them, "Those there, those [women's] associations, they contribute money from their own pockets, and they don't get any pay, but they're the ones who are raising the sons of the nation and arming them with knowledge. What I ask you to do, is to encourage them, so that they don't fall back." And in fact they did help us. Whenever we went in to see a minister from whom we wanted something, we would go with two or three of us. When we sent in our card, saying that we were there to visit him, the minister would come out of the meeting [he was in], and go to the room where he received people in order to show us in. We wouldn't leave his place until we had the paper signed that we had gone there for. We asked the Minister of Education about the students after the school year and during the summer. These students didn't have anywhere to go. I went to the prefecture to make them passports. Noone said no [to our requests]. When I went to [the Ministry of] Education for scholarships, I didn't leave until I had gotten twenty or thirty scholarships for [the students] who didn't have any [money].

Eiwa! The people [then] were patriotic and cared about one another. But today, excuse me, even if there is wealth here in Morocco . . . Unfortunately, I will say this in all truth, in truth, if these rich people gave at least the tithe that God advises, then we wouldn't have any more poor people left to give money to.[8] At least they should give it to those poor students who have nothing, not even enough to live on, and to widows. . . . There are people who sometimes go for two or three days without eating anything, and without daring to ask for anything. And we, hamdoullah, will go look for them. . . . When Morocco wasn't that wealthy, there were loyal people. I told you, a nationalist who had been tortured would say to you, "No, come here. I'll share what I have with you."

And Sidi Aboubakr [El Kadiri] said, "Oh, if Lalla Rqia had been educated, woe unto us!" But in any case, I can read a little bit—an article, the paper, the Koran, hamdoullah. You know, there was this woman who, when we were together and I opened a book, she would say, "But Lalla Rqia Lamrania, you spend all day away, and then you come back and open up a book. Please, let's talk a little and gossip together." But hamdoullah I had a little intelligence, and an empty head. . . .

To tell you that we're still at it . . . [After independence] my son Moulay Abdellah became the director of the central prison, the one in which he had been a prisoner. I was sitting down [at home] one day, when two letters came from the Ministry of the Interior, from the person who took care of things concerning members of the resistance. I telephoned Moulay Abdellah, and I told him, "My son, I just got two letters from the [Ministry of the] Interior, and they are contacting both of us." He said to me, "Go ahead, Lalla; if it's necessary I will let someone take my place here and I'll go, but if there is nothing, you, you know, that's your job." So I went [to the ministry]. When I got there, he said to me, "Where's Moulay Abdellah?" I told him, "Moulay Abdellah is now at the prison where he was a prisoner; he is the director. If you want him, and it's necessary, he'll come here." He told me, "I'm going to give you these papers to fill out, so that you can make a request, because some agréments and also some money will be distributed." Eiwa, God is witness and sees everything! I told him, "Look, my son. As for me, my son worked and he is still working. There is enough for us to live on, hamdoullah. So give that to the people whose parents are dead, and who have been left as orphans; to those whose capital was used up during the strikes, and whose stores were closed for so long that they were ruined. Those there, they deserve it. We, on the other hand, have enough to live on, hamdoullah, and we don't want to be paid. And me, I told you, what am I going to do with an agrément? Hamdoullah, we have enough to eat and to drink!"

Fatima Benslimane Hassar

I met Fatima Hassar in her offices at the Moroccan League for the Protection of Children in Rabat, where she is executive director. An imposing woman, she was elegantly dressed in a business suit, and greeted me in impeccable French. The interview was in French.

Fatima Benslimane was born in 1928 in Fez, into a well-known Fassi family, but grew up and went to French public schools [primary and secondary, all the way to the baccalaureate] in El Jadida. Malika El Fassi came to visit the

7.4

Fatima Hassar (1995).

Credit: Anne White.

Benslimane family in El Jadida once, while Fatima was still a child. Fatima was so impressed that afterwards she went to her parents and said, "I want to grow up to be like that woman."⁹

Fatima passed her baccalaureate in Casablanca in 1949 and studied at the university in Rabat from 1951 to 1953.¹⁰ Shortly after passing her bacca-laureate, she was engaged to be married to Larbi Hassar, a pharmacist, and moved to Salé, where her fiancé lived. They were married in 1952. For the oral history interview, Fatima Hassar started by giving a summary of her early life and then started at the beginning, describing what it meant to her to live in a nationalist home.

First, I had the good fortune to live in a family of nationalists. That's very important. My grandfather [because my father was dead], my grandmother, my uncles, all were in the nationalist movement. I had a grandmother who was extraordinary. She said, at that time, that girls should have the same rights as boys, and that they should have the same education as boys. And I think that it was her conviction that made it possible for me to continue my studies to the level of secondary school and even beyond.

In the city of El Jadida we had a rather significant nationalist movement. It was the Istiqlal [Independence Party]. There was nothing but the Istiqlal, the Istiqlal movement. And our role, the way in which we participated was to give literacy classes to older women. Just think of it! A girl of twelve or thirteen who is teaching classes to older women! That already marks you. At that age, I had already begun to give literacy courses to older women, and afterwards we also gave courses to girls who didn't have a chance to go to a regular school.

After that, there was the speech given by the Princess Lalla Aicha in 1947. It was really a revolutionary speech, a speech which called for the liberation of the Moroccan woman. And I think that for my generation, it's from that point that women's participation [in the nationalist movement] began. That's not to say that women didn't participate in the nationalist movement before that time, in all areas—political, cultural, economic—all areas. But I think that [Lalla Aicha's speech in 1947] was the starting point, for our generation and for the generation that followed us. Because if there had not been that speech, maybe my generation would not have been able to pursue higher education, and maybe we would not have been able to participate as fully as we did in achieving the independence of the country, as well as in the economic and social development of the country.

There was that; and there was also 1948, which made an impression on us: the time of the occupation of Palestine. That made a lasting impression on me. In my family, it was a day of mourning. I still remember that my grand-mother—I always talk about my grandmother because she was an extraordinary woman—my grandmother brought us together and said to us: "For us, as Arabs and Muslims, this is a great day of mourning in the history of the Arab world and the Muslim world. And we Arabs cannot say that we are free from colonialism until Palestine has become the land of the Palestinians again." That marked me. I think that it also made a great impression on others of my generation, but I know that for me it was decisive. And every time we started something after that, [my grandmother] would say, "Don't forget our Palestinian brothers." And then she told us, "Learn the French language. It will be a weapon in your hands; because to understand someone, you have to understand his language and his culture."

Those were two things that really made an impression on me, and that may have pushed me to get an education. Then, since I was the only Moroccan and the only Arab in the class, I had to show that Moroccans were also capable of being among the best, and of having good grades; that they were capable of speaking. When I would speak up during discussions, it was also a form of struggle for Moroccan independence. Oh yes, there were some stormy discussions, especially when the Germans had occupied France. We said to our classmates, "*You're* the ones who are colonized; you've been colonized by another power, Germany!" That lasted for four or five years.

There were also the events of 1944, after the Independence Manifesto. I was in Salé then, and there were demonstrations there at that time. No, I myself didn't participate, but I watched; I saw what happened. There were people from my husband's family—I had no idea that I was going to marry him then—who participated in these demonstrations. And everyone was talking a lot about the Independence Manifesto, and about the demonstrations. There were some women, two of them I think, who were killed that day in Salé.

So after I passed my baccalaureat exam in Casablanca, I became engaged and came to Salé, and that was a change for me. I taught in a free school—translation, French language. My husband—at that time my fiancé—taught mathematics, physics, and chemistry, all in Arabic. It was the first time that those subjects had been taught in Arabic. And the first Moroccan Arab to get a baccalaureat graduated from this school. [This was very important], because we were also engaged in a struggle to demonstrate that the Arabic language could be as precise and scientific as French, and that the schools created by the nationalists educated cadres that were equal to, or even superior to, those that were educated in other schools. So in Salé I had the good fortune to be in a school where all the professors were nationalists. People came to teach without being paid, without any salary at all, and that was very important. Yes, almost all [of the professors]. I am speaking about the school in Salé. We were all there to teach young Moroccans, without being paid. And there were families [who helped to support the school] by paying expenses for the children who came to pursue their studies. That was what made it possible for the school to work. [They paid] for children who weren't from their families; every family paid for one or two children. It was that that made it possible for a great number of children who didn't have the means to pursue their studies. And we encouraged the education of girls. It was there, for the first time, that we had coeducational classes with boys and girls [studying together]. The director of the school was Mr. Aboubakr El Kadiri, and I would say that my encounter with him also marked me; he was extraordinary.

Around 1951, I had begun to take care of the women's section of the Istiqlal Party in Salé, in addition to teaching. So what was our role? My responsibility was first of all to encourage and sensitize parents so that they would send their girls to school to pursue their primary and secondary school studies. We were even able to send the first girls from Salé to the teachers' college in Fez! That was revolutionary at that time! A real revolution! Afterwards, we wanted to do political education, civic education among women. At that time we even began to do some education in sanitation and hygiene, and courses in basic education.

Then, to help young people who weren't from Salé to pursue their studies, we created a place for students to live, for boys who came from the region of Figuig in the south of Morocco, so that they could pursue their studies and pass their baccalaureat in Rabat. Because at that time the school in Salé was the only one [in all of Morocco] which prepared students for the Rabat baccalaureate exam. So there was student housing, and it was the women's section of the Istiqlal Party which took care of housing and feeding these students, without any compensation. Some women took care of managing the house, while others took care of everything else that the boys needed. And at the beginning, when we didn't have the dormitories, we asked a family in Salé to give us a saint's tomb [*marabout*], and we created student housing there. We put two beds in each little room, one for each student.

Above all, that [work to support students in the school] enabled us to raise people's awareness in an area that was very important—education. Because we said, "Now we are fighting for independence, but we need to train cadres for the future." That was in 1951, and [at that point we thought that] the colonizers would only stay for another year or two. So in 1951 things began to move in Morocco; then in 1952 there were the arrests following the assassination of Ferhat Hachad. Mr. Aboubakr El Kadiri was arrested; a great number of people were arrested, [including] several professors. And at that moment we wanted to show—we, the women—that everything that had been started by men could be continued [by women]. And it was, with the help of two young men who were responsible for running the school.

So everything continued [at the school]. At the same time, we created a section of social affairs in the heart of the Istiqlal Party, and we took care of all the militants who had been arrested. We had to take care of the prisoners who were in prison, as well as their families. It was important that the action of the Istiqlal Party continue, as it had been, and that the school continue. Those were four important things, and we succeeded in making everything work.

Then there was the arrest, the exile, of Mohamed V in 1953. I will always remember that day. They came to arrest my husband at five o'clock in the evening, and I had just had a baby, just three months earlier; they searched our house and everything. And then, at two o'clock, we knew that His Majesty had been exiled. Well, the first people who came out into the streets were the women. And both men and women took part in demonstrations in the streets of Salé. . . .

And our struggle continued for all that time: From 1953 to 1956, we kept the school going, as I told you. We stayed involved with the families whose parents were in prison. It was important that the families keep on living just as though their parents were there. And we continued with our political action in the resistance, and with our political work. Here, the Moroccan people—and I don't say this just because I'm a Moroccan—is a people who can set an example of solidarity. There was an extraordinary solidarity—between classes, between men and women—there was no problem. We conducted political action, social action, and cultural action, simultaneously; because it was important that education not stop. At the same time we were able to do something new—to organize the first vacation colony, for girls and boys, in Salé. Me, I took care of the girls, and Mr. Radé, from the UNFP, took care of the boys, and we organized the first [coeducational] vacation colony for girls and boys. It was a real revolution!

Then there was independence, and at that time, after independence, we created—I'm talking about Salé—associations to continue our action in the social arena. All right, the activists had been freed, but now there was a whole other problem, a whole program we had to carry out. We had to continue our action in the area of education. So we created a section for scholarships for children who didn't have the means to finish, to pursue their studies. We were equally concerned about the education of girls, and there were as many girls at the school as there were boys. Afterwards, we also emphasized everything that had to do with the struggle against illiteracy. We began literacy courses for older women; and [as a result] there are lots of women today, who are eighty years old, who learned to read at that time. So, literacy.

Afterwards, [we focused on] the raising of women's consciousness. We were organized into cells, and we started to give courses every week. And it was girls of fourteen and fifteen [who taught the courses]; we gave the girls [the responsibility] of starting that program. Our most important goal was to give these girls a civic, political education [I'm talking about girls of fourteen or fifteen who were going to school]: To say, *here* is the history of Morocco; *here* is how it was during the protectorate; *here* is the nationalist struggle conducted by the Istiqlal Party. It's thanks to this struggle that we have arrived at this point. And you too have a struggle to engage in, the struggle against underdevelopment. You can't just say we're independent, we're here. The struggle for us, for us as Moroccan women, is a continuous struggle. First, against the colonizer,

7.5

Istiqlal Party women's meeting. Rqia Lamrania in front row, far right;
Fatima Hassar in second row, second in from the right.

Source: Rqia Lamrania.

and now, against underdevelopment. Normally girls of fourteen and fifteen who
go to school don't have these problems; but they should never forget that before
arriving at that point, Morocco had to go through several stages. So that was
[what we did] for the young girls.

As for women—those who were in the cells of the Istiqlal Party, fighting
for independence—we needed to show them that it was also necessary for them
to evolve: Thus the struggle against illiteracy. They too needed to continue to
struggle against underdevelopment. For example, women who did artisanal
work could organize themselves into cooperatives, or they could . . . do something. We said to women who didn't have the means to send their daughters to
school, "No! The first priority is to send girls to school. We're ready to give you
a scholarship so that you can send your daughter to school." For the girls who
had arrived at the level of secondary school [brevet], we said to their parents, "It
isn't enough! Send them on to teachers' colleges." As for the young people who
had gotten their baccalaureate, we said to their parents, "No! All you have to do

is come to us, and your children can get a scholarship. The baccalaureate is nothing, [it is not enough.]" You see, it was a whole process of raising people's consciousness about the future.

So we began; we were already organized into cells. Afterwards there was the first congress of the Istiqlal [in December, 1955]. I was there. At that time we had already demanded that women have the right to vote, and be eligible to hold public office, and that women have the same rights as men, already, at that congress. And you see now that the Moroccan woman is a voter and eligible to hold office. Unfortunately there is no woman in parliament, but I think that there will be. . . . The essential thing is that the right exists, in documents.

Then, in 1956, at the same time that we continued to work actively in the Istiqlal Party, there was the creation of the National Alliance for Social Welfare [*Entraide Nationale*]. At that time I was already a member of the national council of the Istiqlal Party. When the Alliance for Social Welfare was created, His Majesty designated the Princess Lalla Aicha to head it [and me to work with her]; and that was what opened up all areas of social welfare work for me, and enabled me to discover them at the national level. And really for me, this was fascinating, and I really flourished in this domain of social welfare. And I think that you can't separate the social from the political or the political from the social; because politics has its roots in a social program, and social work has its roots in a political will. So you can't possibly disassociate the social domain from the political domain. At the same time that the Alliance for Social Welfare was created, the Moroccan Red Crescent was also created, and His Majesty designated me to work with the Princess Lalla Malika in the Moroccan Red Crescent Society.

Then, at that time, I participated in the first delegation of Moroccan youth to go to the first youth festival, held in Moscow. For me that was a sensational discovery; I met youth leaders from all over the world. There were two women in the Moroccan delegation, me and Madam Zhor Lazraq. We traveled along much of the same road. Afterwards, when I came back from Moscow, two months later, there was the first congress of Arab women in Damascus; and I was fortunate also to be designated by His Majesty to accompany the Princess Lalla Aicha to this first congress of the Arab woman. So you see, this was in the space of just two months, and I think that that was *very* important for me, to discover youth on an international scale, and to discover the activities of the Arab woman. We had been cut off from the Middle East, because we were under the French protectorate; so women in the Middle East didn't know about the Moroccans: They thought that Moroccans were illiterate. And we ourselves didn't know anything about the Arab woman. So I think that these two contacts at the same time gave me some new horizons.

So we could say that the struggle for youth is the same all over, and the struggle for women is the same all over; and there we had met women from all the independent Arab countries. There was only Algeria that was not yet independent at that time. No, there was no representative from Algeria. In 1957, Tunisia had just gotten its independence. If you want to say which delegations were the most important, those would be Syria, Libya, no . . . Egypt, and Lebanon. Those were the largest and most important delegations. Afterwards, I participated in several congresses that were Arab congresses, with Arab and African women, to support the Algerian struggle for independence. I remember that the first Arab-African meeting took place in Cairo, and it was the Moroccan woman who fought for the Algerian cause. I was sensitized to the Algerian cause, like all Moroccans, because Moroccans fought for seven years for Algerian independence. After Moroccan independence, we fought for the independence of Algeria. His Majesty set the example, and the Princess Lalla Aicha, and all the political parties; all of them fought [for Algerian independence]. In the Alliance for Social Welfare I took care of refugee Algerian students. These were Algerian students studying in Morocco, and we allowed them to get Moroccan passports so that they could go abroad to do their university studies. So I had a great deal of contact with Algerians; and we also took care of Algerians in [refugee] camps, Algerian families who were in Morocco. And I can assure you that the Princess did extraordinary work in providing aid to Algerian families who were in Morocco. On the moudouana. Yes, there was Allal El Fassi; it was he who reviewed the moudouana . . . you must have read about that. Now there is a group of women who say that we should reexamine some aspects of the moudouana, especially the question of divorce. Because polygamy doesn't exist anymore in Morocco; there is only about .06 percent. There's the question of the age of marriage—now it is sixteen years old [fifteen years and six months or sixteen years] for the girl, and eighteen years for the boy. Something else that's important—before, the bride was not present. Now the bride is present, and she signs the register herself. She can set conditions for the husband, at the time of the Marriage Act, saying that she must have the freedom to work, or that he can't marry a second wife, and that if he mistreats her she herself has the right to demand a divorce. What's more, in the Islamic religion, women have the right to conduct business without the authorization of their husbands. You have only to look at the life of Lalla Khadija, the first wife of the Prophet. The Moroccan woman is independent in everything that concerns her property; she can even designate another person outside of her family to take care of her property. So you see, the Islamic religion gives independence to women in everything that concerns the material side of things, all property that belongs to the woman. What we are asking for now is to put [those laws] into practice. There are several people at the commission [that is reviewing the moudouana] who aren't very well informed; who will tell you that there is polygamy, and talk about the verse in the Koran . . . They tell you, you can marry a second, a third wife, if you put them on the same level, and treat them absolutely equally. And that's not possible. Afterwards they say that the thing that God most condemns is divorce. So I think that the most difficult problem is the problem of divorce; that is the most difficult. Yes, yes, we discussed the moudouana with the secretary general, Mr. Allal El Fassi. At that time then, it was a revolution! And now there are some parties, and [some people] in parliament, who think that there should be an evolution [in women's rights under Islamic family law]. . . . But women already have the same rights as men in public functions. In all areas, in the workplace, women have the same rights. Well, in terms of responsibility in the home . . . Unfortunately even in the United States men don't have the same responsibility in the home as women.

8

Oum Keltoum El Khatib: Casablanca

I remember that when I was still a little child, my grandmother carried me on her shoulders and taught me the patriotic songs that Moroccan women used to sing to put courage into the souls of men at the time of the wars of Abdelkrim in the Rif. The women of this era used to sing, "Lalla,[1] oh Lalla, listen to the sound of the guns across the river!" When they heard the thunder of canons and the whistle of bullets, they used this refrain to signal the others across the mountains. And the others would call back, singing, "The men wear the djellaba, but we, the women, are the ones who have prepared them and sent them to war!" And again, "Lalla, oh Lalla, I still keep my pride, even if the colonizer is here!"[2]

Oum Keltoum El Khatib talked for more than three hours, holding us all spellbound as she wove a rich tapestry of history, memory, and myth. At the end, she herself was surprised by how much she had remembered, how much came back to her as she talked. She said it was the first time that she had ever told all these things in one continuous narrative.

We[3] arrived at Oum Keltoum's villa in Casablanca at four o'clock in the afternoon on March 3, 1992, which in that year was a few days before the start of Ramadan.[4] Oum Keltoum and her husband, Benacer Harrakat, greeted us, and took us into the long rectangular salon, arranged, like most Moroccan salons, with brocade-covered sofas and cushions running along all four walls. We sat down around one end of the room; I explained what I was doing; and then Oum Keltoum began to talk. She was wearing dark-tinted glasses, and covered up in a dark-colored kaftan and scarf. Gradually, through the late afternoon, the light faded, and people's forms blended into the dark background of the cushions, while Oum Keltoum's voice spun out the story of her life.

At one point we were offered sweet mint tea, along with some especially rich Moroccan pastries and cakes that had already been prepared for Ramadan. Later, glasses full of fresh, milky banana juice were served. Two or three times in the session, her husband spoke briefly to clarify a point. We were all surprised, at the end, to discover that it was almost eight o'clock in the evening and had been dark for some time.

Like other nationalist women, Oum Keltoum stressed that Moroccan women have always worked—even those in seclusion embroidered and sewed at

8.1

Oum Keltoum El Khatib, with the author on left (1995).

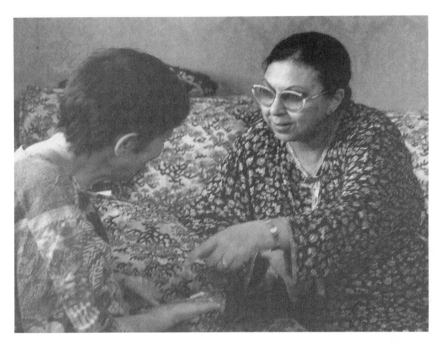

Credit: Anne White.

home—and that women often ended up as the sole support of their families, when their husbands died leaving them with six or seven children. Nor were Moroccan women ignorant, even if they had no formal schooling.

The Moroccan woman knew how to heal people with herbs. . . . As for me, I still use the medicinal herbs that my mother used before me to cure serious illnesses. That knowledge isn't written down; it would be lost without the Moroccan woman.

In the twenties, Moroccan women played a role in the Rif War; and in 1937, when the nationalists were put in prison by the French, women reacted by declaring an end to celebrations and the wearing of henna.

Because henna was a symbol of joy and was worn during celebrations, at women's Chebana parties in the month before Ramadan and on the twenty-seventh day of Ramadan. It was the Moroccan woman who decided not to wear henna or make-up anymore, to go into mourning. They sang, "Don't put on henna! Don't put on make-up! The children of the motherland are in prison!" So there were no more celebrations. If a man got married, it was quietly, whereas before we used to celebrate for seven days, with musical groups and everything. But now, a bride would travel to her husband's house in silence. Another sign of mourning was that Moroccan women no longer wore their jewelry, or at least very seldom. Even when a woman gave birth, there was no celebration, and instead of the presents that were usually given on such an occasion, they took a platter and covered it with a cloth colored red like the Moroccan flag. And people gave what they would usually give as presents to the new mother to the nationalists instead, or to help those who had a family member in prison.

There was a train that passed by close to our house, and when my grandmother saw it go by, she wept, saying that the children of the motherland were going into the French colonial armies to fight in World War II. But when, on the other hand, Moroccan men were going to fight the colonizers, then we were happy. The Moroccan woman was very well aware of the political situation at the time.

And what is special about the Moroccan experience—and what we are most proud of—is that we Moroccans had no help from foreign countries, unlike other countries. Morocco got its independence by itself, and never had any help from anyone, except for some assistance in arms from Egypt in the 1950s.

I was born in Fez in 1935, and moved to Casablanca when I was six months old. The family El Khatib is known for its nationalism. When I opened my eyes, it was in a nationalist home. My grandfather worked as a carpenter and woodcarver. That was hereditary in our family, passed down from my grandfather to my father. When I was born, my grandfather was just finishing building the mosque *l'Mouhamedi* in Casablanca, and in 1935, when the mosque was inaugurated, we moved to Casablanca. I began to grow up, and I am told that I noticed things at a very early age and that I was curious to know everything.

My grandfather worked with the French and with the Moroccan government, under the supervision of French engineers. But my grandfather was a Moroccan citizen, so they couldn't tell him what to do. There was the [French] administrative schedule and the Arab schedule. He followed the Arab schedule, and stopped work every day at the hour of the *assar* prayer to take care of things at home.[5] He would bring together the women and girls in the family and tell them stories from the Arabian Nights and Moroccan folktales. After the *l'moughreb* prayer,[6] he went to the mosque to hear and participate in the talk about nationalist issues, then came back and repeated it to the women at home. My grandfather read the Koran when he prayed, and I would sit next to him, when I was still very young, and would learn from him. Before I was five years old I had memorized a good many verses of the Koran. I was also enrolled in the Koranic School in the street where we lived, just a hundred meters away from our house. There I learned to recite twelve verses of the Koran by heart, but I didn't learn how to read or write.

It was my father who had the idea of sending me to school. This wasn't a common idea in the forties, and there were very few schools in Casablanca. And because of colonialism, whoever wanted to go to school had to wait until there was a vacancy. You have to understand the life we led in Morocco in this period. My sister, who was four years younger than me, entered school before I did because my uncle left school and she took his place. I still had to wait until someone else left to take *their* place. Although he was very conservative, my grandfather finally agreed that I could go to school, but only on the condition that I wear the veil and that I go to a school very close to our home, no more than fifty or maybe a hundred meters away.

The teachers at that time were nationalists. They weren't working just to earn money. They wanted to teach as many people and for as many hours as possible, and to instill a nationalist spirit. There was pure Islamic education like that at the Qaraouine and at the Koranic schools, and there was also basic practical education that included the natural sciences, geography, and several other subjects. They tried to teach in a way that was modern, using the means that were available at the time. There were courses that dealt with theory, and courses on practical, applied subjects. Even in the courses on theory, the professor would send us to conduct practical exercises—and remember, this was in the forties.

You have to understand that the schools at that time didn't even have any books, and everything had to be translated from Spanish or from French. Imagine, it cost more to buy one book than to buy seven gold bracelets! A book then was worth more than 150 grams of gold are worth now! I bought several history books, all by the same author, for the price of seven gold bracelets, or even a little more, which now would be worth about fifteen hundred dirhams [about $160]. Each book would be passed from one person to another. We studied from seven-thirty in the morning to twelve-thirty, and then from one-thirty in the afternoon to seven or eight [in the evening]. The teachers took turns teaching classes. And another thing about the school . . . Not all the classrooms had desks. Sometimes we sat on the floor, like in the Koranic school. But there were some classes where we did have desks, and where the teacher used a blackboard and chalk; these were the classes that were conducted in a modern way.

We had to take turns in class at that time, but we didn't leave school during the day to let the other students take our places. Instead, we went into another room like this one. We sat down opposite one another and the teacher taught us the Koran. We didn't waste any time. There was also recreation, and the hours for prayer were observed. When the hour for prayer came, everyone did his/her ablutions and prayed.

I started school in 1942, but at the end of that year British and American armies came to Morocco, and the French resident general declared Casablanca to be in a state of war, which forced all the schools to close.[7] At that time I went to Fez with my family and studied at the house of the *ma'allma* [a woman who teaches traditional artisanal skills to young girls]. In September, 1943, I returned with my family to Casablanca and went back to school, as the schools were open again. Finally, in 1946, I was ready to take the exam for my primary school diploma. There were a lot of obstacles put in the way of a girl who wanted to take this exam, because the French government did not want this [to happen]. The French didn't want girls and women to go out, to be emancipated. The French thought that if women were educated and became politically aware, it would lead to the overthrow of French colonial rule.[8] Don't forget that in 1944 women participated alongside men, with weapons.[9] I applied to sit for the exam at the end of the fifth year of primary school when I was twelve years old. There was no question of doing it any earlier. Since there was no civil documentation like a birth certificate, you had to have twelve witnesses appear before the judge to present proof of your age.

When I started school, there were already other girls who had started before me, but unfortunately none of these girls got to the level of the fifth year of primary school. As soon as they got to the age of twelve or thirteen, their parents would keep them home. It was *hshouma* [shameful] for a girl to go out of the house once she got to the age of puberty. As for me, I continued in primary school and studied together with boys. For two years there were eighteen boys and me, the only girl. In 1946 I got my primary school diploma. [At that time] there wasn't any secondary school in Casablanca. The first students to finish primary school [all boys] got their diplomas in 1945, but none of them were able to go on, because there was no school. So in 1946, they started up a class at the level of secondary school for those students who had gotten their primary school diplomas in 1945 and 1946.

I enrolled in the class, along with the other students who had graduated from primary school with me. But I was only in school for one day. It created a scandal, and the school was closed. It was *unthinkable* for a girl to study together with boys! The government closed the school and made me leave. And here there was a crisis! What was going to happen, what was not going to happen. . . .

The professors and the director of the school discussed things with my father. They agreed that the professor would come to the house to teach me at night, covering everything that was taught in school during the day, so that the other students would not get ahead of me. And in that way, I was able to pursue my education through secondary school. Just imagine! Professor Si Mohamed Khalid Ben Lahcen came to my house at five in the morning! And especially in the winter, five o'clock seemed very early!

Our studies were serious, and they were also political. The professors taught us from the [Independence Party] newspaper *Al Alam*. That was the text for our analyses, essays, practical exercises, dictations, and so on. The professors were concerned not so much with the amount of material we covered, as with the extent to which we were engaged and politically aware. We grew up with the idea of nationalism and political activism, and we knew there would come a time when we would be called on to sacrifice our children, our very souls, for the motherland. We were being prepared for that; that was why we were educated. And all of the patriotic songs were songs against colonialism. At this point, in 1947, more schools began to open. These were primary schools, paid for by generous Moroccans who gave the land and money for the schools. Noone even thought of building a house for themselves, or traveling abroad, or taking a vacation.

So I continued studying [at home] through 1947 and into 1948, and in 1948 the government gave permission to open a secondary school class for girls. By that time there were several girls ready to enter secondary school. In 1948 they started a class that was called the "continuation class," which was a secondary school class, and I was one of the girls who went into that class. When they were beginning the class, they had to ask parents whether they would agree to their daughters going into secondary school. There were a lot of obstacles for girls who wanted an education. People said that girls were created just for staying at home, working at home—it was the fathers and mothers who said that. So if a girl were to go to school from seven in the morning to seven in the evening, how would she do her share of the work at home? Here they saw— the school administration and the parents—that they had to find a solution, a way in which girls could do both schoolwork and housework. This came mostly from the parents who wanted to educate their daughters. They decided that the girls would stay at home for half of the day. In the mornings, the girls would work at home, then in the afternoons, at two o'clock, they would go to school and study from two until seven in the evening. Since at that time we girls did housework, this was a reasonable solution.

But my father knew another man who was a great nationalist, Si Ahmed Ben Della, who had sent his daughter to receive a modern education to learn how to do machine embroidery with a Singer sewing machine. She was the first who did embroidery on a Singer, and her name was Meriem Ben Della. She is still living, praise be to God. She's the director of a girls' school, the *Taher Sebti* institute in Casablanca. We were like sisters, and my father sent me with her to learn how to use a Singer. In the mornings we went to learn embroidery. The director of the school was a Jewish woman. At that time, there were Jewish and Christian women in Morocco who went out, but Moroccan Muslim women generally didn't. There was only me and Meriem Ben Della. We were the only girls who went out in the street. There were even some people who looked at us through their windows as though they were looking at animals in the zoo. We wore the djellaba and the veil in the street going to school, but I did sometimes lower my veil.

I received my diploma in Singer machine embroidery in 1949, and I also completed my secondary school courses successfully, thanks be to God, even with honors. At that time, my father was getting me a passport so that I could go to Lebanon to continue my studies. Because my father was great friends with a Lebanese family whose daughter was about the same age as me and had gone to study in Lebanon two years earlier. So when I passed my exams, they began to prepare for me to go there to study. But then the political situation changed, and made it necessary for me to get married.

The party that was in the lead [of the nationalist political movement] and that attracted the attention of the colonialists the most was the Istiqlal Party, and the person who was secretary general of the Istiqlal Party in Casablanca was Benacer Harrakat. He had decided to get married, and he needed to find a wife who could be relied on to keep things in confidence. Here you can see the role that nationalism played. In general when you ask for the hand of a girl in marriage the conditions demanded are material conditions. But here, the only conditions were those of nationalism—nationalism included everything.

My father had lost four children before I was born [they all died as infants], so I was the first daughter who lived. That meant that I was spoilt by my parents, who sacrificed everything for my welfare. My family and other relatives were all very concerned about me, and many families of relatives asked for my hand in marriage for their sons. But if any one of the nationalist leaders wanted to decide about his daughter, my father wouldn't object. He said, "This girl is your daughter. Do with her what you will." The way it happened, there wasn't even a final agreement and congratulations; my father didn't even say whether he accepted the offer of marriage for his daughter or not. He let them take care of everything, saying, "These are your children. Do with them what you will." As for me, I didn't have any choice in the matter.

At this point, her husband interrupted, saying,"Wait, let me make a point here! She knew me, and I knew her!" Amina and I joined in, saying, "Ah, you didn't tell us that!"

No, wait a minute . . . We have to get to the proposal of marriage first to say whether I accepted it or not. The rest comes later. Me, I knew him [her husband] at school. I knew him from party gatherings. But to marry him—that was another story! I was in close contact with the Ben Della family, whose house was like the headquarters of the Istiqlal Party. Their son-in-law, Abdessalam Benani Tanjaoui, whom I knew since I was very young, was the one who broached the subject of marriage. My friend Meriem Ben Della also got involved in this matter, and they both advised me, saying, "You're a nationalist, and so you should marry a nationalist. We've been working in politics, and now you should plunge right in and commit yourself. Now things are becoming serious. You studied for a purpose, and you've accomplished that purpose. Now you need to take action." So I accepted the proposal of marriage.

8.2

Oum Keltoum El Khatib with her husband, Benacer Harrakat.

My father wanted to send me to the Qaraouine in Fez. The director of the Qaraouine was related to us, may God rest his soul. [One day] I was upstairs, looking down, when I heard the director tell my father that it was a sin that he still let me go out, especially at my age, and that I had already done studies that were more advanced than those I would get at the Qaraouine. So that was it. The decision was marriage. On the twenty-sixth of June, 1949, I took my exam, and on the same day, the twenty-sixth of June, I was engaged to marry Benacer Harrakat. So, two exams in one day. . . .

Here, Oum Keltoum "opened a parenthesis" to talk about the events of 1944 in Fez, before returning to her own story and to the subject of women in Casablanca in the 1940s.

Moroccan women in Casablanca became very active in the 1940s; I know that from my own experience. I remember very well that in 1945 a group of women came to our home to present their congratulations to my mother.[10] And I remember that they made up a platter covered with a red cloth . . . which was the custom in that time . . . and then people gave twenty *centimes*, which was worth a lot in that period, and sometimes even more. [At that time twenty centimes was what it cost for a student for one month at school.] Why did they give money? For the nationalists!

One day in 1948, a group of women held a meeting in the Ben Della house in support of Palestine. When they passed a platter to make a collection for the war in Palestine, women took off their gold belts—and in this era gold belts were very hard to come by—and put them on the platter. At this time a *serrtla* [a set of seven gold bracelets] was worth thirty-five or forty thousand francs. I knew a woman, Habiba Ben Della, who, when they came to her house, wanted to contribute her serrtla, which her father had just bought for her, to the cause. Her father pulled out a hundred thousand francs and told her to put that on the platter instead, and to keep her serrtla. So she put the hundred thousand francs on the platter, and then, without her father's knowledge, she also took off her serrtla and put it on the platter. She just couldn't keep her serrtla while knowing that other people had contributed, and that the Palestinians needed help.

In Derb Ghelef, which was a lower-class neighborhood, there was a woman named Lalla Fatima Roudania who opened up her house, and got a platter full of *tsabih* [a kind of necklace used at the end of prayer]. She also wore a *tsabih* around her neck, and then called on the women of the neighborhood, and brought them back to her home to give them these tsabih, but also, more importantly, to tell them that the motherland was threatened, the country was at war, and that French colonialism had done this, and this, and this to Morocco . . . and that now it was important that these women know all this and that they begin to take part in the nationalist movement. She would bring in the Koran and made them swear on the Koran. And anyone who swore on the Koran could not give away any secrets after that. [The authorities] saw people going into Lalla

Fatima's house . . . because the colonialists had their eye on any open house where people went in. Why? In order to keep people from having meetings. But this woman was giving away prayer necklaces. And the colonialists had already sponsored *zaouiya* [saints' celebrations] and everything else that would make Moroccans even more ignorant. As long as people were just chanting "Allah, Allah, etc.," it would distract people from what was going on. We first heard this saying from our grandparents and our parents: They said that when the French wanted to come into Morocco, they first sent cards and sugar. Sugar was for the Moroccans' pleasure and the cards for their amusement, keeping them busy while the French occupied their country. And all that to keep the Moroccans distracted. So for them, this woman was just distracting other Moroccan women, so they didn't think they had anything to fear.

In 1946, I was invited by the Chraibi family to their house, where there were regular, weekly women's meetings. I started participating in these meetings, until finally Mr. Abou Ashita Al Jamii decided to prepare me to direct women's meetings. In 1947, he started giving me newspapers to read. Once I had read them I would tell him what I had understood, or what I had learned from the materials. Then he began to send me to women's gatherings to raise women's political consciousness. I continued my work in these meetings for years after that. I never went to these weekly meetings alone: "Dada," an old woman, was my companion wherever I went to organize meetings. She was a woman who was politically conscious, and she occasionally gave me advice. She also left her house and came to stay with me when my husband was sent to prison for the first time in 1951.

Gradually my political work expanded, and together with a group of women I founded "Girls of the Independence Party." We played an important role in helping women to become politically aware, and took part in celebrations which included speeches by women. In 1947, King Mohamed V started organizing a special celebration for women on the nineteenth of November to thank them for their participation in the *Fête du Trône* [a holiday to honor Mohamed V, at that time celebrated on November eighteenth]. I was among the women who took part in this celebration in the palace, where we were officially invited. I took part in this special event in 1947, 1948, 1950, and 1952.

Her husband cut in to say that she didn't just participate; she was the one who led the women and presided over their celebrations.

In the 1940s, Mohamed V would come to Casa in the summer to spend some time there, and he would go to pray in the El Mohamedia mosque. He would leave the palace and go there on horseback, and return on foot, and on his way, the nationalists would cheer him. The French tried hard to prevent this, even bringing in the military, but in spite of that the nationalists were able to bring out schoolchildren, both boys and girls, to sing songs and present bouquets of flowers to Mohamed V. It was like a national celebration.

8.3

Khaddouj El Kadiri from El Jadida.

Source: Oum Keltoum El Khatib.

One day in the nineteen forties—either in 1947 or 1948, I don't remember which—this woman here [showing a photo], El Kadiria, was staying with us at home, and asked to see the king. Although women were generally conservative and didn't go out, this day, the day that the king went to pray at the mosque, was a holiday, and it was a day when women were supposed to go out . . . so this woman went out. She was illiterate, but she had learned the *Hadith* [sayings and doings of the Prophet], because her husband was a learned man [*aalim*]. Her name was Khaddouj El Kadiri. I took her to the celebration, because she had come to visit us from El Jadida, and she didn't know the way or anything. Me, I was standing up front in the row of girls, and she was standing in back, with the other women. Suddenly she started up, all by herself, shouting, "Today, today is the day of mercy and of grace. Today is the day that the French will leave Morocco. Thanks be to the courage of the leader of the Nation!" When people heard that, they began to repeat what she had said, which got the police so angry that they broke up the gathering, using their weapons and arresting a lot of people. The flags were torn . . . there was confusion, and I was separated from her. And when I got back to the house, I found her there. How did she know the way home? How had she managed to get there? Just to show you how courageous she was.[11]

[Let's talk] about the events of 1947 in Casablanca . . . the "slaughter" of Casa, also known as "the slaughter of Derb El Kabir." Women took an active part in this event. Here I will show you the photo of a woman who participated, named Lalla Fatima Roudania, who lived in Ain Chok. The greatest resistance fighter in Morocco. She just died less than two years ago. Fatima Roudania was an illiterate woman, an old woman. In the 1930s, my husband knew of her riding a bicycle. She was from Taroudannt and had come to Casa. She hid several resistance fighters at her home, brought weapons into her home, and saved several resistance fighters. She herself set two bombs. And she was the first person to give weapons to Brahim Roudani. [Brahim Roudani is a well-known resistance fighter who has a boulevard in Casa named after him.]

My husband could tell you about [Brahim Roudani]. He could tell you a lot about Lalla Fatima too, as he was the one who was in touch with her and gave her instructions. It was after he had enlisted in the resistance that I myself got in contact with her in 1950. We used to hold meetings outside of the city, to get away. We went to the orphanage to visit the girls there, but it was really to hold meetings. We went to the outskirts of the city to pick flowers, but at the same time we conferred together. When my husband was arrested in 1952 I became like her daughter.

She was even greater than any of the men. Talk about Brahim Roudani; he kneeled down before her! So this was a great woman. I consider her to be the greatest resistance fighter in Morocco. When members of the executive committee of the Istiqlal Party were arrested, she used to cook meals and take food

8.4

Casablanca resistance fighter Fatima Roudania.

Source: Oum Keltoum El Khatib.

to prisoners in prison in the El Jadida area, even though she herself had no relatives there in prison. She did this on a daily basis. Her husband worked with the French, and she had only one son. In the early 1950s, she and Brahim

Roudani both lived in Derb Martinet, and we lived there too. They had a family tie, but the real ties that they had were the ties of nationalism.[12]

Brahim Roudani sent for her, and said to her and to four other men, "Now, it is no longer a question of political work or words. We need to form a group and find weapons. The only thing we're waiting for is for them to put their hands on Mohamed V. The day that they take away Mohamed V is the day that the armed resistance will begin." That was the order that was given.

Her husband was a guard at the El Aamra prison. At that time, in the forties, before the Americans arrived, the Germans were short of food, but they had weapons. Some Germans came to the El Aamra prison, and they made an exchange with them there. They gave the Germans a meal and the Germans gave them a revolver. It was their thanks [for the meal]. A second revolver was given to her by professor Bouktaya's assistant, who wanted to get rid of it, and so asked her to throw it in a trash can in Ain Chok [the district in Casa where she lived]. What did they do with the revolvers? They took them to Fatima Roudania, a woman. This shows you the character of Moroccan women, and the way they were trusted. But where could she hide the weapon? There was a place in the house where we kept the hot ashes—because we burned coal at home. So she wrapped up the weapon and hid it in the ashes.[13] She threw the revolver down there.

As soon as Si Brahim Roudani said that they needed arms, she took them and brought them to him. . . . Fatima Roudania wore pants, golf pants. She wore a coat or a sweater, like a man, and rode a bicycle. She covered her head . . . I did have another photo where her head is covered like a man. Well, she was wearing these golf pants [loose pants with wide, short legs], and so she took the revolvers, put one in each pants-leg, and tied them in with a string. Then she got on her bicycle and went to his house.

She greeted him, "*Salaam alikoum*,"[14] and he said, "Well, now we need weapons." She lifted up her foot and slapped her leg and said to him, "Here's one." In those days, it was really shameful for a woman to show her legs like that! He began to scold her, and she went on, showing her other leg, and said, "Here's another!" And he continued, saying that he was not joking, and as he was a serious and important man, he said, "I'm going to kill you!" She completely ignored his threats, taunting him, "What will you get out of it once I am dead? You'll be left with my son! Who's going to bring him up?" She said, "You're already worried about the people who have gone to prison and who have left you their wives and children to take care of, and now you want to kill me and my son!" She really had it over him. But he was still angry at her. Then she did like this [lifting her leg], and took out the revolvers. At that, he pulled out the paper he had, and tore it up. He said to the men, "Go ahead, eat that! Here's a woman who brought two revolvers before I even spoke! What do you have to say for yourselves? What are you going to do?"

Bouktaya's servant was also with the resistance. He brought her two bombs. She thought about what to do with them, and then hid them in the decorations around the windows, where you couldn't see them. One day, I remember . . . it was the car belonging to a French colonial professor who was well known for his wickedness. He lived in one of the houses that they had build for professors in the area of the Hermitage, on the hill. She put the bomb in by herself, and lit the fuse. She hadn't quite gotten back to Ain Chok on her bicycle when the bomb exploded and roused the whole neighborhood. And she set another bomb in a place in Ain Chok that they called "The House of the Soldier," for French soldiers. She set the bomb, and it was that bomb that destroyed the house. The day that the bomb went off, she was the one who threw it across the terraces. They didn't know where it had come from. Fatima Roudania was bolder than any man. This Si Mohamed Bouktaya, may God rest his soul, was in hiding, concealed by her in her house. He was a big, strong man. When she wanted to help him escape to the Souss, she dressed him in a haik, a veil, and women's slippers, and she got him out dressed like that.

They arrested her once, and kept her in prison for a month. And it was the worst kind of torture that they used on the nationalists in Casa in 1954. When they asked her for the names of people she knew among the nationalists, she said that everyone she knew was a nationalist. "I am a Moroccan. You, you're not a nationalist, because you're a traitor! You should leave the country. You, you're not a nationalist because you're French." She defied them. She told them that she didn't know how to read or write. She fasted for a month. They put her head in water, telling her to drink, but she refused, telling them that she was fasting. They said, "You're in this condition and you're fasting?" She told them that there was only one God. When they said that they would take her soul, she told them that only God could do that. And she survived, may God rest her soul, and they gave her the card [*carte de résistant*]. Afterwards, we all came to see her. Old and young, everyone came to see her.

[Starting in 1951, the men went to prison.] After that, women played roles in the resistance which were very risky. It's really strange! The first time [my husband] was in prison, in 1951, I had just given birth, forty days earlier. I gave birth on the twenty-third of January, and he was put in prison on the thirteenth of March. The last time he was in prison, he left me pregnant. They came to arrest him on the eighth of December [1952, the day of the general strike], and I gave birth on the seventeenth of January, another girl, the second one.[15] On that day, on the eighth of December, I was proud to dress in Moroccan dress. Before I got married, I wore a [European] dress. But that day—on the eighth of December, 1952—I was pregnant; and I wore a Moroccan kaftan.

I had a stencil at home. I had learned how to use it, and I had practiced writing tracts [for the resistance]. Each time, I had to write them eight to ten times. [My husband] also taught me to write tracts on the reverse side of the paper. We wrote with onions, and then if you held it up against a light you could see the writing on the other side. . . . It was juice from an onion. When you wrote like that, other people could not read it. And you couldn't recognize whose handwriting it was. Because the tracts had to go to various different towns, one to Derb Seltan, one to Khouribga, and another to Fez, and you weren't meant to be able to tell whose handwriting it was.

We had all the equipment in the house; and the French came to the house on that day of the eighth of December [1952]. Things started to happen in the morning, when everyone came to our house. It was my husband who was meant to gather all the information. We didn't have a telephone, so he went to Sidi Ahmed Ben Della's, who lived about fifty meters from our place. So he was at Ahmed Ben Della's on the telephone, and I was at our house. The labor union activists had just brought some news. Those who knew how to write brought it in writing, while those who didn't know how to write came to the house and dictated the information they had to me, and I wrote it down. When he came back around lunch time, he saw all these papers, and put them in his pocket along with the other papers that he had brought.

It was two o'clock in the afternoon when we heard someone knocking at the door. We could always recognize someone from the military when they knocked, because they always knocked with the butt of their gun. They opened the front door, and also the door into the room. The police had come to arrest my husband. He had taken what he had in his pockets and put it in the sugar box. When I saw the papers in the sugar box, I took everything, and I did like this [demonstrates putting it under her kaftan]. I hid everything under my clothes, and stood up in front of them with my big [pregnant] belly out front. The stencil machine, the typewriter, the paper for the tracts, the newspaper, and the tables were all in the room where he had put all of that. There was a sewing machine for embroidery, and I was just working on some little napkins and sheets. The first table was right by the door of the room. It was there, in the drawers of that table, that there were all the embroidery papers and everything. When they came in the room, they opened the first drawer and took out a paper on embroidery. . . .

I was standing there trying to look natural. They were searching for something, but everywhere they searched, they found nothing but clothes. He was taking his time, putting on his things. But I was afraid that he would put on the coat which he already knew had a paper in the pocket. My younger sister was upstairs, and I told her, "Bring down this other coat for him." I looked at him; but I couldn't tell him not to put on the coat. I was afraid they would guess that something was up. So I acted as if . . . They asked him, "What's wrong with her?" And he said, "She's having labor pains." And they told him, "Get the midwife. Take her to the doctor." I said, "No, no. My mother is the midwife. Do you want me? Did you come after me?" They wanted to comfort me, and they gave me a chair to sit on. But if I had sat down, they would have known everything, so I didn't want to sit down. I told them, "If you came for me, I'll put on my djellaba and I'll leave with you. But if you came for him, take him away." I said this with a kind of audacity! As soon as they were about to go out, I said to them, "If you want, I can put my djellaba on and follow you." I wanted to go upstairs so that I could get rid of what I was hiding. As soon as they had left with him, I began to burn things. He had left me a lot of stuff, so it took me forty days to burn it up. But I didn't want to burn everything. As for the letter announcing the strike, I took it and sewed it into the hem of a kaftan. After my husband had been in prison for ten days, the police commissioner came back to the house looking for the strike letter, which was still sewed into the kaftan.

A lot of people were killed, and when we went to the police station to bring food they told us that my husband was dead too. His friends began to look for him. After four days, there was still no sign of him. Here, where . . . they threw the bodies of the dead in the basement of the police station, he had been thrown into that basement together with the dead bodies. And he stayed there for twenty-two days. At that point, everyone said that he was dead. But I wouldn't believe that he was dead until the day I got an official notification of his death. I kept my courage and stayed calm.

One day, I saw the police commissioner coming, the commissioner Diase, together with Guerro and a Moroccan. They asked for the letter about the strike. I was calm, and came inside when the commissioner wanted to come in. But there was a Moroccan from Rabat with him. I told him, "No Moroccans are going to come into this house, come what may! Even when my husband is at home, I wear the veil. It's alright for me to see a foreigner or for him to see me, but it is unthinkable for me to see a Moroccan. If my husband were here, he could bring in as many Moroccan men as he wanted, even a dozen. But no Moroccan man can come into my house while I am here alone, not even if I should lose my soul! Only over my dead body would a Moroccan be able to come in here. But if a Frenchman wants to come in, welcome." The Moroccan stayed outside, because we understood one another, we spoke the same language. He knew my tricks, and I knew his.

I took the paper [that the commissioner brought with him]. I was still pregnant at the time. I read it in Arabic, and it said that they were looking for the strike letter. I asked him, "What do you want?" He said, "The letter about the strike." I asked, "What does the letter look like?" I said, "And my husband is dead?" When I brought food to the police station for him, I kept asking and insisting until finally they told me that he was still alive. He told me, "Look, if you give us that letter, I will bring him to you now." I said, "Go and get him, and I will bring you the letter from the place where it is." And he said, "No, give me the letter. Then I will go and get him." And I said, "What does the letter look like? If it is in French, I don't read French. And if it is in Arabic, Moroccan men don't let their wives interfere with their business. Nothing . . . I just know how to cook and to make bread. And you've already taken him away to prison, and done all that. He wanted to incriminate me too. If you are going to keep him in prison for one year, why don't you keep him in prison for ten years!" And what I wanted was for him to leave the house and go away, because I wanted to burn the letter before they tracked it down.

He stayed, and wore himself out, trying everything to make me give in. Finally I began to cry. I told him, "It's not fair, what you're doing. You've taken away my husband. Bring him back so that he can give you the letter. Bring him back and take me with him." He left, and I went back upstairs and continued to burn documents. I even burned souvenir photos; I didn't want to leave any evidence. And then, the resistance fighters began to come to my house, among them Dr. El Khatib. They came as if they were coming to see me to help me in giving birth. But in reality, they came to take away the stencil, the tracts, and so on, and to help me burn documents.

Benacer Harrakat explained that at this time, after the General Strike on December 8, 1952, all of the Istiqlal Party leaders were arrested and put in prison, as well as all the trade union leaders. So a whole new generation of leaders started forming to replace them.

At this point, they even began to prepare women to work in the ranks of the resistance. For example, I got a passport in 1953. As soon as my husband was put in prison, I got a passport. Because they told me to get a passport. That way, if they needed me to, I could go to Tangiers or to the north [the Spanish zone]. And they put a photo on the passport.

When he went to prison, we brought him food. We began to make contacts in prison. He left the police station, after twenty-two days, and went to prison, after having appeared before the military tribunal. Then they began to give us permissions, and I began to go into the prison. There were ways to get to the prison guards. I bribed them with material goods; I bought the director of the prison with four tires.

After he had gone to the prison in Kenitra, I began to go out at two o'clock in the morning. It was normal to go out at that hour then, and another ten women did the same thing. I wasn't the only one. We went out at two in the morning to take the 4:45 AM CTM bus for Tangiers. And when we got to Kenitra—I had never set foot in Kenitra before, but I went because my husband was in prison there—we found families that were there before us. They put me up, and I spent the night with them. They did more for me than my own family would have done! Men from the resistance, from the Party, would meet us at the gates of the prison, and took us there [to these families]. We found the women making couscous, peeling vegetables—women we didn't even know! There were places for us to eat and drink, and they also gave us transportation and paid the fare for the bus or the train. People then weren't out for themselves. On the contrary, they all helped each other.

8.5

Oum Keltoum El Khatib passport (page 1).

Source: Oum Keltoum El Khatib.

8.6

Oum Keltoum El Khatib passport (page 3).

Source: Oum Keltoum El Khatib.

One day, we were forbidden to go into the prison, after having gone into the prison for two months before that. The crisis deepened. Mohamed V came to his palace in Casa, and the women signed a petition of solidarity with the monarchy. I even brought along my mother . . . I brought her back more than forty times, and each time she signed a different name. At that time [the French] said that there was just one guiding hand for the nationalists, and that it was the people who were now in prison. From now on we were forbidden to go in to see the prisoners. And yet the prisoners continued to change their clothes, shave, and eat, because food came into the prison every day. They lived as though they were at home in their own houses!

Afterwards we were not even allowed to visit. They used to take the prisoners out to work in trucks, so we formed a line around the gate of the prison, and then we put down our baskets and sat down, so that if they wanted to take the truck out through the gate, they would have to drive over us! One day we sat there from eight in the morning until five in the afternoon. They brought some lawyers to negotiate with us, but it was no use! . . . The next day, in spite of everything, they let food into the prison; so we had succeeded! And they allowed us to go into the prison to see the prisoners, but they asked us all to get identification cards. I actually already had one. But it was necessary to have a photo on the identification card—and it was forbidden for us as Moroccan women to be photographed.

So now I said, "We agree to get identification cards, but you'll have to let the men out of prison to make the cards for us. Afterwards, you can arrest the men again. As for me, it's forbidden for me to make an identification card." [And I already had an identification card.] I told him, "It's forbidden for me to take off my veil, and I wear my djellaba and veil when I go into the prison. Let my husband out, and he can do whatever he likes with me. But as long as my husband is in prison, I must stay exactly the way he left me."

But I had to go into the prison to see him, so I used my identification card to get into the prison. I went to the military tribunal, and I got four permissions, one for Monday, one for Tuesday, one for Wednesday, and one for Thursday, each under a different name. Then, each day I went under a different name, and I brought someone with me. Sometimes I was Mme. Harrakat, Oum Keltoum El Khatib, or Oum Keltoum Bent Mohamed, and it was always me. Sometimes I took with me Abderrahmane Harrakat, sometimes Mina Harrakat, sometimes Abderrah Harrakat. But those weren't really the names of the people who came in with me. Mohamed Sergeane came into the prison with me. He was one of the greatest resistance fighters ever known, and I got him into the prison almost every day. We would meet with members of the resistance at the prison gate, and they would ask us to do something for them or to bring them information. The guard who was at the door of the tribunal was a member of the resistance, may God rest his soul. He would tap us on our shoulders, without our speaking to him, and would do whatever was necessary.

9

Amina Leuh and Khadija Bennouna:
Nationalist Education and Politics in Tetouan

Amina Leuh and Khadija Bennouna were both born around 1930, and grew up in Tetouan, the capital of the northern zone of Morocco, which was controlled by the Spanish. Both come from prominent families closely associated with the independence movement. Amina Leuh's mother was from the family of Abdelkrim El Khatabi, the leader of the 1920–26 Rif War. Abdelkhalek Torres, the president of the Reform Party, was Khadija Bennouna's uncle.[1] Both women participated in the nationalist movement, but in different ways: Amina Leuh in the sphere of girls' education, and Khadija Bennouna in the context of the women's organization of the Reform Party.

Living under the Spanish protectorate was much easier than living under the French. The Spanish Civil War was going on during much of this period,[2] which kept the Spanish preoccupied with domestic affairs, and allowed Moroccans to "breathe" fairly freely. In the 1930s and 1940s, Moroccans in the northern zone were allowed to publish newspapers, and to develop national industries. After the king was exiled, in 1953, the Spanish actually helped the Moroccan resistance against the French. During this period partisans could move rather freely between the Spanish and French zones. They used to get arms from the north, and the Spanish themselves also provided them with weapons. Toward the end, the north became a base and refuge for the Moroccan resistance against the French; this helped a great deal in bringing about the return of Mohamed V in 1955.

Amina Leuh

I met professor Amina Leuh through the Institut universitaire de la recherche scientifique, where she is a senior researcher, and where I have been affiliated for several years in the course of this project. Since then, I have met with her several times, at the Institut and at her comfortable home in Rabat-Souissi. For this oral history, she spoke about her own experience growing up in Tetouan in the thirties and forties, and directing a girls' school. Professor Leuh

9.1

Amina Leuh when she got her doctorate in Madrid in 1968.

9.2

Amina Leuh giving a speech.

9.3

Amina Leuh as a young woman.

Source: Amina Leuh.

9.4

Amina Leuh as a child.

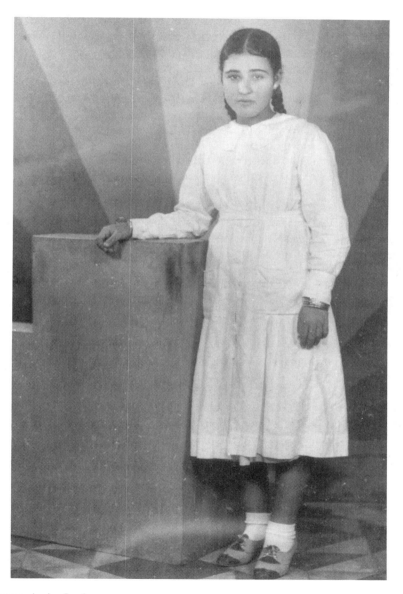

started by telling me of Sidi Mohamed Ameziane, who was the leader of a resistance movement against the Spanish in the Rif, based in Melilia, from 1909 to 1912, until he was killed in battle.

My father was a member of Abdelkrim Al Khatabi's movement, but before that he also knew Sidi Mohamed Ameziane, and used to know every song or poem written about him. After [Sidi Mohamed Ameziane's] death, a song was composed about him, and all the women of the Beni Ouriaghl tribe sang it. It goes like this: "The moon has disappeared/ The stars around it have also disappeared/ Sidi Mohamed Ameziane has disappeared/ And so has his horse."

My mother is from the family of the *Emir* [Prince] Khatabi; he was her uncle. She was young during the Rif War, and she learned the songs that women used to sing at the time. She learned songs in the Riffi language. So I collected songs from her. She had an extremely good memory. She died a year ago now, and my best memories are the moments sitting with her and having her talk about those days. She had such a remarkable style of narration; she made you visualize scenes: the house, the warriors, the details of war. She even remembered the names of some Spanish women who were prisoners at that time. She told about a Spanish woman who came to the house to teach us sewing . . . She remembered her name, but I have forgotten. . . . She would tell me how the warriors would get ready for war, their gatherings, and so on. The oral history of events, as if you were watching scenes from history. And the best of it was the songs. I did record some songs, but very, very few. I always have the impression that we are immortal, and that's a mistake. Only God is immortal.

[Let me give you] one example of the historical value of the songs: The Spanish, toward the end of the Rif War, started using poisonous gas in their attacks. [In fact, if it had not been for the cooperation between the French and the Spanish, the Rif War would have ended in complete triumph for the Moroccans.] So, as I said, here is a song that refers to the use of gas, which was not allowed in battles. The words of the song say, "People, hurry up and hide in the caves/ The enemy is attacking with gas."[3]

Women in the Rif also had a role in relation to the prisoners of war. When they were brought home, it was like an *Aid* [festival], a celebration of the Rif warriors bringing back the prisoners. The Riffi women didn't torture the prisoners; they just expressed their joy at the triumphs of their warriors. On the other hand, some Riffi women were consulted by the leaders for advice. The sister of the Emir Abdelkrim El Khatabi, for example, was older than her brother; her name was Rahma. He sought her opinions and advice on each and every subject, not just family affairs but also political issues, because she was known for her insight and wisdom. He relied heavily on her views because she was usually right. Of course, this is just one example; there were many others. . . .

What were the essential goals and methods of the resistance in the North? (1) To spread national awareness, they used speeches in the mosques, or political speeches, meetings, gatherings, conferences, and connections with foreign countries, especially with Arab leaders.[4] (2) They created free schools, the first of which was created in Tetouan in 1926.[5] (3) They put out newspapers, all of them designed as a means of resistance. The first Arabic newspaper in Tetouan was *Majalet Essalam* [Peace], which started in 1933. After that many others appeared. A publishing house was also created. Theater was another weapon. It really flourished, especially in Tangiers.[6] Theater was a great thing at the time. All of this was done for the purpose of raising the national awareness and destroying harmful practices and beliefs. There was also the establishment of national industry in Tetouan, firms that produced soap, shoes, clothes, electricity—all of these were created in that era. . . . Charity organizations were formed, and played an important role. One of them created the first school for girls, in 1934.[7] I believe it was the first school for girls in all of Morocco.

The Reform Party encouraged all these activities, and the party itself formed several groups, among them one called *fityan* [youth]. They wore similar outfits; I remember they dressed in green. And for the first time girls worked together with boys. There were only two girls, but even that was a symbol of the presence of girls. I remember that when I was in the primary school one of them used to come to the school in the costume of fityan. It was a great event, and there was a famous song about this. What was the role of this group, fityan? The political party had this group which represented the party by songs, and they attended meetings . . . there wasn't any particular role, but this youth was formed for what was to come later.

In 1937, the government created the first modern school for girls in Tetouan, called *Girls' School No. 1*. This school played a central role in Tetouan society as far as girls' education was concerned. The school still exists today, though the name and location are different. In this era there was a national renaissance, particularly in Tetouan. Everybody who was there at the time would confirm this.

I personally lived at home in a special atmosphere, where I heard them talk about Abdelkrim [El Khatabi]. It was just ten or fifteen years after the Rif War, so people who experienced it were still alive. I heard about the battle of Anoual, and such and such battle, so I heard all this at home, and at the same time news about the Reform Party. Also I saw pictures of Torres giving speeches; he was very famous for his gestures when he spoke, so his manners attracted our attention. This was the era in which I started primary school. I'm not from Tetouan; I'm from Al Houceima.[8] But I went to Tetouan when I was just a little girl. My father, God rest his soul, wanted me to study. In Al Houceima there were only Spanish schools. So he sent me to Tetouan where there was this school, Girls' School No. 1; and I went there. All the staff and teachers were Spanish; there were only a few Moroccans. There was a Moroccan director, but that was just a token, because the Spanish had all the power.

Imagine the situation—very few Moroccan teachers, the majority Spanish, a Moroccan director, a Spanish superintendent, and this in the era of the rise of nationalism! The Spanish are at the height of their colonial power and the Moroccan nationalists are at the height of their power among the people, and so the situation is really precarious—the least incident would create an outbreak of confusion and chaos. So you can just imagine the state of affairs! What did the Moroccans do? They started focusing, stressing Moroccan-Arabic culture, because they were afraid that the pupils would become Spanish.[9] So they stressed religion—the Koran—Arabic language, and nationalism—three subjects to fight intellectual colonialism. There was no distraction, there was no cinema, no going out; our only objective and interest was education. That's why our level of achievement was high.

When I was a student, I used to ask a number of questions. I still remember . . . I used to wonder why we live under colonial power; what is the meaning of colonialism; why don't our people enjoy the same freedom as the colonialists? [At that time there was fear, and meetings took place in secrecy.] Why are our women under the grip of ignorance? This was the essential question. I used to ask these questions of my father and my teachers, and I got some interesting answers. I collected a number of interesting observations which allowed me to draw conclusions and to understand the causes of our backwardness—the central reason was ignorance and illiteracy.

Morocco was subjected to colonial rule because of this. At that time I read a poem by a Moroccan poet named El Mokhtar Soussi. I remember the title of the poem: "Rather Death than Ignorance." It's a marvelous nationalist poem, and it had a great impact on me. . . . I was in the last years of primary school, and I noticed that very few girls were in school. Why? Because the girls would only stay in the school for one or two, or three years at the most. They learned Arabic, religion, the Koran, and then they went back to their homes to learn housework in preparation for marriage. That was it. There weren't any girls who reached the level of the primary school certificate.

My father, thank God, was open-minded, and didn't even consider bringing me home, even after I finished primary school. I was going to continued my studies further than this. He wanted to send me to Tangiers. We knew an English lady, who was a friend of the family, Mrs. Arnold. She was extraordinary. She considered my father as her son. So he wanted me to stay with her in Tangiers and go to school. But the whole family stood against this wish—how can you send your daughter to an English school? This is impossible, etc. etc. He said, "Alright. Since there's a school in Tetouan, she'll stay here in Tetouan and enroll there." This is to show you how open-minded he was.

I was really exhausted from all the thinking I did, and I realized that the only way to get rid of the colonial presence was by using its own weapons—that is, by knowledge and education. If they have reached a stage where they can colonize us, then we have to reach that same stage ourselves. But how?

Before mentioning how we went about this, I want to talk about a very important incident that occurred: the visit of Mohamed V to Tangiers. While I was still studying, and still struggling with all these questions, he came to Tangiers. My father insisted on my going to attend the celebrations, because the king brought the Princess Lalla Aicha. At the time she was called the leader of the women's movement. She talked about the education of women, and so on, so all the girls had a dream of meeting her. So I did go to Tangiers, and she gave a speech in three languages—Arabic, English, and French—and she said these are the languages that her father wants Moroccans to speak, men and women, because it's the ideal way to open up to the outside advanced world. There were extraordinary crowds of women there, and the King was there too. He watched us from the terrace of a house, so that he could follow the event. Of course, the speech of the Princess was a trigger, and a confirmation that the women's education was the key.

I returned to Tetouan a different person: no more doubts, no fear. My dream came true—I started teaching. After a while, I became a teacher in a same school where I had been a pupil; then I became the director of the school. That was *the* opportunity I was waiting for. Of course, I needed to arm myself for the battle. I made myself a model of teaching and of behavior. I knew that my teaching had to be brilliant, and my behavior irreproachable, and that I'd be severely judged for the slightest error.

So now I started my own battle. I started teaching at eight in the morning, and went until eight in the evening, just stopping for lunch. I taught classes, taught songs, directed plays, and did research. I chose to do this; it was not an obligation, but for me I was fighting for a nationalist cause. Indeed, it wasn't long before I had educated an amazing group of girls. They had a good level in Arabic, and good national awareness. I took this group from one stage to the next, until they reached the level of the teacher's certificate. I tried to encourage them to continue their studies, because otherwise we'd never achieve our objectives. Now this group of students are mostly teachers and school directors. They were ready right at the beginning of independence. They are still working in the same schools and with the same spirit they had.[10] I was convinced I did my duty; now and then we meet and remember our battles.

While I was teaching, I would get in touch with the mothers of girls in the school. I used to try to convince them to let their daughters continue their studies, because education is good for such and such a reason. But words were not enough; I needed something concrete, visible, to convince them. So I used school festivities to that end—events like the end of the year celebration and religious occasions. I invited the mothers, and I also invited ladies from the great families of Tetouan, so that they could see it all. It was a new phenomenon to have school celebrations; and to have girls appear with boys, give speeches, and so on—this was quite an event! I still remember the first celebration in the school. It was a stunning success! Almost all the great ladies of Tetouan attended, and they were full of praise for this new cultural phenomenon. You know, in Tetouan, there's a lot of gossip; whenever something happens, people talk it over everywhere, in the cafés, in the streets, in the hammam. Our school celebration was the subject of the day. It was talked about everywhere to such an extent that I received a letter of congratulations from what we'd now call the Minister of Education.

So, celebrations were one means of fighting. It was a success, a nationalist success, and the first step in my battle. After a while, the girls improved, and the school celebration became a nationalist event. Now that education was allowed, we had to concentrate on spreading national awareness among people. So the speeches were no longer just about pedagogical matters, they were also about politics and nationalism.

I remember in one such celebration, at the end of the year, we gave people the freedom to say whatever they wanted—statements against the colonialists, nationalist songs, whatever. I was the director of the school, and it was a government school run by the Spanish. I knew that I was responsible for everything that happened, but at that time we were young and blinded by nationalism. Of course the Spanish teachers and staff were all present at the celebration. Everybody was silent, but they took note of everything and reported it to the Spanish national education representative, who was a diehard colonialist. They told him that it wasn't a school celebration that they had attended, but rather a nationalist political event. The following day, he sent me a letter of admonition, telling me that the school was for education and not for horror stories, and that if there were any similar event in the future then God knows what would become of me—this was a kind of warning. Do you think I paid any attention to the letter? On the contrary, I took it as a proof of our success, an encouragement! So, I had achieved something useful. I started becoming famous.

So I was famous. Whenever there was a celebration—wedding party, baptism, family feast—I was always invited; in fact I was the first one on the invitation list. I didn't go because I liked to attend parties, but because parties were a good opportunity to talk to women about the importance of education. Every meeting I had with women, I was sure to raise the issues of the necessity of education—learning and learning . . . nothing but learning. I got lots of applause and congratulations, and I myself saw that I had succeeded. But I shouldn't forget the difficulties that I encountered. I knew I was working on a difficult front, because I was fighting traditions and established practices. There's a proverb in Arabic saying, "It's easier to change your religion than to change your habits." When I entered this field, I was aware of the dangers of traditions and old beliefs. So when people agreed upon the positive nature of my efforts, this was a success.

My teaching, and my contacts with women, allowed me to get in touch with the women's organization [of the Reform Party], despite the fact that I was not a member. As I told you, my world was teaching; but my fame in teaching led to coordination between my work and the work of the women's organization, and solidarity around nationalist issues. To give you an example, I remember that once professor Abdelkhalek Torres, [leader of the Reform Party, was going to return to Tetouan]. . . . There was a decision [by the Spanish resident general] not to let him enter the town, but the people of Tetouan decided to challenge this. The day before his return, I had a visit from representatives of the women's organization [of the Reform Party]. They came to my school and told me that there was going to be a strike the following day, [and they wanted the school to participate]: The girls should not come to school. We agreed on the method of informing them secretly—it had to be so because of the spies. Then I told them, "You may go now; I know what to do." That same day, we received a notice [from the Spanish authorities] forbidding us from having strikes, demonstrations, or anything of the sort on this occasion, and saying that the school directors would assume all the responsibility. Of course we never thought about the consequences.

The following day, not a single student came to the school. The school was empty. The Spanish superintendent came, and asked me, "Where are the girls? Who asked them not to come?" I replied that I didn't know, maybe their parents forbade them. . . . Obviously the news reached the Spanish education representative. Ours was the only school which was on strike. He sent me another letter, reprimanding me, etc. etc., but who cared? If you remember, on that day there was a violent confrontation between the people of Tetouan and the Spanish army. There were many people dead, arrested, and injured. This is known in the history of our country.

So for the Spanish authority, I was a gadfly; I preoccupied them. But I believe that if the Spanish had touched just one hair of my head on that occasion, like expelling me from my work, or . . . that might have caused a revolution for my sake.

I used another weapon—newspapers. I used to write articles in the papers, daily papers and magazines, on subjects concerning women, education, knowledge, the abolition of harmful traditions, etc. I have copies of the articles in Tetouan, in my house there. The fact that I was a woman writing them used to attract people's admiration. That's what I wanted—I wanted people to see a woman communicating with people, men, expressing her opinions, and defending her rights. I also used the radio for the same purpose. I had a weekly program on the Tetouan radio station, which was called "Thursday Talk." This was in the 1950s, maybe in 1954. Sometimes I didn't use my name; I'd say "the youth of Tetouan" if the topic were especially controversial. But everyone knew who had the program.

There were two schools for girls in Tetouan—one high school and one school for teachers, and I was the director of both of them. I continued my work and efforts, but in a slightly different way because things had evolved. This was a critical moment in the history of Morocco—the exile of Mohamed V. That's why I turned the struggle into a political battle. Thank God we had good results concerning the education of women; now I had to carry on with my national duty working in the same school, but in the political field. The fifties were when we had the visits of Arab leaders. The national bodies got in touch with me when these Arab leaders were going to visit Tetouan, so that we could help organize their visits. Of course this was with the agreement of the Spanish. The first thing was the girls: The girls would prepare talks, nationalist songs, questions, condemnations of France, and calls for independence and an end to the exile of Mohamed V. All of these would be presented during the visits of the Arab leaders. Of course they were accompanied by a group of Spanish officials, and when these officials came to the school they would be shocked because of the enthusiasm and strong nationalist spirit—remember, they were Spanish schools. I used to hide behind the girls so that my eyes didn't meet theirs. Once we had the visit of the general president of the Arab League, named Chouqairi. That was a day never to be forgotten! When he came, I didn't expect that atmosphere in the school. I mean, it turned into a nationalist struggle—the girls were chanting, singing, and everything. The Spanish were present, of course. Chouqairi was so affected [he was famous for his eloquent speeches], that when he left the school, he said, "Never before have I seen such a moving nationalist sight organized by women as I have witnessed today in the school."

Of course this statement was a good reason for the Spanish to forbid any further visits to the school. The Spanish couldn't do anything else, because by that time the armed resistance had started all over the country. So there was no point in sending me a warning or anything. They kept silent, swallowed the event. The nationalist struggle ended, of course, with the return of King Mohamed V, and the declaration of independence. At that time the King made a famous statement, saying, "We're moving from a small battle to a bigger one."[11]

So this, in brief, is the panorama of my contribution to the national awakening. I considered my work in girls' education as a duty, and a modest share in the struggle for national independence. I succeeded in what I set out to do, because now I notice that the issue of women's education has triumphed. Now no difference is made between boys and girls in education, and education is the right of everybody, like water, or air.

We don't have to fight against traditions any more; now there are new issues, like political rights and social rights, and women's rights. These are the new issues, now that Morocco has its independence. Indeed battles never end, like the struggle now against cultural imperialism. After independence I had one cause—the Arabic language. I wanted to restore to Arabic its lost value, its place as a symbol of Moroccan identity. It's not logical to accept the dominance of a foreign country, [or a foreign language]. I wish I could speak ten languages. As we say in Arabic, "Each language is a different person." But this should not be at the expense of our language. Whenever I was invited to a congress I would talk about this particular issue. This is what interests me now. Arabic is our identity. I write articles about this.

I was encouraged first by my father, and then by my husband.[12] He encouraged me a lot. It's a rare event when a husband forgets about his own struggles and encourages his wife's education. He was open-minded and knowledgeable, and always supported me, until he died, seven years ago now. I studied in Madrid for five years—at times I came back here, or he joined me in Madrid. In fact I was lucky to have a special father and husband.

The views of men? That's what we were fighting against—the traditional views of men, their conventional attitude to women's lives. I mentioned before that I was prey to rumors and harsh judgment. Very few parents accepted that their daughters should be educated; and even those few did not want their daughters to go beyond primary school. They were scared of Spanish influence in the schools. They said they are going to convert our children to another religion. A lot was said about me. My father encouraged girls' education by using me as an example. He wanted to send the first group of female students to Egypt, but he couldn't get his wish; the parents just refused the idea. I myself was influenced . . . I got my ideas of women's liberation mainly from Egypt, not much from Spain, because we used to get Egyptian newspapers, and there were Egyptian female writers in the paper like Bint Chati, Souad El Qalamawi, Ni'mat Fouat. They presented new ideas to us; I was a devoted reader of these papers and magazines. I was influenced by this, in the first place. Then I also got some influence from Spain, although our relations [with Spain] were poor at that time. Now there is understanding and exchange, but before, colonialism was an obstacle which didn't allow us to discover other things about Spain, beyond colonialism. I understood this after I went to Spain to study and lived together with people of different nationalities. There I opened up to the outside world.

Khadija Bennouna

I had met Khadija Bennouna once before, briefly, at Malika El Fassi's house, as I was just leaving and she was coming in. The impression that stays with me is of a woman charged with intense energy, in movement. Some time later, I went to her home in Rabat-Agdal to record an oral history interview. The Bennounas live in a large airy corner apartment on the third floor

9.5

Khadija Bennouna and author (1995).

Credit: Anne White.

(American fourth floor), looking out over a circle of greenery and open space with a living room furnished partly in the Western style with sofas and stuffed chairs, and partly in the Moroccan style with banquettes lining the walls. Khadija Bennouna was still out when I arrived for the interview; her husband, Mehdi Bennouna, greeted me in perfect English.[13] *After we sat down and Moroccan mint tea and pastries were served, he took the opportunity to give me an overview of the general situation in Tetouan, and the various ways in which his wife contributed to the nationalist movement. A little later, Khadija Bennouna came in, and without even stopping to take off her djellaba, sat down and plunged right into her narrative, picking up where her husband had left off, talking about her own activities in the forties and fifties, especially in relation to the nationalist movement.*

Before the [Reform] Party was first created in the north, women were somewhat marginalized. They heard about and experienced the nationalist movement through their husbands, fathers, cousins, and sons, but they didn't participate directly. When did we think about getting involved in nationalistic action? It was in 1947, when they said that Mohamed V would be going to Tangiers. The male members of the Reform Party planned to offer the king a map. The map was to represent the north of Morocco, which was the Spanish zone, and Tetouan was going to be represented on the map by an emerald. The map was to be made out of expensive material, with Tetouan marked with an emerald and Tangiers represented by a ruby. At that time, I—and may God forgive my use of *I*—I was seventeen years old, but I was already married, because I got married in 1945 at the age of fifteen. I was full of energy and vitality, because I was living with my uncle, who was Abdelkhalek Torres, and his house was bustling with political activity, and friends, talk of nationalism, and committees, etc.[14] I told him, "Lalla Aicha is coming with the king to Tangiers. Why not organize ourselves as a group of women and offer her a present?" He said to me that was a good idea; since Lalla Aicha was also coming, women should also contribute a present. He asked me what we would do, and I replied, "We'll order a diadem from a jeweller, who in turn will bring it from Madrid. It will be set entirely with diamonds. We'll put it in the middle of the Torres house—first we'll put it in a box—and all the women of Tetouan, regardless of their age or class or fortune, will come to see the diadem. Once they know it is for the princess, they will put whatever they want to contribute in another box." That is indeed what happened. For a whole month, we went on collecting offerings and contributions, while the diadem was displayed in the box on very beautifully embroidered cushions. Of course there were women there all the time charged with the security of the box. We collected three times the price of the diadem—three times the price of a diadem in diamonds!— because of the incredible number of women who answered the call. You know that people's hearts used to burn for Mohamed V; they adored him. They also adored Lalla Aicha, who was the leader of young girls and women, and particu- larly *our* leader, as we were the younger generation at that time.

After that, we got the idea of starting a women's association. Since we'd gotten such a positive response in our first experience and so many women had participated, we felt that we should organize these women and do something ` with them. So for the King's visit [to Tangiers] we were in the delegation of the Reform Party. Both old and young women were there. Then my uncle, Abdelkhalek Torres, asked me, "Well, what's going to be done now? Are you going to stop here, after seeing all these masses of women [rallying to see the Princess]?" I told him that of course we weren't going to stop, and that we would create a women's association which would be a part of the Reform Party. I remember that I had spent the night in his house. He used to get up at seven in the morning to read the papers before the rest of the household was up; and that morning I too got up at seven, and he called me. He said, "Come here. We'll talk about how to organize a women's association." I said, "Listen, we're the generation of women that are young and somewhat educated, so our job will be to play a secondary role. But the older women—I mean old respectable women—will be the members of the [central] committee. They will be the face of the association, representing the association to the people of Tetouan. As to us, the younger generation, we will serve as their assistants. That's to say, the president will have a young assistant or vice president, and the secretary general will also have a young assistant. These older women don't know how to read or write, but since they have grown up in nationalism they will be the ones to represent us to the rest of the people. These old ladies have a good reputation and carry an aura of respect and admiration." You shouldn't forget that these older women had good ideas! They were all above their fifties, but they all had lots of clear ideas about nationalism, which, as I said, they got from their fathers, husbands [or other male relatives].

So my uncle said, "Let's start, with the help of God!" Then we defined the objectives that we would aim for, and, after three or four days, we called a meeting. Every woman that we had invited to the meeting was there; they had all turned up. Then we created the central committee, which was made up of the older women [as I mentioned], and each one had her assistant who could read and write.[15] Oum Keltoum Torres, the sister of Abdelkhalek Torres, was the general secretary; her assistant was Khadouj Lakhitiba, the daughter of Abdellah Lakhtib. We made Lalla Fatouma El Wahbiya the treasurer; and her assistant was Lalla Rabia El Amrani, wife of Messfioui. The rest of the women were all named advisors. The committee was made up of eleven older women, and the rest were young. The Relief Committee was made up entirely of young women, as they had to go out and do strenuous work. Then we had a committee for education [all young women] to help girls without the means to pursue their education. We also had a committee in charge of organizing festivities, and another committee for raising consciousness and fighting illiteracy. I was the president of this last-named committee, although I was also the assistant to the general president of the association. I headed the committee because we used to go into the mountains to raise people's consciousness, focusing on rural women.

We would inform the male Reform Party member in a particular rural area, saying that such and such a woman will come to your village on such a day to initiate women villagers [in a campaign against ignorance]. On that particular day, he would gather a large number of women from the mountain villages. All of them would be sitting on the ground, and the woman from the association would talk to them. We made them aware of nationalism, and of the meaning of nationalism. I used to be one of those women who went up to the mountains for this job. We'd explain about colonialism and its consequences. All of this took place in the mountains. Some women would join us after collecting firewood; others would come with their goats or cattle. I used to sit down on a stone or under a tree, anything to make them aware of what was going on, what to do, how to be good nationalists, to love our children and our country, and to work hard for its freedom so that we can do what we want in our own country.

When we went among the mountain women, they were amazed, with wide eyes and open ears. They really seemed enthusiastic and thirsty for information. [People in the Rif had been fighting the Spanish until 1926]; then came a period of inactivity. The townspeople didn't work with them to prepare them, and the new generation grew up inactive. When we talked about nationalism, and said that women were emancipated and had started to work outside the home, doing their duty, they asked us questions like "What can we do?" We'd answer, what you can do now is first of all to know about what is going on. We'll inform you about everything. What we also want from you is to put just one *peseta* (that's how we used to talk about money then) in the box of the party. We're not asking for more than that, but give whatever you can afford to give. In fact the mountain women gave us everything that was left over after providing their children's food. And the reason they helped was that they were recognized as nationalists. Indeed they used to contribute, and they helped, and they opened up their minds. They were able to understand what was meant by nationalism, and also the consequences of their own actions. When we went back to see them, we informed them that their contributions had helped us achieve good results, and that we used their money for such and such a purpose.

There were times when we had to organize demonstrations, hold meetings or collect money. At that time, the party didn't have to worry about finances, because when we in the women's association organized gatherings there wasn't a single woman who came to join us empty-handed. A woman from the committee in charge of organizing festivities would sit at the entrance with a box, and people would put in whatever they could. We would keep some of what was collected for our own expenses, especially to buy school supplies for poor girls, and then we'd give the rest of the money to the party. We were so strongly united that it seemed as though all of the north of Morocco was working with the Reform Party.

We also applied these policies to the Rif, to Nador, El Hoceima, and many other places. It was only Tangiers that didn't join us, because at that time Tangiers was an international city, and the people there were content and didn't really care; they weren't frustrated or repressed, ready to explode [like us]. No, the people of Tangiers were just thinking about their pleasure; so we couldn't succeed there. We succeeded in all the northern area, or Spanish-controlled zone, except Tangiers.

When we took part in demonstrations, we used to be in the front ranks, in front of the men. They told us to go ahead, because the Spanish wouldn't harm women. We organized lots of demonstrations. The biggest one was when Mohamed V was sent into exile. That indeed was the "hottest" and most successful of the demonstrations, so much so that people had no room to walk in the street. Tetouan is a small place, and there were so many people out in the streets that they had to stand still; there was no space for them to move. There were so many nationalist songs we used to sing, lots of marching, chanting, etc. . . .

After this, the resistance started, and the use of weapons. Demonstrations, songs, and shouting were no longer adequate to express our opposition to colonialism, and our anger at the king's exile. Now, serious action was needed. However, not everyone is capable of armed resistance; only some people are up to it. We didn't even tell the older women about the need for action. Even though they held the positions of responsibility . . . we didn't always tell them about everything, because they'd say, "You're like our daughters. You shouldn't get involved; we worry about you." So we left them in the dark, and went about our work.

At that point, the resistance needed not just money, but actual gold. So each and every woman who could afford to give something in gold did so. I remember I had seven bracelets around my wrist, each weighing 100 grams, and as soon as they said that gold was needed I removed them from my wrist and threw them on the table. What we got from people was incredible!—gold, diamonds, and silver [from those who had nothing else], pearls, precious stones. My mother herself offered a diadem in white gold decorated with diamonds. We collected gold that was worth tremendous sums of money. We gave all the gold to the Committee for Resistance, which was in charge of selling gold and the rest of it. . . .

At that time Mehdi Bennouna [her husband] had come back from the United States, and he was not allowed to enter Tetouan, so we went to live in [the international city of] Tangiers. Tangiers was the city that was used for the transit of arms [but not for buying and selling]. When arms reached Tangiers, they were hidden in a special place, and there were certain men in charge of smuggling them into the country. But women too used to smuggle in arms, because nobody could touch women, not the police or officials, or anyone else. As a rule, women were respected, except, of course, those who "go out of their way" [prostitutes], may God preserve us. As for honorable women, it was forbidden for anyone from the police or any Moroccan government official to touch them. We used to take advantage of this state of affairs in order to smuggle arms. Take me, for instance—I don't know of any other person except myself doing this. There was a person I was supposed to meet at eleven in the evening. Each time I went I disguised myself in a different way [I wasn't so fat then]: Once I was dressed as a *Jbelia* [a woman from the mountains], once with my hair tied up disguised as a man, or I wore a djellaba and veil, sometimes with a walking stick; each time I had a special outfit. So, I would knock on that man's door; his entrance hall would be unlit, and I would find as many weapons as I was capable of carrying. I wouldn't see the man's face, but we had a secret password to exchange. For instance, I would say "glass," or "carrot," or "potato," and he'd say, "That's it. Pick up the stuff." So I would pick it up [the arms] and hide it under my clothes. The following night a taxi would come to the door of my house—I know the taximan, he's still alive: Abdelkrim Tangi, may God bless him. [His brother is Si Mohammed Tangi; his son is now the Secretary General of the Ministry of Fishing. This man worked hard for the resistance.] As I said, he'd come to my door and pick me up, just him and me with the arms still hidden in my clothes. Each time, he'd have a particular rendezvous in a special place to deliver what I had. For instance, we'd go a certain distance on the route to Rabat or Tetouan; then he'd stop, signal with his lights once or twice; we'd get the same signal back from the top of the hill or somewhere, and then we'd put down the stuff and leave. I didn't see either the man I got the arms from or the man I gave them to. So I'd go back home as if nothing had happened. And the next night I would start all over again.

This, then, is the work that was done on the political side, the work of resistance done by women in the north. We had some connections with women from Rabat, such as Lalla Malika El Fassi and Lalla Rqia Lamrania. In addition, we were crazy about nationalist songs; we used to memorize a lot of them and sing them in our gatherings and demonstrations; we had a large team of singers.

The women's association didn't limit itself to political issues; it got involved in social matters as well. For instance, we taught embroidery and handicrafts. In each town we would have a center for poor women where we would teach them various artisanal skills. They didn't have to pay anything; in fact we even provided them with all the necessary material. For those who couldn't afford the expense of schooling, we would take care of their education; we'd buy their books, shoes, blouses, and so on, and educate them. We also had health programs; the committee in charge would go to extremely poor areas, and would take care of women in labor, provide clothes for the baby, help the mother with milk if she couldn't breast-feed her baby. . . .

The name of the association meant "heart-on-heart" or "perfect union." When those older women saw our hard work, they became more dynamic. They had some brilliant ideas. You may think that because they're ladies of a certain age with no education, [they wouldn't be able to contribute much]. But they have ideas which are sometimes better than ours, because we're still under the sway of "crazy youth" and we still think about having fun and amusements. They used to give us structure and guide us: They'd say, "Today we have a meeting, and we have to do such and such a thing." We'd meet and exchange ideas; there would be minutes for each meeting, and after the minutes were edited and polished, they would be read at the start of the next meeting. Everything was beautifully organized, up until we got independence.

The Reform Party would send its decisions down to the women's association to guide them, and the women would send the minutes of their meetings to the men to inform them of the activities of the women's association. Khadija Bennouna explained how this liaison worked:

Sometimes certain meetings of the men would be interrupted because information or orders had to be given to the women's association. When they had to decide on something with the agreement of the women's association, there would be two women present in the men's meeting: Khadouj Khtiba and myself. So I would inform our president and Khadouj, in turn, would inform the general secretary; this was one method of work. Because older women used to remain in the dark; they didn't sit together with men; they used to be veiled. But we were used to mixing with men. So Khadouj and I would note down the minutes [of the men's meeting], and then we would inform our women by calling a meeting and working from our notes.

There was no problem with women being free to go out to work with the nationalist movement. There was no woman whose husband would forbid her from going out; there simply wasn't. If a nationalist woman had to go out for a meeting or a demonstration, or for any other thing like working with one of the committees, for instance, or visiting hospital patients or prisoners, such a woman would never be forbidden [by her husband] from getting involved in nationalism. Every man agreed to his wife's working for the national cause.

At this point her husband interjects: "But I used to forbid her from going out!

You didn't even live with me, let alone forbid my going out![18] This was the story then. I'm telling you, as far as work for nationalism went, women were free to a large extent. That's because in the Tetouan, and in all of the north, women were "pure." Young girls from the great families were all respectable and pure. Those women who were not pure [prostitutes], had to live in one particular area of the city; men who wanted them went to that area. These women were not allowed to walk in the streets. So any woman walking in the streets was pure and could *not* be approached by men or talked to. At that time there was a *pasha* who decreed that if a woman screamed in the street and said that this or that man insulted her or "approached" her, the man would get a hundred lashes, and would also have his hair and eyebrows shaved and then be let out in the streets like that. So the city was clean; if a woman went out alone it meant that she was respectable, noble. The area of the prostitutes was known; they weren't allowed to leave it; if they did so it was just to see the doctor in the hospital, and the time of their visit was known. They lived together in their area, and the city was clean without them. So men didn't hassle their wives about going out. [In that era], women and men sat together for family gatherings, such as lunch or supper, and it didn't matter; but for big parties, men and women were separate: for wedding parties, baptisms, and so on. They ate and drank separately; there used to be a day for women and another for men. Indeed [nationalism brought the sexes together]. As I told you, the old women, if they had to sit with men, wouldn't speak or lift their eyes; they'd lower their heads. Not like us; we were different. They chose us, young women, because we were daring—Khadouj Khtiba and myself. [Khadouj is still alive; she is about my age.]

Once we got independence, I decided to carry on working, but to get involved in social work, leaving politics. So that's what happened; I abandoned politics. Up until the present time, I'm doing social work. l work in the Red Crescent, and we have a charity association where we bring up girls here in Rabat. It's called *Jamiyat El Mouassat* [Relief]. I've been working in this for thirty-two years now. We bring up girls whose parents are identified; they come through the police . . . or girls whose fathers are known but incapable of working, or motherless or fatherless girls. We don't accept illegitimate children; and we accept girls only at school age, from five years on. They are entirely taken care of: they are fed, educated, given accommodation, full board, everything until they finish high school and go to the university. At this stage, we try to find them a grant and a place in the university dormitories; then they leave us. Their destiny, in most cases, is marriage. As for those who don't succeed in studies, or don't like studies, we steer them towards professional training or something practical like hairdressing—something that can enable them to earn their living. After a girl gets her diploma in professional training she leaves school and tries to find her own way.

We started this in a house in the medina of Rabat, a traditional house inside the medina. At that time, we brought together thirty-four girls; and provided them with beds and food, and then we started collecting ten dirhams a month from Rabati ladies. The girls started going to school. Then we realized that the house wasn't sunny enough, and that there was no clean air. So we found a piece of land, and we asked the Ministry of Health to give it to us. At first we put American Quonset huts there.[17] It was better for the girls to live in the Quonset huts and have fresh air and some sun. . . .

Khadija Bennouna and Malika El Fassi actually did the work themselves of fixing up the Quonset huts so that the girls could live there.

If there was a hole, we'd fill it up; if paint was needed or cement, we'd provide that. It was much better this way than living in an unhealthy house. Indeed the girls became stronger than before. Now everything is solid construction. You should come to see it. . . . This year we have 128 girls, but all of them have clothes, food, schoolbooks, beds, shoes. Just a couple of months ago, we went to *Macro* [department store] to buy them books. You know how many copybooks we bought? Two thousand eight hundred! We bought everything they needed for school, plus sportswear, tennis shoes. We spend millions at the beginning of each school year. Don't forget that this is an independent institution [*horra*]. It receives a very small help from the government. The rest is from contributions. . . .

I always say, I've been begging since I was seventeen years old. [My husband] was presiding in the Red Crescent committee set up to help Iraq, about a year and a half ago. Letters were sent to people asking for their contributions, but the women involved in the Red Crescent were hesitant about knocking on people's doors. They said they might have to wait outside the door for people's response, which could be positive or negative, or the people might tell them to go away. I told them, "I'm used to begging. Give those letters to me!"

There are a number of people who asked me to write my memoirs. I have never wanted to do so because these are things I've done for myself, God, and my country. But there are people who come to see me, like you, because they want to know about historical events. Well, of course I have no objection to talking about this. This isn't out of boasting. No, it's all done out of love of God and the country. That's all I can say.

III

Women in the Armed Resistance

10

Casablanca and the Women of the Armed Resistance

I was born in Casablanca, and my parents are from the Sahara, from Sidi Ifni. They came to live in Casa. In Casa, we found nothing. There was a French factory that [canned] sardines at the port. Moroccan women worked with the sardines. And the people, the Moroccans, we poor things, we didn't have anything but tents in that period. We didn't get anything for working. There weren't houses or anything.

—Ghalia Moujahide, resistance fighter, Rabat

The Neo-Proletariat

In present-day Morocco there are shantytowns on the edges of Casablanca, Salé, and other urban centers which give some idea of the living conditions of the urban poor in the last half of the protectorate. These shantytowns have no running water, no electricity, no sewage systems, no roads, and usually no gutters. They are just groupings of single-room structures propped up against one another, made of dingy white-painted *pisé* clay or other miscellaneous material, with sheets of tin or plastic, anchored with stones, for the roof, and packed dirt for the floor, each sheltering an entire family. Sometimes, as in Ghalia Moujahide's example cited above, there isn't even a semi-permanent structure, but only a tent to live in. The shantytowns and working class districts were prime recruiting areas for the Istiqlal Party, and then for the armed resistance. Located apart from the European settlements, they were not easily subject to administrative control or supervision. Moroccans in the shantytowns lived at a subsistence level, with variable and uncertain income. More and more, they began to feel that independence would not only liberate the country, but would also give them a better life.

There were several waves of rural-urban migration, starting in the 1920s, coinciding with either good times or bad in the economy.[1] In years of drought and famine, peasants were driven out of the countryside by economic hardship; in boom years they were lured into the cities by the promise of industrial employment. The first great wave came in 1926–31, boom years in the

Moroccan economy, when largescale construction projects created employment
for men who had moved from the countryside. The next wave of migration
came in 1936–37, years of drought and famine in the Moroccan countryside
which were followed by the worldwide great depression. The year 1942 was
another one of special economic hardship, brought on by World War II; it is
remembered by many Moroccans as the "year of the ration coupon." Then, in
1947–50, there was the biggest economic boom in the entire history of the
protectorate, a period of rapid economic expansion centered in Casablanca and
other coastal cities. This time, the expansion also created jobs for women,
leading to an increase in the female proletariat.

   This second period of economic expansion may have been created by the
colonial authorities at least partly for political reasons, so as to remove nationalist economic arguments. But by this time, the rise of the nationalist movement
and the escalating cycle of colonial repression had gone too far for rational
argument; 1947, when the economic expansion gained speed, was also the year
of the "Massacre of Casablanca," the year in which the Moroccan king aligned
himself definitively with the nationalists, and the year in which a small group of
nationalists in Casablanca started preparing the armed resistance.

Working Women

   It is notoriously difficult to gather accurate statistics about women's work.
Much of women's work, unpaid and in the home, is not counted at all, and even
women's work outside the home is usually underestimated. When I talked with
women and asked them whether they had worked outside the home before
joining the armed resistance, they would often say no, and then later in the
interview refer to work outside the home that they hadn't thought worth
mentioning earlier because it wasn't full time or continuous or in a factory. Most
analysts seem to agree that only a rather small minority of Moroccan Muslim
women in Casablanca worked outside the home,[2] a number that was even further
reduced in the period from 1952 to 1960, mostly because of unemployment
among men.[3] The Moroccan Muslim women who did go out to work were
generally from the poorest proletarian families. Many worked as domestic
servants (30 percent), most of them in European homes; others were factory
workers (20 percent), worked in processing wool and making carpets (13
percent), as seamstresses (7 percent), teachers and nurses (1 percent), and in
seasonal work (29 percent).[4]

   What is really surprising is that the percentage of women working outside
the home is not much higher. While that may be due partly to biases in
reporting, it also speaks to the difficulty of finding employment, the heavy
burden of household chores, and the pressure on men to emulate the bourgeois
model of keeping their wives in seclusion inside the house. Most of the families

of the Casablanca neoproletariat had recently migrated to the city from rural areas. As we have noted in earlier chapters, rural women in Morocco work hard—doing housework, cooking, getting wood and water, grinding grain, making butter, weaving, and helping with the harvest. Their dream is to *not* work when they move to the city, and this is also their husbands' dream. Many sayings and proverbs attest to this: "It's a dishonor for a man to make his wife work." "A happy woman is one who stays at home and is fed by her husband."[5] Women's work outside the home was only justified, or at least excused, on the basis of unfortunate necessity.[6]

Among the women I interviewed who worked outside the home, some seem to have enjoyed the income and sense of satisfaction that their work provided, others were matter-of-fact about their jobs and the necessity to work, and still others saw work outside the home as one more burden in an already overburdened life. Women who stayed at home usually did so either because they were very young (girls as young as ten years old were sometimes married), because there was no work available, or because their husbands kept them in seclusion and would not allow them to work outside the home. Here too, some women were pleased not to have to go out to work, while others were matter-of-fact about being confined to the house.

Economic pressures "emancipated" working women in the new urban proletariat. Women who worked outside the home moved around freely, contributed substantially to the household income, and might, if they were factory workers, participate in strikes and union meetings. But their economic emancipation did not necessarily translate into a change in social status or freedom from being controlled by their husbands. In fact the opposite often seemed to happen. It was still not respectable for a woman to go out alone.[7] Therefore the husband (or brother, or father, or even son) of a working woman would monitor her behavior even more closely, and she would be punished or repudiated by her husband at the slightest suspicion.

Women in the Proletariat—Growing Up

A 1949–1955 study of proletarian family structure shows that these families were essentially nuclear and monogamous.[8] Polygamy was a luxury, and most men in the proletariat could not afford to support more than one wife. The extended family, where it still existed, usually consisted of a nuclear family with one parent.

The study also showed a marked instability in proletarian families, and other studies confirm that there were high divorce rates in working class neighborhoods.[9] In the shantytown of Ben Msik in Casablanca, sociologist André Adam found that 51 percent of the women were in at least their second marriage, 47 percent of the men were in their second marriage, and almost 7 percent of the men had been married more than five times.[10] These circumstances also led to a new type of family, headed by a single woman, usually widowed or divorced. An analysis of the 1951–52 census revealed that more than 12 percent of the women in Casablanca were widowed or divorced, while in Morocco as a whole the figure was 14 percent.[11] Among the women I interviewed, only about a quarter were raised by both parents. Some were raised by one parent and a stepparent; but the largest number were raised by their mothers alone.

Women from the armed resistance who grew up in working class households tell of difficult, short, and unhappy childhoods. Even very young girls did heavy manual work, fetching water from the well or in large, heavy cans, cleaning, washing, and running errands. In the oral histories, women speak in sad detail about their experience growing up. But they speak most vividly of an interior life—dreams and incidents that gave them intimations of a more heroic life to come. Here the women shift into an entirely different register, the same voice in which they tell stories of their participation in the armed resistance. Fatna Mansar talks of seeing photos of Palestinian women bearing arms; Saadia Bouhaddou, as a child, loved to gaze at the stars and think; Ghalia Moujahide is steeped in the tradition of her tribe, the Ait Ba'amran, resisting Spanish colonialism in the Sahara.

Women in this milieu were married at very young ages, sometimes even before puberty, to men they had never met who were much older than they. Fatna Mansar was married at the age of ten to a man of twenty-five; Saadia Bouhaddou was also only ten when her father married her to a man of thirty-five who had already had six wives before her. A 1953 study of Derb Ghallef, a working class neighborhood in Casablanca, showed that almost half (42 percent) of the women had been married before the age of fifteen, and almost all (80 percent) of them before the age of twenty. On the other hand, only a small percentage (20 percent) of the men in the same neighborhood were married before they were twenty.[12]

Casablanca was a new city, built by the French protectorate. In the last half of the protectorate especially, it was the site of two fundamental and large-scale social transformations: urbanization and modernization. For the Moroccan Muslims who migrated there from rural areas, the move to Casablanca was often a wrenching experience. They were peasants who had to adapt to city life; they were uprooted from small tribal communities and traditional societies, and had to relocate themselves in a large, shifting, rootless population, in a society that was rapidly modernizing. Women in rural areas were used to working in the fields and to considerable freedom of movement. The veil was something that women wore in the cities, where they were likely to run across strange men, not in the countryside. In the cities, on the other hand (with the possible exception of Tetouan), respectable women did not usually go out on the streets at all, and if they did they were heavily clothed, wearing a *haik* or *djellaba*, a head scarf, and a veil, and escorted by a male member of the family. Some women, recently migrated from rural areas, found it difficult to adjust to these new restrictions.

Some of these recent immigrants reacted to the trauma of dislocation by reaching out for connections with the societies they had left behind. A 1951–52 study found that 30 percent of the men in one Casablanca working-class community had married a woman of their same tribe.[13] One way or another, most members of the Casablanca neoproletariat were searching for new forms of community life; indeed, this was a large part of the impetus which led them to join the independence movement. In the forties, men and women of the Casablanca proletariat were recruited in large numbers by the Istiqlal Party; later, some of them joined the secret cells of the armed resistance.

Women in the Armed Resistance

Many women participated actively in the 1953–56 armed resistance. Some joined the first resistance cells as they were being organized in the late forties, and more joined later, after the armed resistance broke out in August of 1953. Some men would not allow their wives to go out of the house, but even in seclusion, women played significant roles. They kept watch while meetings took place, hid arms in their houses, and supported the men who fought in the resistance and those in prison by cooking for them, washing their clothes, and performing other essential functions. These activities within the home don't qualify a woman for status as a veteran of the resistance, and some of these women, when asked, say that they didn't do anything much. Others stress the scope and importance of the work they did, as well as the hardships they suffered because of their husbands' resistance activities. This was the case with Aicha and Mina Senhaji, co-wives of resistance leader Abdellah Senhaji, and it is why I included them in the oral histories—in order to expand the definition of what women's contributions were significant, admirable, and even heroic.

In the shantytowns and working-class districts of Moroccan cities at this time, many husbands did not allow their wives to leave the house; it was most unusual for a man in this milieu to share secrets with his wife or to allow her to participate in any political activities. Thus it was no small accomplishment for a woman to be trusted with secrets, and it was even more extraordinary for her to join a resistance cell, and to be given important responsibilities. However, it is important to note that Morocco was and is a patriarchal society. Women were brought into the armed resistance, not because men thought that women in general were capable and trustworthy, but because men decided that some women were *needed* for particular tasks such as carrying messages and arms. Most women joined the resistance after their husbands or other male relatives were already actively involved and worked under the direction of their husbands, and it was the male resistance leaders who determined which women would participate and what responsibilities they would be given. The women who participated in the armed resistance took on extraordinary roles because there were extraordinary circumstances. And when things were back to normal, the women went back to their normal, traditional roles.

The oral histories tell several different stories about how women joined the resistance. Ghalia Moujahide was brought into a resistance cell by her husband. Saadia Bouhaddou, on the other hand, joined the resistance without the knowledge or permission of either her husband or her parents. And Fatna Mansar forced her way into her husband's resistance cell against his wishes. None of this disproves the general statement that men were in command, but it does show how a strong, resourceful woman could impose herself and challenge the norms of traditional society in the extraordinary circumstances of the resistance.

There are about three hundred women currently registered as veterans of the armed resistance,[14] in contrast to approximately thirty thousand men who have the same status. Clearly this is not an accurate reflection of women's participation. Just as the roles of women in Moroccan society and history in general are consistently overlooked and downplayed, so women's roles in the resistance have been minimized and official statistics distorted by persisting gender distinctions. Marie-Aimée Helie-Lucas writes about this minimizing of women's roles in reference to the Algerian liberation struggle:

> If a man carried food to the armed fighters at great personal risk, he was called a "fighter." A woman doing the same thing was called a "helper." If a man risked his life to hide armed fighters or wanted political leaders, he was called a "fighter." A woman doing the same was simply performing the female task of "nurturing." Nor was she considered a fighter when she collected fuel or food for the fighters, or carried their guns, or guided them through the mountains. She was merely helping the men. Only the French army acknowledged her action by imprisoning and torturing her in concentration camps and killing her.[15]

Another factor that prevented women from getting recognition as veterans of the resistance was the application process itself. In order to be considered for a card, you had to compile a substantial dossier, with written testimony and corroborating testimony by witnesses. Women were illiterate; some were not allowed to go out; and they were generally intimidated by dealing with official government bureaucracies. I spoke with many women who took an active role in the armed resistance and yet had still not succeeded in getting their card and its accompanying benefits.

Because the resistance organization was made up of secret cells, the women who were involved did not know what other women were doing at the

time. Every woman I interviewed stressed that. It was an entirely new experience for women to work directly with men, especially with men other than their
husbands or other close male relatives. It was also new to be isolated from other
women, and to be sworn to keep secrets from those they would normally confide
in, including their own mothers. Even now, forty years later, most of the women
don't identify so much with other women in the resistance as they do with the
other members (usually men) of their resistance cell and organization.

These women are often reluctant to talk about their experience growing
up before they entered the resistance, and even more reluctant to talk about
their lives since independence in 1956. As might be expected, this is especially true when women are talking in a more public forum, in a group of other
women. Instead, they talk as though their real lives started when they became
politically aware and joined the resistance, and ended in 1956 when they went
home. It is this heroic life which the women remember and relate, using a
strong "I"-centered narrative, and setting their stories in an historical continuum of other wars that Moroccans have fought against foreign invaders and
colonialism. The rest of their lives seem to be marked by discontinuity and
disappointment.

The central myth of these oral histories is a heroic myth of the Moroccan
woman, steadfast, active, and courageous (often even braver than the men she
worked with) in the struggle for national liberation. This resonates less with
traditional ideas of Moroccan womanhood, which stress self-sacrifice and acting
for others, than it does with a character archetype of Moroccan folktales: a strong,
smart heroine who outwits the men in authority to get what she wants. And the
form that the oral histories take—detailed, dramatic accounts of missions carried
out during the armed resistance—is reminiscent of the Moroccan folktales which
are traditionally told by older women in the family.

When I first listened to women talking about their experiences in the
resistance, I wasn't sure what to make of what I was hearing. I was impressed
with the scope of women's roles and activities, and I was able to gather a great
deal of detailed information about the particular operations each woman had
carried out. Yet once I had interviewed a certain number of women, subsequent
interviews didn't yield much new information. There seemed to be endless
stories, with extraordinary detail, of going to get arms and ammunition, of
hiding them from the police, and of being dragged down to the police station,
being interrogated and beaten. Much of the narrative was in the form of dialogue, with conversations repeated word for word. When I interviewed women
more than once, they came back to the same stories they had told me before,
repeating them in almost the same words. The stories were compelling in the
way the women told them, but what was their significance as history? The
particular incidents began to seem much the same, just with different characters
and different numbers and kinds of weapons.

Then I began to pay attention to the stories themselves, including all the repetitions, the formulaic expressions, and the archetypes of character and plot, and I realized that these stories opened up much larger questions about the meanings to be found in oral history interviews and about oral history's complex relationship to both history and myth. The women's stories of the resistance are repetitive and lacking in variety because in a sense they are all telling the same story—the myth-biography of a female hero of the resistance.[16]

All of the oral history texts in Part III include material drawn from at least two separate interviews. When women talked in the more public forum of a group meeting their narrative focused almost exclusively on detailed, dramatic stories of joining and carrying out missions for the armed resistance. It was only in a second interview, in their homes, that women were willing to talk about more personal matters, and to look back over the whole spectrum of their lives. Even with women whom I met first in their homes, a second interview was useful to clarify points of fact, and to expand on some subjects. In presenting the oral histories, I have kept the sequence of the interviews in order to show the *difference* in women's narrative strategy depending on the setting—public versus private, formal versus informal. In the oral histories, the women are presenting themselves in at least two distinct persona: the heroic story/myth of a woman warrior in the resistance, and the life history of a woman growing up under the double oppression of poverty and a restrictive social order.

All of the women from the armed resistance punctuated their narrative with "I'm not lying to you," or similar expressions, and with various oaths, calling on or swearing by God. This was so striking that I asked various Moroccan colleagues what they thought it signified. The most convincing explanation came from a young man who had been doing research on families in rural areas around Taza. He said that because Moroccan popular culture portrays women as liars and minimizes their roles in history and society, the women themselves may feel that they have to buttress their stories, to "prove" that they participated actively in the resistance, by swearing to God as witness and by repeated assurances that they were not lying.

I have tried to keep the women's distinctive speech patterns, and to keep the drama and passion of their stories. I feel a special responsibility to the women of the armed resistance, because the women themselves were so concerned about their oral narrative and how it would be translated into print. They wanted to be sure not only that they had spoken accurately and truthfully for the record, but also that they had spoken well, that their words had been eloquent and well chosen.

The seven women in the oral histories speak for themselves—and they also represent the hundreds and thousands of unsung heroines of the Moroccan resistance. Here they talk about their lives, their experience in the armed resistance, and what it meant to them.

11

Fatna Mansar: Casablanca

I first met Fatna Mansar at the Casablanca home of Professor Soumaya Naamane-Guessous, together with Soumaya's mother and her father, resistance leader Thami Naamane.[1] When I first met Fatna, she was wearing a djellaba and head scarf, and her eyes were hidden behind tinted glasses. As she spoke, I was impressed with her poise and eloquence.[2] We started the interview by asking Fatna to tell us about her life as though she were telling a story. She spoke for about an hour, with frequent interjections by others to check on the names of other people in the narrative and whether they were still alive, to clarify certain points, and to ask about the participation of women in general and before 1953, and about her experience of colonialism.

I was still a child when the war of Palestine began. . . .[3] I went and I saw women carrying machine guns, climbing mountains, in the East, in Syria, Lebanon, and Palestine. I saw it in the [Istiqlal Party] newspaper *Al Alam*. And here I didn't know that a woman could leave her house. That was what I was taught—that a woman left the house of her father to go to her husband's house, and left her husband's house to be taken to the cemetery. And when I saw a woman like that [holding a machine gun], and I was young, I just stayed there like this [amazed, mouth open].

Once I said to the man in the newspaper shop, "Khou Said?" [calling his name] He said to me, "Yes?" I asked him, "What is this woman [pictured in the newspaper] doing?"[4] . . . I was still young; I was only seven years old. He told me, "She's a Muslim." "And what is she doing?" "Oh, my girl, those Jews did this and this and this, and so on . . ." [explaining the conflict between Jews and Muslims in Palestine] until I could understand. Because I went every day to look at that paper for a long time, and to contemplate that woman. And after that I got an idea that stayed inside me. . . . Inside myself, I asked myself, why do they tell Moroccan women one thing, and there they tell women something different and they act like that? I had the idea that she must be a woman and a man at the same time.

I was born in 1931; my name is Mansar Fatna. I was brought up in a four-person family—mother, sister, and brother. Because my father died when I was six years old, it was my mother who brought us up, who worked. We also

11.1

Fatna Mansar (1995).

Credit: Anne White.

had a bit of land for agriculture. We were an extremely poor family, on the edge of penury.

Talking about life in Casablanca under the protectorate, before the 1953 exile of Mohamed V, Fatna blames French colonialism for all the inequities in Moroccan economic and social life, and for the lack of opportunity for the common people:

We were smothered; there was no liberty, no human rights. Those who were with the French, or the French law, had everything they wanted; and those were not were deprived of everything. Like education, for example. It was the children of the upper class who were able to study, and not the children of the common people. For example, in the medina[5] there was only one primary school and one secondary school, and even the secondary school was not for the children of the common people, just for the children of high-class people. As for the farmers, what happened was that when the wheat was ready, [the French] came to the place where there was a good harvest, and they weighed all the wheat, and the farmers had to give whatever the government asked for.

Fatna was married when she was only ten years old to a man of twenty-five, who came from a family of farmers in the province of Taza. He had fought with the French army during World War II, and had been wounded. At the time of their marriage, he worked in Meknes as a merchant, dealing in women's clothes, makeup, and sundries.

I was married when I was ten years old. When I was married, we went directly to live in Meknes, and I stayed with the man, who locked me in the house, because I was too young, and I didn't know anything at all.[6] I played all the time—sometimes I fell asleep in the middle of the house or somewhere else—until he came back and opened up the house.

The first family [who weren't relatives] that I knew was the family El Assafi, and that was when I was fourteen years old. After that we used to discuss politics, like that, up until 1950 when we were exiled from Meknes. We were exiled because of politics. The armed movement didn't exist yet, but there was the party, the Istiqlal Party. And when the French discovered that people were involved with the party, they exiled them [or put them in prison]. Because my husband was a veteran of the French army, they didn't have the right to imprison him, and when they exiled him he was free to choose the city he wanted to go to. Besides us there was a group of professors and a school director. Each one left for a different city: Rabat, Salé. Me, I was from Casablanca, so we came here.

I knew Rqia Lamrania and Fatima Hassar through the party. There was coordination between the different party bureaus. This group of women [that I knew], for example. We got to know each other through [Istiqlal Party women's] meetings. Yes, I went out with my husband for meetings, but I went to the meetings alone. Women went out alone when they were going to meetings [held in women's houses]; they weren't going to get lost. There were meetings here in Casa, but the center of the women's movement was in Salé, in Rabat and Salé.

Touria Seqatte was with us in Meknes; she was exiled to Salé; and then she got in contact with the party women's movement in Salé. Me, I went to Salé to have meetings with the representatives of the party down there. I took the bus by myself. I went to see women whose husbands had been arrested. We visited the prisoners who were from Casa and who didn't have anyone to visit them. We held meetings in Touria's house. Her husband was in prison [at the time].

El Assafi came one year to take an exam here, at the school of Mohamedia. And that was the first time in my life that I went out without my husband.[7] When El Assafi had finished the exam, he asked my husband if he could take me with him. After ten days, I still remember it, there was lots of coming and going at the house of El Assafi. Once the people had left, he came back to our place and said to us: "What on earth is going on? There are rumors that they are threatening Mohamed V." Eight days later, it was officially announced that Mohamed V was going to be exiled. I began to go out, me and Touria. Here I will bring other people into the story, as I told it to myself yesterday.[8] What should we do? It was decided we should go [to the mosque] to pray, all of us dressed in haiks, in order to go see the official goings on. We set out from here. All of the political leaders had been arrested. One day they exiled Mohamed V, and the next day there was a revolution in Rabat, and afterwards there was the revolution in Salé, and after that we went out and took part [in the demonstrations]. Yes, [women went out into the streets], and I still remember, the first woman who was hit, who got hit, was the wife of Cherkaoui.

I stayed there fifteen days, and then I went to the prisons to look for El Assafi; to see if there was someone who could give me some information. Finally I located El Assafi in an underground prison in Salé. I got in touch with a policeman [at the prison], and I began to cry in front of him, and I still remember, he told me, "Follow me," and I followed him, and then he brought El Assafi out from the basement through a little door. El Assafi came out, and he couldn't stand on his feet; he had wrapped them up so that he could lean on them. And he scolded me for having come to see him. And then I stayed there until we came back to Casa, and each of us began to think about what we should do. Meanwhile the resistance continued.

Joining the Resistance

Some months after the exile of Mohamed V, in early 1954, Fatna realized that her husband and some other men had formed a resistance cell.

They had formed an organization, and some of them were meant to carry out operations while the others were meant to distribute leaflets. As for me, because I was a woman, they hadn't given me any responsibilities at that time. I didn't know that then, but when I sensed it, I stepped forward and imposed myself. I told them that either they would let me join the group or else I would carry out an operation on my own, which might end up being something that was wrong. And they still refused to let me join the group, so I went ahead with my own operation. I formed a group of women, and we collected money to buy food and clothes for prisoners who had come from outside Casablanca and didn't have any family members in the area.

Then one day, in 1954, there was a strike, and there were two big wholesale grocery stores in Derb Gnaoua [that didn't close for the strike]. So I called two women from our group to burn down the two grocery stores, and this was our first operation. What did we do? I said, "We'll pour gasoline on them." Who was going to do it? I told them, "You go stand next to the door . . . You, you go here; you there, and me, I'll go in." But one of them said, "No, that one will go stand next to the door, and that one will go in and ask for something, and you, you'll light the fire." We left to carry out the operation, but we didn't succeed. Just when I took out the match to light the bottle of gasoline that I had put in the cloth, the woman had started to argue with the Jew [the Jewish store owner]. And there were several other Jews standing by the door. He said to her, "I won't do business with you! Get out!" While he was busy trying to make the woman leave, I got away from the grocery store. The police came. Tazi [my husband] found out about it. There was someone who followed us, who saw us. At that point they called me, and they gave me a responsibility, which was to transport arms.

Fatna's account of forcing her way into her husband's resistance cell doesn't necessarily contradict the general statement that men were in control, but it does show how a strong, resourceful woman could get her way and take on important responsibilities in the resistance in spite of opposition from her husband and other men. Fatna herself explains this contradiction:

Women didn't have any freedom in relation to men—unless the woman was stronger than the man. I told you that I was turned down, even though they were facing the threat that I would carry out an operation all by myself if they didn't let me into the group, and even though I knew everything. But for them "I knew everything" was just a figure of speech, because I saw the comings and goings and I wanted to talk. But when I carried out the operation; at that moment they changed their minds and gave me some responsibility.

She went on to describe her role in the organization, and the significant level of responsibility it involved.

I carried arms from Meknes, and after I had carried out that operation without any mistakes I became the person responsible for arms. My role was to give the arms to the people I had information on. When they finished their operations, they gave the arms back to me, without knowing either where I had gotten the arms or where I put them. When we suspected that they were going to arrest someone, I took what there was in the house. Sometimes the director of the group was there, but whether he knew what was going on or not, I had the authority to take care of the arms that I had hidden. I took them on my back, here [showing how she put them on her back], or I put them in a basket and I put vegetables on top of them. These were the sorts of things that women did, me and the others.

[I was never caught], but that wasn't because of me or because of my power; it was the power of God that saved me. One morning while I was sitting around, a man came and told me that Abdellah the butcher had been arrested at Sidi Harrazem. Farida had told him, and she had sent him to ask me to bring her son Zakariya's clothes to her. Me, I was at someone else's house; an operation had just been carried out and the partisan had brought the weapon back to me; and I hadn't had time yet to hide the weapon. What I used to do with the arms, so that noone would know where I put them, was: I dug out a hole in the wall, and then I brought a brick and fit it to the hole. Then every time that they needed something, I took out the weapon and I closed up the hole with the brick and some mortar, and that way noone knew anything. But I needed some time to carry out this operation. So that morning I just put the weapon in my handbag. There were also some resistance tracts left in the bag, those that hadn't been distributed the day before. So I put the bag in the suitcase with Zakariya's clothes, and I picked up the suitcase and took it without realizing what I had done. As soon as I arrived at the door of the Mohamedia school, I ran into a member of the French legion. He called me. And at that moment I remembered my bag! But there was nothing more I could do. Inside my head, I said something. I told myself: "When they begin to beat me, I don't know what I'll tell them, but I won't talk. If I say anything at all, I'll just keep saying: '*Allah, A Rassoul Allah*' [Allah, Prophet of Allah], until I die." I put down the suitcase. He asked me to open it. He spoke in French; me in Arabic. I told him, "Me, I opened it when I was getting ready to leave the house. You open it yourself if you want to see anything; me, I opened it before, when I wanted to." He said: "Open it." And I said, "Open it yourself." He spoke in French and I spoke in Arabic—until finally a man appeared [who could translate]. He told him: "She said that she had opened the suitcase when she was getting ready to leave the house, and that now you should open it yourself if you want to." He opened it. Boy, are they scared! *Ouilee*! [an oath] They die! The suitcase wasn't locked, so as soon as they touched it, it opened suddenly, and he jumped! But they do have one thing, and that is respect for women. When he found my handbag, he took it and did like this [gestures putting the bag aside]. He started searching the suitcase, until he discovered that the clothes were just baby clothes. Then he gave the bag back to me and gave back the suitcase, and he told me, "Excuse me." He put the bag there, with the weapon, the resistance papers, and everything.

In general, women participated in an important way; women had big responsibilities in the resistance. Because it was very difficult for a man to carry weapons and to get by the authorities. . . . Once, when they had searched the men in the bus, [the Moroccan policeman] said, "You go ahead and search the women yourself. I'm not going to search them." There were some women, but not me, who put weapons on their backs, and then strapped their babies on top of the weapons. As for me, when I carried arms, I didn't wear the djellaba; I engulfed myself in a haik because it was roomier. Most of the time they didn't search women.

Thami Naamane added to this point:

"And besides that, women were veiled, and even for a passport or iden-tification card—which women could get made and which enabled them to go anywhere—they still didn't take off their veils. In that era, women were not allowed to have their photograph put on official papers. Moroccans [especially husbands] would not tolerate that. It was at the time of independence that that was allowed for the first time."

Women did things during the resistance, and some of these women were known and some were unknown. Me, I know a woman who had only one foot. She limped, and what's more, she was an old woman: the Haja l'Batoul, may God rest her soul. She had neither sons nor daughters. She was always at the door of the prison, bringing food and clothes [for the prisoners]. She was dark-skinned; she went to all the prisons; I often went with her. She didn't have anyone. . . . And [in other areas of Morocco] women participated actively, both those who were politically aware and those who weren't. They collected money for those children who had become orphaned and for those women who had lost their husbands. And women went all the way to the Sahara to go to the Moroccans who had been exiled there.

The Dossier

In 1959, like many others who had participated in the armed resistance, Fatna applied for, and eventually received, an identification card certifying her participation in the armed resistance and giving her certain benefits. In the early seventies, the commission began a review of all the dossiers, and in 1974 Fatna began the process of requesting her second card. Hers was a controversial case. At the first review session, in August 1975, one witness confirmed that she was the wife of Mohamed Tazi and the sister of Mohamed Mansar, both known members of the resistance, and that her husband had arranged for her to bring arms from Meknes, but he did not mention the name of the man in Meknes who gave her the arms. Another witness said that Fatna and her husband used to accomplish many things, and that some of the people there knew her. This testimony was judged to be inconclusive.

11.2

Fatna Mansar (ca. 1960).

Photo from dossier.

11.3

Fatna Mansar as a young woman.

After she had been notified that the commission's Casablanca branch was "not convinced by the evidence included in the documents," Fatna wrote to the director of the Commission to strengthen her case. In this letter, dated April 1, 1977, she first lists the members of her resistance cell, as well as other partisans who "set up activities." The rest of the letter is devoted to detailed descriptions of Fatna's participation in several resistance operations, including the exact numbers and kinds of weapons she got and the names of other people involved. In her oral narrative, cited above, she just mentions her first mission to Meknes, and puts the emphasis instead on the significance of her role as "the person responsible for arms," trusted to act with or without the knowledge of the director. In her letter, on the other hand, she gives all the details of that first mission as evidence of her active participation:

When the cell started its activities, I was ordered to go to Meknes. When I got there, I went to the Dior Jdad mosque. I found a man at the entrance, and gave him the arranged signal, and he entered the mosque and I followed him. He went to a stack of fertilizer bags, and started moving them, until he got to the last bag. He opened it, and took two guns from it. There were two machine guns and thirty bullets. These are the activities I did inside my cell. After independence, I knew the man's name. It is Al Haj Mohamed Ziad.[9]

In a second review session, on February 14, 1978, one witness said that she was Mohamed Mansar's sister, and that she knew about [resistance] operations [another witness confirmed this], but that she herself did not carry out any resistance operation. Some of the other people present at the meeting said that if she did carry out any operation it was along with her husband, who was a known partisan. One witness said that she did bring two guns from Taza in early 1955. In a third review session, on July 6, 1978, one witness said that she was a well-informed woman, and confirmed that her husband had sent her to Meknes and that she brought two weapons and some bullets from there. This seems to have decided the case in Fatna's favor, and she received her second card.

The controversy over Fatna's request for a second card illustrates some of the problems that women faced in getting recognition for their participation in the resistance. Most of them worked directly under their husbands and other close male relatives, who were thus the only people who knew what they had done, but whose testimony on their behalf was suspect precisely because they were relatives. In Fatna's case, her husband had died [killed in an automobile accident] in 1957 and so was not available to testify. The burden of proof was heavier on a woman, to convince the commission that she had carried out resistance operations on her own, as there was always the suspicion that she knew the details of operations because her husband had been involved. As for her brother, Mohamed Mansar, while the testimony in the dossier implies that he brought Fatna into the resistance cell, in fact it was the other way around:

I was the one who brought *him* into the movement. I received a lot of guests, men from the movement, and I hid them at my place. My brother saw that and didn't understand [what was going on]. I was afraid that he'd tell other people what we were doing, so I proposed to the directors of the organization that we bring him in with us. He was a high-school student; he was like my son. He distributed tracts for the resistance.

When I asked Fatna about relations between men and women in the armed movement, she responded eagerly:

There were such good relations; you can't imagine! There was an enormous difference [from before]. The relations were really excellent! You didn't sense that there was any difference [between men and women]. I was seventeen, so I was young, and the men [were young] too. But sometimes, when my husband happened to have gone out of the house, I would receive twelve people [men], and they would treat me like their mother, sister, daughter. It was like that that they saw me. . . .

[Were there some subjects that the men didn't want to bring up when women were there?] *Excuse me!* In the armed movement *noone* talked to another person when they were in a large group, and noone knew who among the others belonged to the armed movement, except for the three other people who were in the same cell. In a group, they were just friends, but there was no discussion [of resistance matters] among them. When there was an order from the director to execute a mission, it was only passed to three people, because otherwise, if one person was arrested, everyone might be hurt. In my cell, I received some orders; I was responsible for guarding the arms. There was one man who knew that, but even he didn't know where I had hidden the arms. So if he was arrested, and I was also arrested, I wouldn't give away the secret of where I had put the arms.

I learned [these methods of doing things] by myself and from the directors. Every person had his own method of working. Once we had received the orders, we figured out for ourselves how to execute them. For women, most of the time a woman would mingle in the crowd as a partisan, a man, was passing through. I would go with the partisan, and he would give me the weapon, and I wouldn't tell him where I had hidden it. I would hide it on my back, my stomach, behind my back—where I hide it is my affair—in my pants, in the bag of vegetables, in the bag of things to take to the hammam, all depending on the circumstances. You keep these ideas to yourself; otherwise, if I tell them to you and you are arrested, maybe you will give away the secret. No, everyone has his own way of executing the orders. But you have to carry out the orders or else they will execute you. The information given in the orders is the exact time, the people involved, and the place. It was obligatory to execute the orders. Several times [someone was executed because he didn't carry out the orders]. Because once he had the information, he might tell it to other people. If a person wasn't reliable, he was dangerous!

After Independence

In 1957, Fatna's first husband was killed in an automobile accident; and in 1965, she married a younger man, someone she chose for herself. (Her second husband had actually participated in the armed resistance in Casa, but they didn't know one another during that period.) They have one son. While Fatna's personal life seems to have turned out well, she is disappointed with the direction that the country has taken since independence. Of all the women veterans of the resistance that I talked with, Fatna was the only one who had concrete ideas of political, economic, and social programs that might have come out of the national liberation movement, and she was the only one who had stayed involved in politics after independence to try to make this happen.[10] She also discussed the relationship between party politics and the women's movement, and the current situation of the women's movement in Morocco and in other Arab countries.

[After independence] we began to try to organize associations. Unfortunately I can't talk about that. . . .[11] In 1963, when the leadership of the UNFP were arrested, the party dispersed, and the women's movement too. They weren't able to hold meetings like before. . . . There were some professors and students, but not [a political party or movement] the way it was before. . . .

The other organizations have a relationship with capitalism, but not with the common people, because that isn't in their interest. I'll give you an example. My party has never come to power, except once for nine months, and then it proposed an economic program that would have unlinked the Moroccan currency from the French currency. In fact the program that we are following now is the program that they proposed before.[12] And it happened that they cut salaries from top to bottom [from rich to poor], in order to have everyone participate in economic reform. I remember there was someone important, and before getting his salary he looked to see if the law would affect him, and before signing the law he took his salary check. But all the parties that succeeded [the UNFP] do nothing but talk—blah, blah. So our party hasn't gotten into power to be able to govern and to put its ideas into practice. All the party has done is to sacrifice lots of activists, and to provide victims for the prisons. In fact, there's no other party that has given more than us, if you want to talk in terms of the dozens of party activists who have been repressed, arrested, and killed.

[If the UNFP had gotten into power], it might have addressed women's rights and reform of the moudouana [Islamic family law]. But at least in our party, we try to achieve some equality between men and women in the family. For example, if I want to go out without telling my husband, he won't say anything about it. And if he comes back late, I'm not going to ask him, "Where were you?" If you want to reform the society, you have to begin by reforming yourself.

There is an invisible hand . . . I didn't say this before, but now I will say it: There is an invisible hand that keeps women down. I mean to say that men are afraid that women will get ahead of them. Men imagine that women will be dangerous to them if they are educated or if they are emancipated. But really the opposite is the case. The man can't move ahead in life without the woman; she is always at his side; one hand can't clap . . . .

Men are afraid of women, and won't let any women's movement develop except for the movement that comes out of the Palace. We work [in the party] and we bring intellectuals together to have conferences; and we participate in conferences outside of Morocco . . . But it's always the men who represent the party. I think that on the one hand women don't want to wake up, and on the other hand men exploit women for public relations. But on women's issues we never find ourselves united and in agreement. This is true in all the Arab countries. Women represent the parties, but they don't constitute an autonomous movement. The women's movement that exists is directed by the state and financed by the state. The same thing is true of the other movements in Arab countries. Men, even if they reach a high level of evolution themselves, do not want women to evolve. Men will always hold on to this old idea.

12

Saadia Bouhaddou: Casablanca

I first met Saadia Bouhaddou in a group of ten former members of the armed resistance in Casablanca who had been brought together by the Casablanca delegation of the High Commission for Veterans of the Resistance.[1] The session started with a lot of confusion, as the women gave me written material and documents relating to the resistance, gave their names, showed their identification cards, and greeted me and my colleague, Amina Fahim, and each other. Then we settled down around a large table, and each woman took her turn with the microphone and talked for as long as she wanted. Sometimes other women challenged and interrupted the speaker, and at the end of each woman's narrative everyone applauded. Later in the session, after most of the women had talked [and a few had left], things became increasingly chaotic, with everyone shouting to be heard, and some women bursting into patriotic song. It was a lively meeting, rather like the parties that Moroccan women give for other women in their homes, where there is music, dancing, and lots to eat and drink, and women tell stories and jokes. At the Casablanca meeting, Saadia Bouhaddou was the second woman to have the microphone, right after Touria Ouezzani had finished, and this is the story she told:

Greetings. We're very pleased to have this meeting, as it gives us a chance to relive the resistance. People didn't know each other much during the resistance. I was known by only four people, and I only knew four people. Because I was the guardian for the arms at my house. . . .

So I will begin at the beginning. I was a nurse with Dr. Ouerzazi. Here is the identification card that I had in that period. I was nineteen years old when Mohamed V was taken away. When they said that Mohamed V had been taken away, I was roused by the nationalist spirit. I didn't know what to do anymore.

They used to come to us there at the clinic, at Dr. Ouerzazi's. All of the members of the resistance organizations came there to have bullets removed and to be taken care of. But I didn't dare tell anyone that I wanted to do anything. My doctor had confidence in me; he didn't hide anything at all from me, but I still couldn't get up the nerve to say anything to him. So I just kept going like that.

One day, I went out in the evening and I was at loose ends. I had just come from work, and I went out at night and met up with a man. . . . Yes, excuse

12.1

Saadia Bouhaddou (1994).

Credit: Alison Baker.

12.2

Left to right: Fatima (daughter), Saadia, Kautar (granddaughter) (1995).
Small photo left to right: Saadia's mother, her grandmother, and Saadia herself.

Credit: Anne White.

12.3

Saadia with her granddaughter, Asmaa (1996).

Credit: Anne White.

me, during the day I'd seen the man and he was threatening someone because of a cigarette. He was asking him why he was smoking, using French merchandise. That evening, I was bored, I went out, and I met him. I ran into him and I recognized him. So I followed him. When I followed behind him, he stopped, and when he stopped, I stopped. When I got tired I became more daring, and I finally caught up with him and said to him, "Please, I would like to talk with you." He asked me, "What do you want?" I told him, "Next to the Malika Cinema, just a while ago, I saw what you did, what happened . . . and I didn't dare talk with you then, so I've been looking for you." He told me, "It wasn't me you saw." I said, "No, it was you." In short, I wouldn't let go of him. He finally said to me, "O.K. Where are you going now?" I couldn't think of what to tell him, so I said, "I was going to the movies." He said, "Go into the movie theater and go back out the exit." I went into the theater . . . What did I say to myself? "The bullet will come and hit me in the head; the bullet will hit me in the head because I've gone too far; I've overstepped the bounds of curiosity." I left the theater and I walked about two meters, and then I found the man again behind me. He asked, "Are you the one who was looking for me just a while ago?" I said, "Yes." He asked, "What do you want now?" I said, "I too want to fight for my country. I haven't been able to sleep thinking about it." He said, "Alright. Tomorrow we'll meet at ten o'clock." Oh no! He told me, "You'll go somewhere with me."

We went to a garage. There was another woman there, and we left her alone while I went to take the oath. In the oath we said, "It is a promise to God and to the nation, that I will be true to my nation and to my people, my king. And that I will be true in all things. I will sacrifice myself; I will sacrifice my father and my mother if I find that they have strayed from the path." It was the truth. . . . Oh, lady! After I took the oath, this woman, do you know what she said? She suspected that we'd gone to have fun, to laugh, and she said to me, "Aouili! You left me here all alone like Aicha Qandisha [a female demon]!"

So I took the oath . . . and the next day, we met at ten o'clock. He told me, "You know, we don't have any women now, but I'll take you to a man where there *are* some women." He took me to the Secret Organization for the Victory of Mohamed V . . . the name's written down there.

Afterwards, when I went, I found [the man] who was our president, and who still is, up to the present time.[2] I went, and there was a woman whom they called "Rabiaa from Oujda."[3] I took the oath [again] with them. I continued my work, and I was in contact with them. Finally I said to my president, "I don't want to continue like this. I want to go out into combat!" Because at that time in Algeria [in the Algerian war for independence] women were armed and everything. As for me, when I saw women wearing jewelry, that didn't do anything for me. But when I saw women carrying machine guns, I trembled with excitement. To sum it up, he finally told me, "Alright, when the time comes, you can go." So I went on like that, working at my job at the same time that I worked with them.

One day a man named Bouchaib El Ghazi, who was with us in the organization, got out of prison. [He was the one who started up the incident in the train to Oujda. He killed four French policemen, and he died a martyr.] He got out of prison and asked himself what he should do next, and so he told the others, "Let's go see this house that I told you about." He asked, "Who shall we bring along?" and the president told him, "We're going to bring Saadia along." So they came to me. The man who came, this Bouchaib El Ghazi, his feet were all ruined because of the beatings he had gotten [in prison]. He came and told me, "Now we want you to go out into combat. You wanted to go into combat; now we want you to. But you've got to quit your job." I told him, "No, I'll keep on working and at the same time I'll be with you." The man was a little nervous, and he spat out, "Say yes or no!" I told him "Yes," and he said to me, "At eight o'clock this evening [we'll come and take you to the house]. Just bring a bed, a mattress and a wardrobe."

12.4

Saadia with Salam Al Bachir, president of her former resistance organization (1995).

Credit: Anne White.

So that's what I did. I came to my place, and I said to them, "Mother,"—because she had noone but me—I told them, "I'm going to start sleeping at the clinic. Don't come looking for me; just wait until I come back." I went with them to this house. There were now three men with me and one woman, but the woman withdrew. I didn't see her anymore after that. We lived in this house, and I swore another oath on the Koran. And there, lady, they gave me the poison pill, which stayed in my possession. They brought in arms there, and I remained as guardian of the arms. I stayed officially, me and Bouchaib. The others didn't do anything but bring and take away the arms, but as for me, I was officially there.

What did the neighbors say to me? They said to me, "That man that you have there, what's he doing?" I told them that he was my husband, even though he wasn't my husband or any relation to me. I told them, "My husband's a contractor, and those men are workers coming to him to settle the accounts." Once I had gone to see these neighbors there were no problems.

One day, we were in the house sitting down, while another member of the resistance who lived upstairs was there too. He belonged to the secret resistance, but he belonged to another group, called "The Sword of God." The police came to look for him. And me, I had papers from the resistance, lots of them! Eiwa! I can't say here what I did with them. In a word, I hid them. . . . I had an infection in my stomach as a result of hiding those papers. So I kept on like that, working with them.

This Bouchaib El Ghazi, one day he was handling a revolver. I was in front of him, like that. He thought that the revolver was empty, but a bullet shot out. The shell was fired from the gun, and the bullet came out and scratched my head and then hit the wall. Oh yes! It hit me! In fact I have a certificate here . . . Eiwa, Lalla! When the bullet hit, it only just scratched me on the head, so I didn't feel it much. It was more that I felt the smell that it left in the house. The Senegalese were surrounding us, and I couldn't find anything to use but sugar, so I threw sugar on the fire to mix its smell with that of the gunpowder. I held my head like this [putting her hands to her head to demonstrate], and started running to Dr. Ouerzazi's all in a sweat. He took care of me, and I stayed there.

My husband was an Algerian. At that time I didn't call myself Saadia anymore, I called myself Farida, because we had to change our names. So my husband was coming on leave from Algeria. What was I going to do? What was I not going to do? I said to the boys, "You've got to leave the house while my husband is here." And he didn't know that I was with them.

We had to carry out an operation to eliminate a man who was a mason and who had ninety-nine people working under him as spies [for the French], with him the biggest spy of all. They were all Moroccans. And the day that my husband was arriving was the day that we wanted to take care of him, at seven o'clock in the morning. Because when the boys wanted to carry out an operation, I would bring them the weapons, and when they were finished they would give them to me and I would bring them back to the house. So this man was executed, at seven o'clock in the morning. We had taken the things and then had put them back in their places. The boys took them . . . actually I don't remember anymore whether it was I or the boys who took them. I stayed at home for a period of a month, and while I was at home during that month my husband came. He found that my name had been changed. When people asked to see Farida, he asked me, "When did you take on this new name?"

At this point, Touria, who spoke earlier in the meeting, interrupts: "Don't stray from the subject!" Saadia continues.

I know what I'm saying. I'm following my narrative, and I . . . That was the way that it happened. Excuse me! And if by any chance you don't want me to say that, no problem! It's not serious. You, you talked as much as you wanted to. . . . [Touria interrupts again: "Alright, keep going!"]

My husband came and told me, "People call you Farida, why do you have a new name?" In short, my husband was there. One day, when he was about to travel to go back to Algeria from his leave, do you know who he ran into? It was Bouchaib El Ghazi that we met! You know, my story is like a film. . . . It's not fair . . . He met Bouchaib El Ghazi.

Touria cuts in: "We should make a film! And Alison will be our director, and Amina too. . . ."

He met Bouchaib El Ghazi in the train. [Bouchaib] told him, "You know your wife, here's what she is doing . . . here's what she is doing . . . ." And he told all the secrets that there were. My husband said to him, "I'd like to help you too, in Algeria." Because at that moment there was the Algerian [independence] war going on. Bouchaib gave the resistance papers he was carrying to my husband, and he put them in his bag. Then they separated.

The police climbed into the train. When they got in, they said, "Give us the papers!" Bouchaib didn't have any papers, but he had a revolver in his pocket. He also had my poison pill, the pill that I always carried with me.[4] He took the pill. And it was with that that he died, because it wasn't the bullets. The bullets didn't hit and kill him, so it was with that poison pill that he killed himself. They grabbed him and demanded that he give them the papers, and he pulled out his pistol and began the incident with them in the Oujda train. During the struggle, he killed four French policemen. The poor guy, when he couldn't find any way out, he put the poison pill in his mouth. They took him to the hospital in Oujda, and he died three days later there in the hospital. Salam Al Bachir and Rabiaa were there with him, and Bouchaib told them, "I know I'm going to die. Please tell my family, Farida, and all my other colleagues."

They took my husband off the train in chains, together with Bouchaib; and they arrested him and took him to the jail in Oujda. My husband told them that he had been visiting his wife while he was on leave, and all that. Then the police came to interrogate me. And me, all that I just told you, I didn't know it at the time. I wasn't in the know about anything. You know what I thought? That one of the partisans had been arrested and that they'd come to take me away. There was no point in having them rough me up outside in the streets, so I got in the car with them and that was it. I got in, and the Christian said, "No, we just want to question you." And he asked me, "Who is Zinanni Youssef? What relation is he to you?" I told them, "He's my husband." He asked, "What was he doing here?" I answered that he was on leave, and so on. They said, "Alright. That's all." And they left.

One of the other partisans[5] came and said, "My condolences, Bouchaib is dead." I asked, "What happened?" He told me, "This, this and this happened, etc. . . ." I said to him, "That must be why the police came to question me, because he took the Sunday train and my husband took the same train and they met one another." He asked me, "And now, what are you going to do?" I told him, "I'm still ready." I left with them, and I stayed with them. That was how it was. That was it.

I stayed with them, my girl, right up to the last minute in 1956. When Mohamed V came back, at his command, we put down our arms. He asked us to do that. And now we ask the all-powerful God to make us rely on Moulay Hassan, Hassan II, our king, our country. And we ask God that our young women raise their consciousness the way we did ourselves, and we also ask God that they should be as courageous as we were, and that they should be our successors in struggle. We also ask God to protect the Crown Prince and Hassan II, and the people in charge, His Majesty the King, and everyone. And that is what I have to say, and what I've said, that's to say what I've summarized.

It was almost two years later that I got back in touch with Saadia Bouhaddou to record her oral history. In spite of the time that had passed, she had no trouble remembering me when I phoned. She said she would be pleased to see me again and to have me record an oral history, and set up a time for me to visit her at her home, giving me directions to get there on the bus. Saadia lives with her family in a multistory house; you climb several flights of stairs in order to arrive at the main floor with the guest livingroom. At the top of the stairs Saadia greeted me with a warm embrace, welcoming me into her home. She is a compact woman, with bright, expressive eyes and an intense, luminous presence.

Saadia was born in 1934. Her parents were divorced, and had each remarried. She had a sad and difficult childhood, painful for her to recall.

Every time I remember my childhood it's with tears in my eyes. . . . I lived with my father, but I was always alone, relying on myself, because my stepmother was very strict with me. This scar that I have on my forehead is from the time she hit me because I asked for some bread. I was always hearing my father talk about the Jews who wanted to seize Palestine and about the [second world] war.

My stepmother's son used to send me out at midnight to buy him some *kif* [a drug similar to marijuana]. I was crying when I went out, but if I hadn't gone he would have slapped me. Imagine, one day I went out to buy him the *kif* and I lost the money. He really hit me then. . . . I've been courageous ever since I was a child.

When I was eight years old, a man came to ask for my hand in marriage. He gave my father some money in bills, and I asked my father if I could have the bills to make a bed for my doll. I thought the bills were photos. Papa told

12.5

Saadia (about thirteen years old) with her daughter Fatima and her first husband.

Source: Saadia Bouhaddou.

them he couldn't marry me as long as I couldn't even tell the difference between money and photos.

My father was a fqih, so I studied [the Koran] at home. But after two years [at the age of ten], I was married to the father of my eldest daughter. [Saadia stayed in her father's house for a year after she was married, then went to live with her husband. She gave birth to her first—and only surviving—child, Fatima, when she was twelve.] He was thirty-five years old and had already been married six times, but had never had any children. I was his seventh wife. I was only ten years old, my girl! I didn't know the man; it was my father who made me get married in spite of my wishes. I did everything I could to leave him. I wanted to get an education. . . . What was he like? He beat me, from the very first day [we were married]. You know, being a child I didn't like to get up early. So he slapped me the very first day.

[He repudiated me] three times,[6] and in the meantime I had a boy and another girl. [The boy, Si Mohamed, died at the age of 14 or 15 months, and the girl, Mina, at the age of 18 months.] When the divorce was final, I was seventeen years old. After my divorce I went to see Doctor Ouerzazi and asked to work with him as a nurse. . . . Oh yes, I forgot, when I was divorced I was pregnant, but there were complications, and I lost the foetus and went to the hospital. When I was on my way back to my place from the hospital, with my two girls [Fatima and Mina], I met a girlfriend who was about my age and who was going to school. Seeing her made me sad, and it also made me furious. I decided to give the two girls to my husband so that I would be free.

I began to work [bandaging, cleaning] at the doctor's. There weren't many Moroccan surgeons then. And when Mohamed V was exiled [in August 1953], there was something deep inside of me that stirred. What I had heard when I was a child about the Jews creating a state in Palestine and the second world war all came back to me. All my heart was with Mohamed V. I didn't see it myself, but I heard that after the exile some women saw the face of Mohamed V appear in the moon.

The clothes I wore then were modern—jeans, dresses. There was a French woman who asked me why I dressed like that. I liked civilized life. I even rode a bicycle.

As a child, I loved to gaze at the stars and to think. The doctor often told me, "You're a very intelligent woman. I don't know what you would have done if you had gone to school. You would have been someone."

Saadia's second husband was an Algerian, someone she chose for herself. She showed me a photo of them together, as well as a photo of her with her cousin, and one of her with her mother and grandmother. In all of these photos, she was wearing European dress.

After my first divorce, I no longer wore traditional dress. I made my own dresses—like the ones I'm wearing in the photographs.

12.6

Saadia with her second husband, Zinnani Youssef.

Source: Saadia Bouhaddou.

12.7

At the beach (left to right) Fatima, Zinnai Youssef, Saadia, a friend.

Source: Saadia Bouhaddou.

I wanted to record Saadia's oral history in order to hear about her life before and after her participation in the armed resistance, and I was interested in pursuing some questions that arose out of her narrative at the Casablanca meeting. I asked her about going off to live with Bouchaib El Ghazi in the house where they kept the arms—how she herself felt about it, and how it affected her relations with her family and the neighbors. In the context of Moroccan mores of the time, and even now, for Saadia to leave her family's house to go and live in the house where the arms were kept was shocking behavior. It is unthinkable for a young woman to act independently, without the knowledge or permission of either her husband or her parents, and to go and live in a house together with other men (particularly with just one man) not related to her. She explained:

I had always been independent, and I wasn't close to either of my parents, because they were divorced and each had remarried. When I told my mother that I was going to sleep at the clinic she didn't object, because my mother didn't bring me up and so she didn't have any power over me. [At that time] I lived at my grandmother's. I didn't have anything to do with my father. After what he had done to me [marrying me], I didn't want to go back to his place. Oh, before I forget, I was married [a second time] before the period of the resistance. My husband was an Algerian, and he went back to Algeria a lot. Because he was a trader, he went all over the place, here and there. He couldn't leave me alone [in Algeria], so he gave me permission to work at the doctor's. I earned twenty dirhams [$3] a week. . . .

I think my mother may have had her suspicions [that I was working with the resistance], because I distributed notices right to her house criticizing her for eating food produced in France, and using [French] gas and cigarettes. After she suspected that I was the one distributing those notices, as soon I came up the stairs to her house she would say: "God takes care of all of us, so it's not up to you to pass judgment on others." She may have told her husband who sent the notices, but even if she did, that's her problem. When there was any trouble I just hid on the terrace of the house and spent the night there. Finally my mother and grandmother left the house for three months because they were afraid [of the threats in the notices from the resistance].

Even the doctor didn't know [that I was working with the resistance] at first. The way he found out was that one day we had taken in a wounded partisan who belonged to our resistance cell. The doctor told me, "Saadia, that one there [the wounded partisan] belongs to a secret organization; so don't give away his secret!" At that point the wounded man sat up and told him, "But who do you think you're talking to? She's a member of our cell!" The doctor was really amazed, and he asked me, "Why didn't you tell me that?" I answered him, "Listen, doctor, that's part of the secret. If I had revealed that to you, I could just as well have told someone else what you were doing here [taking care of members of the resistance]! Those are all things that can't be talked about."

I asked her what it was like living and working as the only woman among men, especially since none of the men in her resistance cell were members of her family. She said this wasn't an issue.

I was used to working with men, since I took care of sick and wounded men at the clinic. I was used to being with men. There wasn't any difference. They were like my brothers.

Even though Saadia told the neighbors that the man she was living with was her husband, there was a lot of gossip about her among women in the neighborhood. One woman, whose son was actually a member of Saadia's resistance cell, spread stories about what Saadia was up to receiving so many men at the house. It was not until after the return of Mohamed V that her son explained things to her.

[He said] "The stories that you are telling about Saadia aren't true. She's a member of the resistance." His mother, Fatna, called me and told me that she was sorry about the ideas she had had about me. I answered her, "It's lucky you thought that was what I was doing. If you had known my real work, maybe you would have given me away to the police."

I wondered too about the month that her husband spent with her on leave—how she had felt about that, and whether she had really managed to keep her resistance activities secret from her husband for an entire month. She described her state of mind while separated from her resistance "family" during the month that her husband was there.

I told my colleagues [that my husband was coming] and they said they were going to leave the house and remove the arms. The day my husband was coming, they were going to carry out an operation against a contractor, whose name I don't know, who directed ninety-nine informers. . . . I had to accompany them, and then go to meet my husband at the train station. I justified my moving away [from home] by a quarrel with my family, and I took my husband to my house. It was surrounded by my colleagues, but he didn't notice. I was very upset then, so much so that I sometimes cried all night, because my contact with my colleagues was interrupted, and I didn't even know if one of them might be dead. I became like a baby after weaning.[7]

One time before independence I went to Fez to get some weapons—five pistols and two machine guns. I spent the night with colleagues, and then they sent me on alone with the arms. In the bus, the police began to search the baggage. This time I hadn't brought my poison pill with me, because I was just doing a favor for someone from another resistance organization. They searched all the baggage except for three suitcases, among them my suitcase [which had the weapons]. After that the police got down from the bus. My colleagues didn't come until the next day, by car; I didn't go with them because there was the risk that they would be searched. On the other hand, people didn't pay any attention to women.

One day I went with a colleague to the garage to get some pistols repaired. The Senegalese spotted us, and I said, "That's it! We've had it!" But we pretended to be drunk, and the Senegalese said to me, "Go ahead. Get out of here." Women had more of a chance of getting through to transport weapons, because at that time women weren't educated, and the French thought that Moroccan women were not capable of anything. Getting back to our story . . . When I got back, I couldn't go straight back to the house, so I spent the night at a hotel. By coincidence, my husband had come back on leave. When I got back home, I told my mother not to touch the suitcase [which had the weapons]. My husband heard what I said, and he was curious, so he looked through the suitcase and found the weapons. He didn't say anything, and I gave the suitcase back to the men.

The photograph in Saadia's file at the High Commission for Veterans of the Resistance, taken in 1959, shows her wearing a traditional djellaba. When I asked her about that, she explained that this was one of the things that her Algerian husband had insisted on when they lived together again after independence in 1956.

After independence, my husband told me, "You've proved yourself capable of doing all that. Now it's time for you to stay home." I went back to

12.8

Saadia Bouhaddou (early 1960s).

Photo from dossier.

12.9

Saadia Bouhaddou's *Carte de résistant*, issued in 1984.

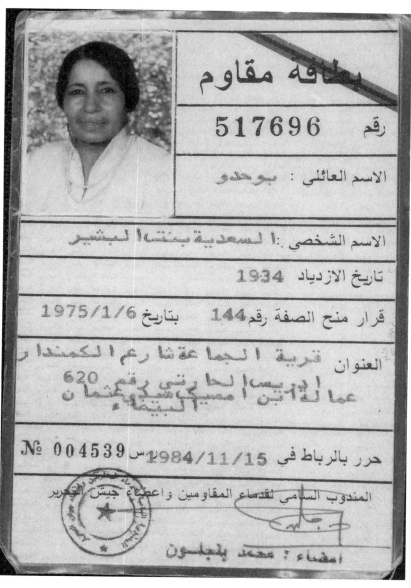

Source: Saadia Bouhaddou.

Algeria with him. When Ben Bella was arrested I went for seven months without even leaving the house. At that time I really missed the work that I used to do. . . . Afterwards we came back to Morocco. We fled Algeria because my husband was a member of the Algerian resistance. But my life didn't change.

I didn't even have to ask for my card; I filled out the papers, and I got it automatically, because my work in the resistance was well known. I didn't need any witnesses; there was noone who raised objections.

After Algerian independence in 1962 we went back to Algeria and stayed there until 1974. After the events of that year I couldn't stay in Algeria, especially since I didn't have any children with him. I couldn't have any children after the incident with the papers.

Saadia and her Algerian husband got divorced, "because [they] didn't have any children together," and she married a third time. It was apparently a happy marriage, but her third husband died of cancer in his fifties. Photos of her first and third husbands are displayed in the salon. Saadia also keeps a photo of Bouchaib El Ghazi, who lived with her in the house where the arms were kept and died a martyr in the incident in the Oujda train. It was one of the great tragedies of Saadia's life that he died so young.

12.10

Saadia with her second husband.

Source: Saadia Bouhaddou.

In the meeting with other women in the Casablanca resistance, I had asked Saadia whether she ever told members of her family about what she did in the resistance.

Oh yes, I often tell these things to my granddaughter [my daughter's daughter]. I have just one daughter. Since the time that I told you about, when I hid the papers, I had an infection and I couldn't have any more children. It was the end of my being able to give birth. I now tell all that to the granddaughter who is with me, and she is like me. My daughter doesn't resemble me, but my granddaughter does. One day I took her to a Doustour [Constitutional Union] women's meeting, and Maati Bouabid was there.[8] He was saying that women are not marginalized in Moroccan society today. I told my granddaughter to say something, to speak for me. And she went right up to him and contradicted him, Maati Bouabid! She was sixteen years old, and she told him, "No sir, I disagree! The Moroccan woman is still marginalized, both here [in the city] and in the countryside!" And she insisted on that point! Bouabid couldn't think of any good answer to what she had said.

Now Saadia presides over a large household, occupying two floors of the house, including her daughter, an adopted daughter and son, and several grandchildren. Asmaa, the granddaughter that Saadia says has inherited her revolutionary spirit, was eighteen years old in 1994. She is the only girl in her Akido self-defense class, listens to Dolly Parton and Cat Stevens tapes, and thinks of going to study in America. Saadia seems comfortable with that; she understands that Asmaa will have to find her own voice and her own path into the future.

13

Ghalia Moujahide: Rabat

I first met Ghalia Moujahide early in this project, in a gathering of ten women from the resistance held at the offices of the Rabat-Salé delegation of the High Commission for Veterans of the Resistance.[1] At the beginning of the session, the women were somewhat shy and uncomfortable, and so was I. The official setting, the presence of a male representative from the delegation, and the women's uncertainty as to who I was and what I wanted all contributed to this. As the meeting was held on a morning in the first days of Ramadan, the Muslim month of fasting, there were no refreshments, and the women were also a little tired and hungry. I opened the meeting by explaining that I wanted to record the history of women in the resistance in order that these important and heroic activities on the part of Moroccan women would not be forgotten. Then I asked each woman in turn to speak about her own experience.

As I was there to listen rather than to pursue a particular agenda of questions, there was no real interrogation or intervention, and each woman had the floor to herself for the duration of her narrative. The core of each woman's narrative consisted of a detailed, dramatic account of missions which she carried out during the armed resistance. Ghalia Moujahide was the ninth woman to speak. A tall, angular woman, with a commanding presence, she told her story in a strong, deep voice, using dramatic hand gestures. She began by telling how, in the late 1940s, she was brought into one of the first resistance cells in Rabat by her husband.

The first time when they wanted me to take the oath, they asked my husband, "And your wife? Do you really trust her?" He told them, "I brought my wife home [married her] when she was very young. I educated her. And you know her family is of the Ait Ba'amran tribe. . . ." And they said to him, "Be careful that when we're doing a job she doesn't go and give us away!" They took me to swear an oath of allegiance. That was the first time. We swore allegiance. At that time I was still very young, and I had two little girls.

You know the resistance. A liar would be lying to you if he told you that that person knew that other person. Nobody knew anybody else. No question of that! . . . Me, I worked with men, I didn't work with women. . . . What can I tell

13.1

Ghalia Moujahide raising high a picture of the late King Mohamed V.

Credit: Anne White.

13.2

Ghalia Moujahide (1993).

Credit: Ann Jones.

you—Now that we've gotten old, we don't know how much we can remember. We remember the weapons and that's all.

My husband began to send me [on missions for the resistance]. The first time, he sent me to Zaer, to Ben Zine's place. At that time there were Americans in that area. And you know there were arms hidden in the country. Anyway, he sent me to Ben Zine's place and told me, "Go tell him to give you the revolver." So I went. I took my two girls with me; they were very young, with just a year between them. I went even though it was raining and he lived in the forest.

He asked me, "What do you want?" He knew me. He said, "Go away and don't come back until you bring some money." I told him, "We'll bring you money. Anyway, who do you think we're doing this for? We're doing it for our king and our country!" He told me, "I don't know about that. Just go and bring me some money." He's now dead, the poor guy, may God rest his soul. I came back at him and asked, "How much?" He said, "Sixty dirhams." And you know what sixty dirhams was worth at that time! [It was worth a lot!]

The next day . . . you know, we went in this bus; the French put us on the top . . . Ah, you laugh! The next day I went, and I brought the money, and I took my little daughters with me; they were like twins. I went and took a basket with me. The bus let me off, I went to his place and I told him, "Alright, here's the money." He gave me an eight-shot revolver. I said, "How about the bullets? There aren't any." He told me, "Go away until after I've finished what I have to do." I said, "What do you have to do?! May God bless your parents, at least give us something to load the revolver to start with, and if there's something more later, I'll come and give you whatever you want for it."

The police along the road were searching everywhere. Do you know where I put the revolver? I wrapped it in a piece of cloth and put it in the basket next to my legs. The girls were very small, and they were in my arms. We came up to the . . . at that time we called it *Zafati* (word for police station). . . . We got close, and then the police climbed into the bus to search us. I took the revolver and hid it against my chest, and held the little girls in my arms on top of it! There is only one God and Mohamed is his prophet![2] Isn't that right! They searched the basket! They saw that the girls in my arms were very small, just a year between them. . . . My daughters now are grown up, with the blessing of God. The police got down. And then the bus let us off, just on the other side. It was far away. From there, I don't know, we got a kind of [horse-drawn] carriage. And I came back home.

My husband didn't do those missions. Instead, it was me that he sent into the fire. But God exists, God protected me. I won't lie to you. [When I got back from the mission to Ben Zine's place], my husband searched the basket, and he asked me, "Why didn't he give you any bullets?" I told him, "He only gave me a few; I don't know how many." So he told me, "Tomorrow, you need to go back to him, and tell him to give you [more bullets]."

[This time] I left the girls; I didn't take them with me. The next day I went back to his place. . . . And my father lived near there, and people told him that his daughter went to see so and so and that he was a thief. Of course, [Ben Zine] wasn't a thief, but neither my father nor my mother knew what was going on. Who would you tell these things to? You don't do that except with people who are capable [of keeping the secrets of the resistance]. It wouldn't do any good, once the police came, to hit someone who gave everything away with your fist. No, [then it would be too late]; no question of that!

Si Abdellah Cherqaoui used to come to our place riding on a sports bicycle.[3] He would park it by the house. We knew each other and understood each other. He brought me . . . he filled the lamp of the bicycle full of bullets. He would come by the house to deliver the ammunition; then he would say, "Goodbye," and I would pick up what he had left, and he'd go off. My husband didn't come home until late. You know why he didn't make an appearance until later? It was so that if there were a problem, it would be me, the woman, who would be arrested and I'd have to manage somehow. Right?!

One time someone working with us said to my husband, "Be careful! Your wife might be arrested by the police, and beaten by them." And it was another one of the group who spoke up, a man named Si Slimane, may God rest his soul. He said to them, "Look! You don't need to worry about this El Ghalia! On the contrary, what I'm afraid of is that one day they will arrest a *man*, and that *he* will give everything away! But Ghalia won't do that!"

We kept on working, thanks be to God, and we ran around, and he sent me again to Salé. . . . I went again, and I knocked on the door of a house, and I brought a revolver and what was needed. At Casa it was the same thing. I didn't go anywhere without bringing something back. Thanks be to God. I'm well known; people know me and what I did. And thanks be to God we did our work for our king and for our country. Thanks be to God! We were beaten and mistreated, and there wasn't a single police station where they hadn't taken me.

At that time we had black tin cans; we called them "American cans." We filled one with hay, and then put revolvers in it. . . . But the man in whose house we hid the revolvers was arrested in the revolt of Akkari.[4] When I heard that, I went running, and I got those weapons and took them to the house of that lady in white.[5] Because they wouldn't question her; they had seen that her husband was dead and all that. So we left the arms at her place. And we went on, like that . . . I told her, "Be a little careful, and don't trust anyone!"

One day Mohamed Djayji,[6] a spy, came to our place, together with some others. My house had two doors. They knocked on one of the doors. My uncle's wife was drinking coffee. My husband came and said to me, "Give me some *lodo* [special water for ablutions before prayer]." I asked him, "What?" He said, "I must make my ablutions." I said, "Do you want some coffee or do you want to do your ablutions?" He said, "I want *lodo*." So I heated the water for him, and I gave it to him. Just then the spies came. Djayji knocked on the door, and I looked at him through [a window]. The house had two doors, and some people were standing there, and some were standing over there. I asked him, "Who is it?" He told me, "El Ghalia, open up!" I asked him, "Why, A'Sidi?" He said to me, "Look, that . . ." [He told me the same thing that the partisans had just finished telling me: that Cherkaoui had been arrested.] I began to shout. I recognized him, so I began to shout. I asked him, "What are you going to do to me?" And meanwhile my husband was there doing nothing! "You, you just stood there, listening to that, and doing nothing!" I can tell him that to his face, even though he's old now. "At that moment, all you had to do was to fire with the two loaded revolvers, and whatever happened would happen." So I shouted, and told Djayji, "Oh Sidi, I am just a woman, I don't go out to men's places." He said to me, "Open up, take that." I told him, "I won't open up. I don't take anything and I won't give you anything. I don't know what you are talking about. And my husband doesn't let me go out." I told him, "Go to his shop if you want to find him." He told me, "We did go to his place, but we didn't find him there." I told him, "I'm just a woman, and I won't open the door." They hit the door once hard and bashed it in, and they came in. He said to me, "Pay attention and be quiet." He asked, "Where's l'Houcine [her husband]?" I told them, "He's not here." But he had betrayed me. Ask and you will see. Ask him himself. When they saw my husband, they began to slap me, while saying to me, "Why did you lie?" and especially that one, that son of a bitch Djayji, the one who should have taken pity on me. He said to me, "Go on, you bastard!" He told them, "This woman here is a bastard! She should be killed." They began to slap me. They said, "Go on out." All of a sudden the legion came.

They took my husband away, and they took the 40,000 *rials* [almost $300] that belonged to us, and the 60,000 *rials* [almost $400] that belonged to the resistance, and also some bracelets that my father had given me after my marriage. When [Djayji and his men] left, they said to the legion, "Look, it is that woman there who is his wife, and those there are just guests. And be careful to seize anyone who comes to the house." They locked the door and took away the key. We stayed in the house. As for my children, I didn't see them. I don't know where they went. Eight days, day and night. Me, I thought that all of Morocco had been arrested. The legion stayed with me. When one group left, another group took their place. And they said, "Be careful of that woman there."

And what can I tell you! For eight days, day and night, the legion was with me. Ask someone to tell you about me and you'll see! Thanks be to God that we are still here today! Because people like us, it's unbelievable what we did! We didn't care about money, or food, or even saving our lives. What happened to a few people would have to be seen to be believed! All we can say is: "Thank God that we're still here today!" We worked, ran, took action! And finally, what can I tell you!

My husband finally gave everything away, and said to the police, "Go to my wife's place so that she can give you the revolvers." Are you a man, to betray me like that?! They came to my place, and Djayji said to me, "Cursed woman! Go get the revolvers from where you put them!" I said to him, "What revolvers are you talking about? What are they like? I don't know those revolvers." He told me, "You, you don't know?!" I told him, "Let the person who told you to come and look for them come himself to look for them. I don't know anything about revolvers, or even what you mean by revolvers or bullets. I don't know anything. Me, I don't know anything!" He began to slap me. He asked me, "Doesn't your husband go out at night?" I answered him, "No." He asked me, "He isn't anywhere around?" I told him, "No." He said to me, "You don't know what he does? How many children do you have?" I told him, "Two." He asked, "Where are they?" I told him, "They aren't here." They held on to them, and the poor children didn't know anything. I told him, "Look, among us Moroccans, the husband can never let his wife in on a secret. Because from one day to the next they might attack me and hit me, and then I'd tell

13.3

Ghalia Moujahide with one daughter (1962).

Source: Ghalia Moujahide.

everything. He doesn't tell me anything. I didn't see anything." So they left to look for my husband. . . . They brought him to the house, and he said to me, "You! . . ." And I said to him, "You, and you are a man, and me I don't know anything about all that, and you betrayed me!" They brought him, and he took two [revolvers] out from where we had hidden them, all loaded, as we had loaded them, and the bullets that we had brought, and then they left like that.

The legion stayed with me night and day. It is not as though they left me alone or anything like that. They changed the guard—if twenty left another twenty would come. Ask what I had to put up with there! Then they went to look for my husband again. [When he came with them], I told him, "Bless you and thank you [said with heavy irony]; whatever happens happens. You only die once. Do I know something, so that you send them to me every time?" He went to look for the bullets, and they took away the cupboards, and they photographed them. Then they photographed us, and they photographed everything. Those men left, and other men stayed with me, so that if anyone knocked on my door . . . But who would knock on my door? Everyone had escaped. Our poor neighbors, all the people in the neighborhood had run off. I don't know. Eight days went by, day and night. And this woman in white, poor thing, she came and said, "No matter what might happen to me, I'm going to go see if Ghalia is still alive or dead." They went to tell my parents that I was dead and that my children had been thrown into the sea. They watched me all the time, so noone knew if I were dead or alive. But then the woman in white told them that I was still alive, and afterwards some other people came, I think they were Algerians. One of them said to me, "Lalla, what are we going to do? Open the door." I looked for a key to open up, and a Christian came and said to him, "Why are you opening up for her there? This door is not supposed to be opened, and you are not supposed to go near her." And the door wouldn't open anyway. So we stayed there, [and the people kept on saying]: "She is dead, she is this, she is that. . . ."

After God decided to free me, they opened up, and took away all the money in the house. *Ouallah a Sidi* [oath]! By the time they were finished, they didn't even leave me a crumb to eat, nothing! They took away the money that belonged to the resistance, and they took away our money. *Harram* [it's a sin!] if they left me a single rial.[7] They took everything, opened up the place, and photographed us again. And me, I went out, and I had the feeling that I was looking cross-eyed, because I hadn't been out for eight days. They took my husband away again, and that was it. God had liberated me, because they were no longer there with me. I told them all in the street: "What are you looking at? You're looking! If you are men and women, and you are that, then throw stones! Throw stones and clods of earth [at those soldiers]!" And two from the legion came up to me and slapped me. I told them, "Hit me, kill me, do whatever you want!" [Even after the legion left], they continued to watch over me wherever I went. If you just talked with me they would take you away! When I went out to do errands, noone could talk to me, because if they talked with me they'd be arrested.

One evening they came and took me by surprise, and they made me go out all naked [without a *djellaba* and scarf—proper street clothes], and took me away. It was Ben El Arrabi, the *mouqqadam*.[8] He came and said to me, "A Lalla, you've got to go out." I asked him, "At least let me get dressed." But I had to go out without even getting dressed. At that time, the headquarters was commanded by a Christian captain, a Frenchman. And I said to him, "These little girls, I just want to take them to the mosque or somewhere." He said to me, "No!" "A Lalla, come in front of me!" [shouting] They took me to the headquarters like that without letting me get dressed. I told myself that they were just going to talk to me. I sat down and said to him, "Please, Ben El Arrabi, could I go in to see the captain to find out what he wants with me, so that I can go and take my children away." He told me, "You can't leave; you can't take away your children." I went in, I sat down, [silence], until some inspectors came up to the headquarters, in two Jeeps, like that. My stomach turned. I knew it. They had gone in to see the captain. They had taken my girls away from me, and thrown them into the ocean! May God recompense this person, who I will never forget, the one who took my girls [and took care of them], may God rest his soul. They took me away, and I went with them. They took me to this damned big police station that's here next to the maternity hospital. I told them, "Me, I don't know anything. If my husband told you something, then go get him so that he can give you what is left [hidden arms]. As for me, I don't know *anything!*" They beat me for three or four days. And finally, when they let mè out [of the police station] at night, it was raining and cold. I had gone out without getting dressed, and I didn't know how to get back home. I'm not going to lie to you. Someone who had a car, I don't know who it was, saw me walking, and he said to me, "What are you doing, Lalla?" I told him, "Mister, I was at the police station." And he said to me, "Come on, get in. Where are you going?" I told him, "I'm going to the village [where I live]." He took me in his car, the poor thing. He asked me, "Where is your house?" I told him, "Near the ocean, in Douar Koura." I don't even remember any more what I told him. When we got there, I told him, "Wait, A Sidi, I'll give you some money." He said, "It is up to me to give *you* money! Go on!" That was it. He left me.

They came to get me the next day. They took me back to that police station, the same one as before. They beat me, of course, because they had found some weapons at my place. My husband had told them, "Go to her place. She has a trunk full of weapons and of bombs." Actually that was true, but they shouldn't have said it. Lies!

And they took me away again, and also my girls, in the night. My girls were very young, the poor things. What hurt me especially was these girls. Three cars of police went with me. That was the only way I would come! The beatings I got! Then they put me across from my husband, while they lied about him. I said to him, "Me, I have weapons? I know that there is a trunk full of weapons? What is that? Where is it?" He said to me, "What weapons?!" I said to him, "It is because of that that they brought me here. What do I have to do with that? What do I know, me?" He said to me, "There's nothing to all that." You should have seen it! They interrogated us all day long. And with the prisoners standing up. What worried me was these little girls that they had taken away from me and left outside. They hadn't let them come inside. The interrogation continued. It was raining, and it was very cold. I don't know how to tell you, it was maybe eight o'clock in the evening or nine o'clock before they let me go.

The next day they came back, and they took me to the police station that is next to our place down there. They said, "Your husband said that you have, you have, you have, you have . . . I told them, "You know what you should do? If you want to kill me, go ahead and kill me. Do whatever you want. My husband told you something? Si Abderrahmane or someone told you something, and the other one told you something? . . . Let them come and take whatever we have. I don't have anything. I am only a woman, and I don't know ANYTHING!"

He said to me, "Sign here." I asked him, "What am I meant to sign? What for?" You know, "Sign what?" They took the money, and that way they made it look as though *I* was the one who took it. He told me, "Sign for this money, and then you take it." We were fasting [during the month of Ramadan]; it would be impossible for me to forget that. I signed. What did they do? They gave me a paper from the central administration in Casa, and they put it in an envelope for me and told me, "There. There's your money that you signed for." When I looked, I only found the piece of paper.

And, blessings from God, we worked, and worked, may God bestow barraka [blessing] on the king, our health, our children. All gratitude and thanks go to God. And then there are lots of things to say, and thanks be to God we have survived. All of that is by the grace of God, for our country and our king. You heard, for our country and our king. You know me, nothing hurts me, I won't lie to you. Me, it is God who gave me this courage from the time that I was small. And hamdoullah, thanks be to God, we never informed on anyone, no matter what. We were roughed up. They beat me and brutalized me, and there was nothing left that they didn't do to me. The thanks and gratitude go to God.

We wept that day of Ramadan. I wept on that Ramadan. Look, look now at my girls! Because they were small, and they saw that, they tell me now, "Please, Mama, don't talk about that anymore." Now they are forty-four years old and their children have grown up. One has become a dentist, and the other a doctor of law. They beg me not to bring back memories of that era. The people who know me, they tell me, "Look, you should just laugh and make fun of all that you have seen. Talk as though you have just been born." The gratitude and thanks goes to Him, and thanks be to God we don't have any more prison. I won't lie to you. We were always afraid. There was the legion with me at the

13.4

Ghalia Moujahide (with her veil lowered) and her two daughters.

Source: Ghalia Moujahide.

house. Ask anyone and you'll see. Thanks be to God that we are remembered like that, so that people know what happened. And we are always ready if there is anything more. Moroccans didn't like the submission, the indignity [of colonialism]. And Moroccans have something to say, right? We, we love our country, our king. And we thank you [speaking to me]. Another time we will have a party and you are welcome. Thanks be to God, we, we love our country and our king. Long live the king! You hear. We love our nation. And we have men and we have capable women, among the best. And the Sahara, we will have it sooner or later. Long live the king, and the Sahara, it is my own country [*bled*—where I come from], my country, my country, my country. The country of everyone.

Later, I went to see Ghalia at her home, a small ground-level apartment in a working-class section of Rabat. Unlike most of the other women I interviewed, who are always surrounded by family members, Ghalia lives alone, and the interviews in her home were with her alone. I asked her about her life growing up under colonialism in the period before she joined the resistance.

My parents are from the Sahara, from Sidi Ifni. . . . They came to live in Casa, but when they came here they found *nothing*. There was French colonialism, and they had a factory which [canned] sardines at the port. Women worked with the sardines. And the people, the Moroccans, we poor things, we didn't have anything but tents in that period; we didn't get anything for working; there weren't houses or anything. We had very, very little. My father and mother told us that. It was there that I was born [in 1927], in Casablanca. We were six girls in the family.

I worked with the French from the time I was little, and I earned ten francs a week. Afterwards, my parents married me, at the age of sixteen. . . . I came here, to Rabat, with my husband. There wasn't much, just a shanty. We took it for twenty rials [about $.15]. And me, I went to the area where they process wool, at Bab Laalou, and I worked processing wool. At first, my husband didn't do much in the way of work . . . then he got a job with a Jewish woman selling drapes. We had a little money, and we rented out four shanties, here. Afterwards, I brought Fatna and Fatima [her two daughters] into the world, and they grew up a little.

She speaks about her participation in the resistance not in the context of her own life before and after the resistance, but rather in a mythic and historical continuum of Moroccan national solidarity against colonialism, especially focusing on the courage of the people of the Ait Ba'amran tribe, the tribe of her family.

The French came to colonize us and to exploit our lands and our resources, but they found a people and a king who were strong and united. And we did everything, until we finally succeeded in liberating our country. . . . I was very young, but thanks to God I was mature and politically conscious, and I had inherited courage from my family. My origin is from the Ait Ba'amran tribe, and we were colonized by the Spanish. My grandfather rode on horseback to fight the Spanish, and my grandmother followed him. We were courageous in our tribe.

In every interview, Ghalia would come back to stories of her participation in the resistance. She herself felt that she was repeating the same things, and, at one point told me, with some exasperation, "I've already told you that three times! What more do you want from me?" Sometimes she told about incidents in exactly the same words she had used before. Gradually several themes emerged out of these repeated stories. First, the resistance did not choose just anyone to participate, and they were especially careful in choosing women. So Ghalia was one of a very select few chosen for her courage and her ability to keep secrets. She was also special because she joined the armed resistance in the 1940s, when the first cells were being formed, whereas most women didn't join until after the exile of the king in 1953.

They began to contact people, but not everyone, maybe only 1 percent. Little by little they contacted each other and got together. And those people that got together at your house, they were chosen because you already knew them; you already knew their worth and whether they could stand something or not. You understand? Si Abdellah Senhaji [one of the first leaders of the resistance] came from Casablanca. There were others who came, lots of them, here in Rabat. He would pull people out and tell them, "You must . . . I want you, and you, and you, and so on . . ." Until finally, out of one hundred people, you had found two or three for the resistance.

These few who were selected swore allegiance to the resistance on the Koran. And even after that there wasn't total confidence in them. The conversation with these people was ambiguous at first, without mentioning the arms that were hidden. And after having observed them, and how they behaved, and their movements, then they might be asked to swear for a second time on the Koran, to swear their allegiance to God, to the people, and to the king. This happened in different cities all over Morocco.

You know the resistance. The resistance is not this or that. The resistance is work and weapons. The resistance is an ideal. The resistance was for those who were capable, and for the people designated by God.

Si Brahim [a resistance leader] told me, "Let's go." I asked him, "Where?" He said, "We're going to someone's place." He took the Koran and put it down. I asked him, "Why?" He told me, "My girl, from now on, we're going to rely on God and on you." I asked him, "Why me?" He was also a Berber, like me. He told me, "I know you. Even though you're young, you have good sense. Now, my girl, you have taken an oath. If someone catches you and beats you . . ." I asked him, "Why would someone beat me?" He told me, "I've warned you about it. That won't happen now, not yet. That will come later." I told him, "If we die, we'll go to heaven, because we haven't done sinful things. We are working for our country and our king." He told me, "We'll do this, we'll do this, we'll do this . . . but not now. You shouldn't tell this to that woman, and [from now on] don't get together with women." I told him, "No, I won't get together with any women."

Another subject that came up several times, was what Ghalia's parents, neighbors, and other women thought she was doing, when she was really carrying out the work of the resistance. This gives us some insight into what was normal behavior for a young woman in Ghalia's position at that time, and the ways in which her behavior transgressed those societal norms.

[After I had gotten the bullets], I put the box down here, and I put on a belt and went to my father's and mother's place down there. I lived quite far away from them. My father asked me, "Why did you come, young lady? What are you doing here?" I told him, "I came to see you two." He said, "No you didn't. You came to do other business here. Did you come to see what you were going to steal?" He thought that we were thieves. May God rest and have mercy on his soul, poor thing.

Then he sent for my husband. Papa sent for my husband and told him, "Who is my daughter coming here with?" Because we didn't have any family down there, there was only my husband's family there. He told him, "Everyone says that your wife comes gadding around here with a Christian! Aren't you her husband? And the girl is still young! And you let her go out alone so that she can come here with a Christian!" My husband told him, "Oh you know, father Moujahide, all she did was to come here with a man who was lost and was looking for a house here, and he wasn't a Christian!" [Actually I had been riding with my husband on his scooter, and he was wearing a hat like a police hat, so they thought he was a Christian.]

Another time, my husband said to me, "You should learn to ride a bicycle." So he brought me the bicycle and taught me how to ride it at night next to the seashore. But we weren't really doing this so that I could ride a bicycle; we were really going out there to try to see if the revolvers worked or not by firing them into the ground. When the women in the neighborhood saw him teaching me to ride a bicycle, they said, "Why not us? She's learning to ride a bicycle, and we'd like to do it too." And so they too began learning how to ride a bicycle.

In her narrative at the meeting with other women from the resistance, and in other sessions when we were alone, Ghalia traced her changing relations with her husband during the period of the resistance. This was most unusual— no other woman even mentioned her relationship with her husband, and certainly noone else criticized her husband the way Ghalia did. Her narrative starts at the time when her husband brought her into his resistance cell, and "everything came from [her] husband." A little later in the narrative she brings up several instances in which her husband doesn't appreciate her ingenuity and courage in carrying out missions. She goes on to more and more pointed comments about her husband's timidity and her own courage; and finally tells about confronting her husband with his "betrayal" of her in telling the authorities where they had hidden the arms and money. A good deal of this may come from Ghalia's bitterness at having been divorced by her husband soon after independence. Some of it may also be the bravado with which Ghalia approaches everything, the way she talks and the way she lives.

After successfully completing her very first mission, to Zaer, Ghalia returned home only to be told by her husband that she had to go back the next day to get more bullets. Her immediate response was this:

"What? Do you want to kill me?" He said, "What do you mean, do I want to kill you?" I told him, "You, you stay at home, and you send me into the fire!"

She returned home after another difficult mission, having diverted the attention of the police by putting henna on her hands so that they would think she was just visiting the wife and having a celebration rather than transporting ammunition.

I was late in getting back to my husband. And when I came in, he slapped me twice. He asked me, "Why did you come back late?" I said, "So that's my reward! You hit me!" Here I didn't know how I was going to get back with the bullets, and the streets were full of police, and there was a lot of confusion, and yet I still managed to get through without anyone stopping me.

Later, in an incident cited earlier in the oral history, her husband does nothing when he has a chance to shoot some of the police who are coming to the house to arrest him. It isn't clear from what Ghalia says whether she confronted him at the time or whether she just thinks of doing it now.[9]

I can tell him that to his face, even though he is old now. "At that moment, all you had to do was to fire with the two loaded revolvers, and whatever happened would happen." [*And another time:*] If you only knew what I did to my husband! I told him, "*Hshouma!*" [Shame on you!]

Maybe my husband got together with some friends in prison and they agreed to admit to everything. They talked about everything: the number of weapons we had, and also the money. [The authorities] brought him [to the house], and he said to me, "You! . . ." And I said to him, "You! And you are a man! And me, I don't know anything about all that. And you betrayed me!" He had betrayed me. Ask, and you will see! Ask him yourself!

Ghalia was proud of the fact that she only worked with men, not with women. On the other hand, she says that she herself, and women in general, were often braver and worked harder than men.

Women worked hard, even better than men, who went into hiding, and I am telling the truth, and if there is anyone who wants to contradict me he should come and confront me!

Like many others, Ghalia applied in 1959 to be given official status as a veteran of the resistance. When Ghalia's husband divorced her, soon after independence, she took on the full responsibility for supporting her parents and a brother who was mentally ill, as well as her two daughters. What's more, the beatings that she had received at the hands of the colonial authorities had ruined her health, especially her eyes, so she couldn't work. A note written in 1968 asks for urgent review of the dossier so that she can get some help with housing, and a taxi medallion [so that she can have some income]. One year, she asked for, and received, some money to help purchase a sheep for the Aid Kabir.

Ghalia has had a hard life, before, after, and during her time in the armed resistance. But she doesn't complain. On the contrary—now almost seventy and still vigorous, she is "always ready if there is anything more." As she says in ending one of the oral history interviews:

Thanks be to God that I am still alive, and I can say that even at my age I am still ready to defend my country right to the end!

14

Aicha and Mina Senhaji:
Co-wives of a Resistance Leader

Aicha and Mina Senhaji are the widows of resistance leader Mounaidil[1] Abderrahmane Ben Abdellah Senhaji, known as Abdellah Senhaji, a Berber from the Senhaja tribe[2] in the south of Morocco who organized some of the first cells of the armed resistance in Casablanca. It was through Aicha and Mina that I discovered the existence of several overlapping networks of women who had worked in the resistance and liberation army. I also learned about the important roles played by women who stayed at home, in seclusion, and began to understand how bitter and angry some women are about what has happened to them since independence.

After the December 24, 1953 incident of the bomb in the central market of Casablanca, many of the resistance leaders from Casablanca tried to get to the northern, Spanish zone. Senhaji was able to reach Ksar El Kbir, thirty-six kilometers southeast of Larache, in the northern zone, under the Spanish protectorate, where he joined with thirty-four other members of the resistance who were already in the area, and organized a group that was to form the core of a new liberation army. The resistance leaders who went north to create the liberation army had decided that eventually the urban armed resistance would not be enough; it would take a well-organized and well-equipped army, operating out of the Rif mountains, to finally restore the king and liberate the country. This effort was greatly aided by the support of the Egyptians, after Nassar came to power, and above all by the cooperation of leaders of the Algerian resistance. The Spanish who controlled the northern zone of Morocco by this time had changed their attitude towards Moroccan resistance leaders fleeing from the French zone; they treated them as political dissidents and gave them every facility for organizing commandos.

The immediate goal of the liberation army was to force the French to bring King Mohamed V back from exile and to recognize Moroccan independence. The ultimate goal of most of the liberation army leaders was to liberate all of Morocco, including the Spanish Sahara, and also to help the

14.1

Aicha and Mina Senhaji (1995).

Credit: Anne White.

Algerians in their continuing struggle to be free from French control, thus completing the liberation of the entire North African Maghreb.

Mina Senhaji describes the essential roles that she and other women played in the liberation army—cooking, washing clothes, tending the wounded— providing all the support services necessary to keep a guerrilla army fighting in the field.

Aicha Senhaji is a Berber, born in a small town outside of Essaouira, on the Atlantic coast north of Agadir. She grew up in her brother's house in Casablanca, where she was married to Abdellah Senhaji when she was thirteen years old, in 1950.[3] Because Senhaji was one of the principal leaders of the Casablanca resistance, Aicha also became involved. Her life was taken up with work for the resistance—hiding arms, collecting money, cooking food for prisoners—all of this while confined to the house in strict seclusion. Senhaji was wanted by the French, condemned to death, and so Aicha too was always in hiding or on the run; she used to keep a large straw shopping bag filled with household utensils, so that she was always ready to escape at a moment's notice and set up house in another location. For a Moroccan woman whose whole

14.2

Aicha Senhaji at her daughter Malika's wedding (1996).

Credit: Anne White.

14.3

Author, Mina Senhaji, and Malika Senhaji (1995).

Credit: Anne White.

world was her home, it took extraordinary courage to flee the house and leave
everything behind. And Aicha did this not just once, but again and again.

When Senhaji went to the north in 1954, Aicha couldn't go with him,
because at that time her first daughter, Fatima, was only one and a half years
old and she was already three months pregnant with her second daughter,
Malika. So Senhaji went alone to the north, and after some time there married a
second wife, Mina, in Ksar El Kbir.

When I asked a Moroccan colleague, who had known Senhaji well over a
period of years, why Senhaji had taken a second wife in Ksar El Kbir, without

even consulting his first wife, he told me that I had to try to imagine that particular time and place. Women were "nothing" then, and particularly in wartime, what was most important was the war effort. Senhaji needed a wife to take care of him—cook, mend clothes, and run the household—as well as to perform these functions on a larger scale for the soldiers of the liberation army. It really wasn't even his decision, but rather that of the people around him who felt that Senhaji needed a wife in order to be effective in leading the army. And certainly Mina's description of what she did—cooking three meals a day for sixty or seventy soldiers, washing their clothes, and tending the wounded— makes it hard to imagine how Senhaji could have managed without her.

Aicha and her daughter Malika pointed out that it was the other liberation army leaders who insisted that Senhaji take a wife in the north, and that they were the ones who chose Mina for him. Indeed, Mina was the niece of Abdellah Naciri, a member of the group, and also a cousin of the wife of Chtouki, another member. In finding a wife for Senhaji, they were looking for a girl whose family and reputation were up to his level, someone who was mature and who could be relied upon to keep secrets.

I met Lalla Aicha first, before I met Lalla Mina. Aicha must be almost sixty by now, but looks much younger. She impressed me with her extraordinarily sweet smile and her soft voice, and I felt that she was a woman of enormous patience and strength. After we met that first time, Lalla Aicha invited me back to her home to talk with her and some other women who had participated in the resistance with her husband.

The women's gathering at Lalla Aicha's apartment showed me several important aspects of women's participation in the resistance that were new to me. First, I discovered that there were networks of women from the resistance, in this case two distinct networks, both centered around Abdellah Senhaji—one made up of women who had worked with Senhaji [or whose husbands had worked with him] in Casablanca and Rabat, and another of women who had worked with him in the liberation army [either with their husbands or on their own] in Ksar El Kbir and Nador in the north. When I went back to Lalla Aicha's to meet with her and the other women, several of the women had already arrived; I was delighted to see that one of them was Ghalia Moujahide. Aicha's co-wife Mina was also there, as well as Assila M'Barka and Halima Ben Moussa, whose husbands had both worked with Senhaji in the resistance in Casablanca and Rabat. Later, I found out that Rabiaa Taibi, whom I had met in Oujda, was a good friend of both Mina and Aicha Senhaji and their families from having been with them in Nador.[4] And I discovered that Assila M'Barka had not only worked with Senhaji, but also with Mohamed Zaim,[5] a resistance leader from Casablanca whose daughter was a friend and research assistant of mine. So I was discovering several overlapping networks of women who knew each other from the resistance, usually with men as the connecting links in the chain.

The other important discovery was more problematic and much less comfortable. The group that Aicha had gathered at her home to meet with me was full of strong personalities. I started the meeting, as I usually did, by asking each woman to speak in turn about her experience in the resistance. But everyone began shouting and interrupting before even one woman had had a chance to tell her whole story, and the meeting soon was completely out of control. While there were some stories and some jokes back and forth, and some very interesting arguments about who was telling the truth about what had happened,[6] the general tone got more and more angry, as several of the women began cursing and shouting about how they hadn't gotten anything in return for their sufferings during the resistance.[7] What made it uncomfortable was the realization that I couldn't do anything useful for these women. Certainly writing a book about what the women had done was not going to help them in any concrete way. Even though the women weren't angry at me directly, I was somehow implicated, linked with that whole bureaucratic/academic world that claimed to honor the resistance but didn't actually do anything for the women themselves and their families.

In spite of the uproar, I did manage to have some conversation with Aicha and Mina Senhaji. Their stories were significantly different from any I had heard before. Aicha spoke softly, as before, but she knew what she wanted to say, and even the shouting and interruptions didn't stop her. She insisted on two things: that she was in strict seclusion, confined to the house and not allowed to talk to men or visit people outside the family, and that she had worked hard and undergone great suffering in order to support her husband's work in the resistance. Here is Lalla Aicha's story as she told it to me at that first meeting.

Aicha Senjahi

Me, my husband followed the custom that there was no question of us [wives] meeting with other men. You heard, he worked [in the resistance]. The problem that we had was at home. For example, there were guests, there were arms [hidden], there were people for whom we had to prepare food. It was that that we, our job . . . .

In Casablanca he didn't allow us either to talk with people or to go to their houses; nor did he allow them to come to my place or allow us to meet them. We kept the arms in the house. I didn't see anyone. The house was always locked up and I stayed inside. Every man who came would give me what he had to give me and I would hide it in the room in the house. That is all that I [did] . . . I didn't go out with him, or take out the arms and go somewhere with them. No, not me. The main thing is that we had our work at home. There was the preparation of food, the housework. He brought money which I hid. Women brought gold, bracelets, and clothes [to support the resistance] . . . [*There is an uproar in the background, as everyone talks at once.*]

Men came to the house, but I didn't see them. [*Turning to her son, Mohamed:*] You know your father. I didn't go in where there were men. Me, I never went in where there were men. But I was always there in the kitchen. I gave them [things], but I never saw any of them in the street. I didn't go out. Me, I never went out, from the time the resistance started, I didn't go to anyone's house except my brother's, until he left for Nador. Then I stayed, me, for two years and two months, at my brother's house.

Later, Aicha explained exactly how she had spent those two years and two months at her brother's house. She and her little daughter Fatima lived for all that time in one room, a little cabin built on the roof terrace of the house. There was no electricity; she could only look out through narrow cracks between the boards that made up the cabin walls, and when it rained the drops made a loud noise—ta-ta-ta-ta-ta—just over their heads on the sheet of metal that was the cabin roof. When the sun beat down, it heated up the metal and made the room unbearably hot and stifling; in the winter it was dank and cold. The only people who knew that she was living there were her brother and his wife. They brought her food, and once in a while her brother gave her permission to come down into the house. She did give birth to her second daughter, Malika, in the house downstairs. Aicha was embarrassed at first in telling these details, afraid that there was something shameful in what she had endured.

[*Aicha, continuing her narrative at the women's meeting:*] I didn't ever go in or out until after he sent for me. He left me with one girl and one three-months along in my stomach; he left me for two years and two months. After that he sent for me, and I went to Nador, to [Senhaji] in Nador. These people took us to Nador; we went through Oued Melwiya; we crossed the river. Me, I never saw people or went to their houses; he would not allow me to do that. I didn't see anyone, because he was afraid that they would make me say something or . . . . Me, I was always at home. Excuse me. The work that I did, me, I prepared lots of food, and I sent it to the prisoners. I prepared a lot, and they transported it in trucks and took it to the prisoners. That was my work, me, always at home. They took the food to those who had been captured, the members of the resistance who had been arrested. That's what I did at home.

Later I went back to Lalla Aicha's house to do another interview with her separately.[8] She had invited Mina again, and several of her daughters and grandchildren who had come home to visit were there, including her second daughter Malika, who has a particular interest in her father's history. I asked Aicha about where she was born and her experience of growing up.

I was born near Essaouira, and grew up with my mother, as my father died when I was seven. I have a brother in Casablanca; he brought me up, and I lived with him in Casa. I took care of the house, and never went out anywhere. You know, at that time, there were strict traditions. So when my husband came along, the men of the two families met and agreed on the marriage. I was thirteen when I married him. At fifteen, I gave birth to my daughter, Fatima. We got involved in the war after that, after Fatima was born. We were not rich, and all the money we had went for the resistance, for fighters, and cooking for them or for prisoners. We also helped poor families. We collected money, gold and valuables to sell them and raise money. My husband used to keep all this in the house; we had just one room and we kept the weapons in it. I never talked to the neighbors or anybody. Nobody came to visit and I wasn't allowed to talk with anyone or to see anyone except for my family, my brothers and sisters—I could go and visit them. This was our life during the struggle for independence. People used to meet at our place and talk about the resistance, but they were all men and I was not allowed to be with them. I used to stay somewhere else until they had left.

So that was my life. We used to have to escape [from the police] and hide in different houses. We had a house in Casablanca on Avenue El Fida with my neighbors. You can come to visit it if you want, but [the neighbors] are dead now. Their children still live there, if you want to visit.[9] So that's my life since my marriage. I had the house to look after, the children, and the members of the resistance. That's it. I had nowhere to go, and that's how it is still.

When he went away, I didn't see him again for two years and two months. This is my life. He left this [daughter] Fatima when she was one year and six months old, and I was three months pregnant with [my second daughter] Malika. This was my life. I had contact with nobody.

[I finally made it to Nador.] It was after the king's return [in November, 1955]. That same week, a man called Lahssen came to get me—but I don't remember him any more. We left Casablanca at nine one night, and traveled the whole night to arrive in Oujda at seven in the morning. He took me to a house in Oujda, where I hid for the whole day, from seven in the morning until six in the evening. The woman we stayed with in Oujda was scared, so she told her neighbors that I was her son's wife, and that I was coming to rejoin my husband whom I married in Casablanca some years ago. So I spent the whole day with those people. Then, in the late afternoon, they took me in a taxi, and it dropped us off at a certain point; then we had to walk up into the mountains until we reached the Melwiya river; then we crossed the river on foot somewhere between Nadaj and Oujda. Again, I stayed with some people there for a week. Then a man named Haj Bouboul came to get me. By then I was really confused; I had no idea who all these people were; I just let myself be dragged along. [Haj Bouboul] got permission from the authorities to cross into the Spanish zone, and he took me across with him. It was then that I finally got to see my husband in Nador. When I got to Nador I found them all there: Abbess's wife, Amina [Senhaji's second wife], Hajja Rabiaa [from Oujda], and all the other friends and people from the resistance. I stayed there three months and then returned to

Casablanca after the Spanish expelled the liberation army people from the area. [At that time Mina also went back to her parents' in Ksar El Kbir.] I stayed in Casa until things got better, and then he came back to take me to Nador again. This is my life.

I gave birth to my son, Mohamed, in Nador. We stayed there for nine months; my husband, Haj Senhaji, became the first governor of Nador after independence. We stayed for nine months, and then came back to Rabat. That's it; that's my life.

Mina Senhaji

At the first meeting, Mina was increasingly frustrated with the other women talking, and made several efforts to get her own story told. Finally she managed, and this is what she said:

You know, this is a lot of talk! And the person who took care of the [liberation] army, and of feeding the liberation army [was me]. My girl, don't even talk about it! . . . You didn't see it. I prepared the food for sixty to eighty people sometimes, and with my stomach sticking out in front of me [pregnant with Khadija, her eldest child]. . . .

We were at Nador. We, we formed the liberation army. At that time, my husband was the president of the liberation army. He took care of the headquarters and [Commander-in-Chief Abbess] took care of the mountain [bases]. The liberation army [was deployed] in the [Rif] mountains, and [Senhaji] took care of the headquarters. Abbess would send the army back to headquarters, sixty people, seventy people a day, and I was the one [together with Rabiaa and the maids] who prepared food for them—lunch, dinner, and breakfast. Sixty people, seventy people, they would arrive in trucks. And the next day they would leave and some others would arrive. My husband was the one who took care of supplies and finances for food, for martyrs, and for . . . Me, at that time I was pregnant with my first girl, my oldest, the first. I was pregnant with her, and I took care of the [cooking] fire and everything. The girl was born mute.[10] We took care of everything until the return of Mohamed V. While we took care of food, of the army, they also brought us the wounded and the dead and we cared for [the wounded] in the basement below. And we stayed there until the return of King Mohamed V. At that time, what did [my husband] say? He said, "Me, I will present my army to the king." Mohamed V came to our place, and [Senhaji] presented the army to him, gave him the army. After that, we didn't have the army anymore. The Haj [Senhaji] was called by the king, who made him governor [of Nador], and after that the army was finished. We, at that time, were content to have worked for God, content that our king had come back to us, to our country. That was what we wanted. But the people of the [Commission for Veterans of the Resistance] didn't do anything for us; they did nothing for us.

When I came back to Aicha's apartment to talk with Mina and Aicha,
Mina started right off, almost as though she were just continuing the narrative
she had started at the meeting more than a year earlier:

Rabiaa [from Oujda] was with me. There were many women from the
north, Nador and other places. When we went to live in Nador, the Haj [Senhaji]
and Abbess got involved in the liberation army. He was trained and taken to
fight in the mountains. Rita, the wife of Abbess, and I lived in the same house. I
used to cook for soldiers in the mountains. Abbess lived in the mountains; that's
why his wife was with us. Abbess used to come just once a week. He'd take a
shower, shave, and change clothes; then he'd go back again to the mountains
[where] he took care of the soldiers. When they came down from the mountains
they would stay in the basement of our building. There were about two hundred
soldiers, and I had to do a lot of cooking. At first we wanted to hire some people
to help with the cooking, but then we were scared [they would give us away], so
Senhaji brought an old woman, named Mi El Ghalia. Poor woman; she's dead
now. She did the washing up and helped with the work. I was pregnant then—
my daughter was born when Mohamed V came back from exile.

The soldiers would [generally] stay two days. There were about sixty or
fifty or forty of them. We'd cook for them, offer them tea, and so on. Then the
Haj [Senhaji] would take them up to a room much bigger than this one which
was full of weapons, clothes, belts, hats, and djellabas. All of this was there just
for the army that was fighting for the return of our king. So when the soldiers had
stayed two or three days, and had rested enough, they would start getting ready to
leave. They would spend all morning in that big room finding ways of hiding
weapons either under their belts, or on their backs, or somewhere else. Then
trucks came to take them away—forty soldiers per truck. And they would all start
praising the Lord and the Prophet Mohamed, and then they would take off.

There were many caids in the mountains with the soldiers, Caid Allal and
many many others. The caids too used to come with the soldiers for food, rest,
and so on. We lived this way for about two years, until our king came back, and
then the Haj [Senhaji] took his soldiers to see the king. We also had to take care
of the injured and the wounded and little children. Hajja Rabiaa was very moved
at the sight of these suffering people. She used to cry a lot and say: "Our Muslim
brothers, the poor soldiers, are dying!"

Dr. El Khatib would bring medicine for these poor injured soldiers, or, if
there were very serious cases, they would be taken to the hospital for care. Hajja
Rabiaa used to help a lot. She would nurse them, clean them, and give them their
medicine. We even gave them our clothes when they needed them. We were
really sorry for them all: soldiers, women, and children. We had no time to go
out or to go to the hammam; we just stayed at home and cooked and so on.
There was this man named J'ha [an Arab folk figure famous for his wit and
cupidity]. Ahmed was his real name, but we called him J'ha. He used to run

errands for the Haj [Senhaji]; get boxes of vegetables, potatoes, and so on, two or three sheep . . . so that we could cook for the soldiers. Aicha was still in Casablanca then with Fatima and Malika. [She stayed there] until King Mohamed V came back from exile; then she came back [to Nador].

[*Aicha:*] I stayed in my house with my brother. In fact we used to move from one house to the other so that they wouldn't catch [Senhaji]. When he finally fled [to the north, to Ksar El Kbir], I went to [my brother's] house, and that's where I stayed, never going out, because the French were after [Senhaji, and it was important that they not find his wife]. I never went out, for two years and two months, *never* saw the street again for all that time, and never talked to anybody or saw anybody. I was all alone, by myself, from the time he left.

[*Mina:*] When [Senhaji] came to the north, she couldn't come with him. He married me in Ksar El K'bir. We went to Tetouan; we spent the night there in the house of some partisans. . . . There were lots of them, some are still alive and others who have died.

[*Aicha:*] So I stayed behind, and was completely cut off from the rest of the world. . . .

[*Mina:*] From Tetouan we went to Nador. Abbess, his wife, and myself, we all lived in the same house. Then Hajja Rabiaa came along. She had smuggled some weapons, and the partisans helped her to escape [from Oujda in the French zone into Nador in the Spanish zone], and brought her to the house. They had also helped another woman named Fatima [Benchekroun]—she is in Taza now, but she too lived with us then. She brought her little girl, who was about ten or eleven years old, with her and left the little girl with me. Abdellah [Senhaji] told her not to take the girl with her into the mountains. He said, "You can go if you want to." She said she wanted to go up there to help the commandos, cook for them, and so on. So Fatima went into the mountains. She is in Taza now and still comes to visit us now and then. Poor thing, she is very sick now. They [the commission] gave her nothing.

I got married in 1954. I was born in Ksar El Kbir. We stayed at home all the time, because girls couldn't go out in those days. At home we were taught needlework and other handicrafts. One day a man came to ask my father to marry me to a member of the resistance who had escaped from Casablanca to the north. My father accepted the proposal because he was an old man. . . . When I married him, I was eighteen,[11] and we lived in Ksar El Kbir for six months. After that I noticed that he used to stay out late, go to cafés and other people's houses for political meetings. People would come to join them from Casa, Marrakesh, and Rabat, and they often used to meet very late at night, for fear of being discovered. When I asked him where he was, he answered that it was none of my business; that there was no need for him to tell me.

One day he told me: "Pack up our belongings; we're going to Nador." I asked him why we were doing that, and he said, "We're going to Nador to organize the liberation army and send soldiers into the mountains." I told him, "No, I'm not going with you." Then he said, "This is impossible! It's bad enough that I left one wife in Casablanca because she couldn't figure out a way of joining me. And now it's your turn to leave me to go alone! No way!"

My father was also against my going away. He was worried about me, and about everything that was going on then. Times were really hard. I told my father, "I'm not staying here. I'll follow my husband wherever he goes. If he falls into the fire, I'll die with him. I won't stay here!" Then my father said, "If that's the way it is, then good luck and may God bless you."

We went straight to Tetouan, and we stayed with the wives of partisans there. . . . There were about six or seven wives of partisans. Some of the husbands stayed there [with their wives], and others stayed in other towns. Si Abdellah and Abbess were going to Nador to find a house and train and organize an army to liberate the country. We, the wives, spent about four or five nights together, while our husbands would get together in a room to talk about their own affairs.

Then the Haj got ready to leave. Said Bou Niilat took us in his car, at night. We passed El Houceima and so on until we got to Nador, where we found Abbess. His wife, who was from Fez, joined us later. She was afraid of traveling alone, so [another woman, Mi Fatna Tarzoutia] went with her. They asked me whether I wanted to go with her too, but I said no, so I went by car with my husband. It was Said's car—they used to give people in the resistance cars and everything else they needed. When we got there, we found that friends had already rented a house. I had brought a mattress and a pillow with me, and when we got to the house that was all that we had for sleeping; there was no other furniture in the house. So that's where they used to meet. They formed an army and sent soldiers into the mountains, and I stayed behind with Abbess's wife.

It was four to six months before Hajja Rabiaa came to stay with us. After a while another woman came; they sent her into the mountains to help them there, by doing things like stealing weapons and taking them to the army. I just stayed at home with Abbess's wife. [Our job was] cooking, that's all, cooking all the time. We didn't even have time to wash ourselves and comb our hair until very late in the evening when all the work was done.

Life went on and on like that until the king came back and we got independence. We were very happy when we got independence. Si Abdellah went to see the king to give him the army. After a period of two or three months, Abbess came to spend the night with us. My daughter, who was still a five-months-old baby, just adored Abbess; she was five months old when Abbess died.[12] He spent the night with us, and was going to join his wife in Fez the following day. He was on his way to Fez, poor man, when he was arrested. They killed him and buried him. The Haj [Senhaji] and Hassan II, the crown prince, went to look for him in the mountains. Everybody loved him. Aicha and her two daughters were in Casa then; I was in Nador. After Abbess left the next day [after he had spent the night], a man came to the house and told me that the Haj and Hassan II were looking for him. It took them three or four days to find his body; they sent the body to Fez, and the Haj came by to take me to Fez for the funeral. We stayed there for three days, and then we went back to Nador. [Abbess died in Agdir, Tiziousli, in the Rif, and eventually was buried there, but the funeral right after his death was in Fez.]

The king sent for the Haj and appointed him Governor of Nador [in 1956], and other people who were with the Haj in the [liberation] army became governors too.

[*Aicha:*] I have six children: five girls and one boy [Mohamed], the one that you saw the other day.

[*Mina:*] I have nine children: six boys and three girls. Two of the girls are married and one boy is married. The other two boys are in Canada.

This is life. The Haj died. We suffered a lot; we went through a lot, but it was all for a good cause. . . . After independence, everyone went their own way. Some people made a lot of money—yes, they did—but our husband never wanted to [make money]. Abbess too was never interested in money; he always believed in his duty, in his country. [Senhaji] was exactly like his father [in that]; his father [fought against the Spanish] in the Sahara. He is from Foumzghid, a few kilometers from Taznakht on the road to Ouerzazat, from the Senhaja tribe in the Sahara.

At this point Malika, Aicha's daughter, explained to me in French what had happened when Aicha arrived in Nador and discovered that her husband had taken a second wife.

My father was obliged to take a second wife. At that time he couldn't have a cleaning woman or have contact with other women or anything, because he was wanted by the Spanish as well as the French and had been condemned to death seven times. That meant that he had to take a [second] wife; so that is what he did. Later, when my mother came to rejoin him in Nador, the two wives discovered one another. So both of them were faced with a *fait accompli*. That is to say that [my father] didn't do what he did with any bad intentions. So it came about that Lalla Mina and Lalla Aicha, my mother, had to accept things the way they were. And then [my father] never made any distinction between the two wives or between the children of the first and the children of the second wife. No, he never preferred the first to the second, or the second to the first. He made them understand that he had been obliged to take two wives. So there; that's how it was. And now we are a family that is very united. For us, there is no difference between our father's second wife and our mother; it's the same thing for our brothers, *Hbibti*'s children.[13] So we are really all very close as a family; the proof of that is that we still live on the same street; we see each other every day; we talk to each other on the telephone every day.

14.4

Aicha and Mina Senhaji (in the 1950s).

Source: Rabiaa Taibi.

14.5

Aicha with her eldest daughter, Fatima.

Source: Rabiaa Taibi.

After this explanation, Aicha continued, concluding the interview with thanks for the good things that happened after independence.

When the king came to Nador, all of the members of the resistance expressed their joy. They came from all over [to see him]: from Tangiers, Tetouan, Taza, and other places. It's over forty years now since we got our independence. Our children are good, thank God. When our husband died [in 1985 in an accident], the king was generous with us: He gave us a salary, which is what we live on.[14] Our husband died about ten years ago.

After I had written the chapter to this point, I asked Aicha and her daughter Malika for their comments and corrections, and in this process I realized that there was more to be said, especially about the period after independence. So I recorded an interview with Malika, Aicha's second daughter, who was born in 1955. She spoke about her memories of the period after independence, starting in the early sixties, about her father, and about her mother.

From 1956 to 1958 my father was governor of Nador. Then, in 1958, he returned to Rabat and took off his uniform [gave up his position as governor]. . . . He stayed in Rabat until 1963. The uprisings of 1963; that I remember very well. At that time there were [these uprisings], and people set a trap for my father. My father was adored; he was loved and adored by His Majesty—that was indisputable—he was loved and adored by His Majesty. But they set a trap for him. Someone came to him and said, "You'd better go to Algeria, because otherwise they'll have your hide!" So he went, and then the others went to His Majesty and said to Him: "You see, he's [part of the plot] against you. The proof is that he fled [to Algeria]!" It was really a put-up job. So my father went to Algeria; he lived there for a year, and we came there after him and stayed there with him for another year, which meant that he was there in Algeria from 1963 to 1965. His Majesty sent for him, to bring him back, [and he returned to Rabat in 1965]. . . .

I remember well how we went to Algeria. First, we escaped from Rabat. Lalla Mina had already gone [to Algeria, with her children]. About a week or ten days later, the police came and broke into our house. . . . I remember one evening, our road . . . It's simple, our road was closed off, like that, by the police. [We lived] in Rabat, in the rue de Sebou, just behind the street we live on now; [in those days] it used to be called the rue de Béarne. [The police] entered [the house] at three o'clock in the morning, storming in as though they were expecting to find a whole commando group. When my mother opened the door they rushed in, and they beat her, right in front of us. My sister Fatima bit one of the cops who was there; she gave him a good bite on his backside. They had woken us up at three in the morning; we were all crying, howling! We were very young—I remember Fatima was twelve years old, I was ten. And then imagine the others—they were only eight, seven, six, and so on. So there we were with

14.6

Mina Senhaji, Tleitmas (wife of Caid Allal Touzani), Aicha Senhaji.

Source: Aicha Senhaji.

14.7

Malika Senhaji, dancing with her husband at her wedding (1996).

Credit: Anne White.

my mother. It was terrifying! I will remember it for all of my life. When the cops came and hit my mother, they asked her, "Where is your husband?" She told them, "Listen. My husband has abandoned me." "And where is his other wife?" "His other wife was always fighting with me. She left together with him. As for him, he has always abandoned me. He left; he's abandoned me, and I don't know where he is. He left me with my children, and I don't even have anything for my children to eat." And since they knew that he had married two wives, it was a reasonable explanation [that she gave]. . . .

They went off [through the house] as though they were looking for—I don't know—a commando group of criminals, or as though my mother had done something [terrible], or my father, whereas after all he was someone who had fought for his country, who had always loved his country. Well they came; they did all that. They dragged my uncle off [and kept him] for a whole month, using torture to try to make him talk. They tore up the furniture looking for arms, as though it were possible that there would be arms in the house, something that was really unimaginable! And then afterwards, there were cops stationed at the corner of the road who watched us. Not only that, but there was another policeman who lived across from us who also kept watch over us all day long. In spite of this we still managed to escape to Casa, and then we stayed in Casa for two months, and after that we went to Algeria to rejoin our father.

We stayed in Casablanca for two months, for two months, in hiding. We lived in a poor neighborhood, where there was no water, no electricity. We only had candles. My mother never told anyone who she was, and she told us never to say who we were. That I remember, because I lived through it. Afterwards, I remember that our departure was arranged for one evening. One evening we took the train—at ten at night, I think, or eleven—and we left Casablanca for Oujda. We arrived in Oujda, and someone was waiting for us; I don't remember who it was. He took us somewhere outside of Oujda; we spent the night there, and the next day, early in the morning, he got us across the frontier [in a car]. We found our father there on the other side of the Algerian frontier. So there we saw our father again, after a year in which we hadn't seen him.

After we met our father, we left directly for a little town in Algeria, Rio Salado [El Malh in Arabic], where we then lived for one year. We were living in what was practically a palace, a house left by the [French] colonialists [*colons*] who had left Algeria [after Algeria's independence in 1962]. And we lived well there; for one year we were treated like kings. And all the time [that we were there] people came to see my father, people sent from [Morocco], from His Majesty, to tell my father that he should come back to Morocco. So [this shows that] His Majesty certainly always knew that Senhaji was someone who had always loved his king, his country, his king and everything. Then we came back; we came back in 1965, in September, 1965. Everyone came back, the whole family, including [both wives and their children], everyone. My father left us in Oujda, at the home of Commander Miloudi [and his wife, Hajja Zohra], who are close friends of ours. We stayed there, I think, for fifteen days, the time that it took my father to come to Rabat and rent a house here and buy some furniture so that we could come back.

So we always started back at zero after a certain time. Until very recently we never had real furniture, or a real house. [My parents] were in Casablanca, then they left for Nador, then they abandoned everything in Nador and came back to Rabat, then we left for Algeria—to Casablanca first, and then Algeria—then we came back. So you see, there has always been a certain instability for all of us. And when we came back [in 1965], my father had eleven children (later, four more were born); he had two wives; and in addition to that there were two male cousins who were with us, plus one female cousin who helped in the house. So there were three additional persons. When we came back from Algeria, my father wasn't working—he had no work at all. The government gave him a thousand dirhams [a little more than $100] a month. With eleven children, plus three others he was responsible for, plus two wives! We lived like that from 1965 up until 1973. The first parliament was in 1973, I think. At that time, my father was elected as a member of parliament. He was also [appointed] vice president of the Liberation Army; the president was Dr. El Khatib and the vice president was my father. [This was the High Commission for Veterans of the Resistance and the Liberation Army, which was created at that time.] That was the first time that he had a salary; it was the salary [that he received] as a member of parliament. No, he never took any salary as vice president of the Commission; he never took anything. Afterwards, in 1974, they created the *Parti de l'Action* [Action Party], and [my father] was the secretary general of the party. . . .[15]

And after that, [my father's] dream was to write a book on [the history of] the resistance in Morocco, on everything he lived through, from 1947 to 1956. . . . And the last page [of the book][16] was written on the day of his accident, at eleven in the morning. And what he said to me then, he said, "For me, today, if death wants to come, let it come. I wanted to write this book before I died." He said that in the morning, and then just after that [at 12:30 that day] he had his accident. [He was hit by a bus.] He stayed in a coma for a week, and then he died.

Malika talked about all that her father had done to help former members of the resistance and liberation army—working on their papers (for the Carte de Résistant), letting them stay in his house for a week or ten days because they came from distant places and were poor, paying for their stamps, giving them bus fare, and sometimes even giving them one or two hundred dirhams [$10–$25].

And when there were holidays—you know that for Muslim holidays parents buy new clothes for their children and everything—my father would tell us: "I can't buy you any new clothes. There's not just you; there are others who come here and who don't even have enough to eat." And he gave to the poor. He was always surrounded by veterans, and he always wanted to help them; he always wanted to give and give. He never stopped giving. It was because of that that our house was always full. Often there were about a hundred people; and this was true every day, every single day. My mother was always there to help people, to receive people, to do the cooking. It was like this all the time. It never stopped, right up to 1985 when our father died.

My father was a man who was very tolerant, very indulgent, very kind. He never hit his children. When he wanted to correct us, he always took a newspaper, and when we did something naughty he would hit the paper against the table like this [*Malika demonstrates hitting a newspaper on the table next to her*], and say, "Eh, you silly little thing!" He was someone you never heard shouting, never. Never angry, never shouting. On the other hand, my mother was very strict. It was she who was in charge [at home]. Yes, it was she who was in charge, and she was very severe with us. When I say severe, I mean [we had] a strict upbringing. We had to behave according to strict rules; there were things we couldn't do. We couldn't get back home late; even when we went to the movies sometimes, we had to get back on time. While my father would say, "Oh, come on now, let them be! They're with their girlfriends at the movies. If they don't get home until six or seven it's alright." That is to say that my mother had complete control over the education and discipline of her children. She didn't wait until our father came home to tell him, "Look, your son did this, did that." No. No.

In spite of all the moving we did, we all went to school. My sister and I went to the French school. We all went to school; there was no problem at all with that. In both Rabat and Casa. In Nador no, because we were very young, but I think that Fatima was sent to a little nursery school. As soon as we got to Rabat we studied with the French. We lived in a neighborhood where there was almost noone but French people, so even though my father had been fighting against the French. . . . He was never against [French education]. . . . After all, [my parents] did try to give us a life that was more or less normal. We [also] went to school in Algeria; there we had problems because the level wasn't the same and they did everything in Arabic, whereas I had been in a French school where most subjects were taught in French, so I had trouble following. Also we had to repeat a grade, which made us lose some years, etc. etc. But in general we didn't have too much to complain about in that. . . .

Later, I asked Malika what she thought about her mother's story, about what her mother did and what she suffered. And I asked her what she herself drew from her mother's experience.

It's very simple. I believe that I take everything from her—well, "everything" in the sense of the spirit of resistance. I take everything from her and from my father, and me, I continue [in their path]. I think that my mother is a woman who had a great deal of courage. She was very young when she was married, and she married a man who was much older than she. She was thirteen and he was about thirty-three or something like that, which is already difficult. She is a woman who never really lived a [normal] life with her husband as a woman, because she never had that opportunity. When he left [to do work] for the resistance in Casablanca, he left her all alone; he couldn't do anything else. He married again; when she arrived [in the north] she found another wife with another daughter. In sum, I believe that she was a woman who, in her suffering—she did have some moments of happiness [too], so [it was] not even in her suffering, but rather in [the course of] her life that was so very eventful—she was a woman who never had a life, a real life of a married woman. They moved very frequently from one city to another, from one house to another. She is a woman who really never had anything she could call her own. Every time that she could finally say, "I have this that belongs to me," she had to leave it, to leave behind everything that she had.

We talked about the other women in the book who participated actively in
the armed resistance, and I suggested that what her mother did was in some
ways even more courageous than what those other women did.

Absolutely! Because she was forced always to be in the background. She
couldn't be out in the field; that wasn't possible because of her age, because she
had children, and, above all, because my father did not allow her. He didn't
allow her [to participate in a resistance cell] because of his way of life and his
way of seeing things. First, he couldn't allow his wife to be together with men in
the field. Second, he couldn't because he himself was always in hiding, so he
didn't want people to see his wife, because at any moment she might say
something, even without wanting to, or this or that.[17] Because he was a man who
was always being pursued, and he had a price on his head. So she was a woman
who didn't start breathing [freely] until after her return from Nador. No, not
even then, and not even after her return from Algeria. . . .

My mother didn't have a calm life until after the death of my father.
About fifteen days before his death—it was as if he knew it was going to
happen. . . . You know that we live in the same street, Hbibti and my mother.
We have a big villa; you've never visited it? It's a villa, the villa in which we
lived for a long time all together. My father never wanted to separate his wives
and his children, so we always lived together in the same house. And an
extraordinary thing: Fifteen days before his accident, he took the apartment
where we now live for my mother, just as though he knew that he was going to
die. He rented that apartment [for her]. It was . . . well, she wanted a little more
space, and the children were growing up, and when you're young you can sleep
together four in a room, but once you get bigger, the girls need their independence, and the boys are getting bigger too so they need their own room and
everything. And we had too many people, and my mother had begun to
complain, saying [to my father], "The day when you're no longer there, noone
will bother to come by to see if your children have anything to eat or not."
Because she was too tired. Every day breakfast wasn't finished until noon; the
midday meal was finished at four in the afternoon; at four they started up
again—the kitchen never closed up—after four there was tea; and then dinner
lasted until midnight or one in the morning.

I can assure you of one thing—we could never see my father. Every time
that we needed something, we wrote him a note and gave it to him; then he read
the note, [which explained] why I needed to buy a pair of shoes, or a book, or
this or that. We wrote it in a note, even though we were in this room and he was
in the room next door. But I assure you . . . And in the morning, people woke
him up. Before he was up at seven in the morning, there were ten cars in front of
the house. And in the evening, by the time they all left, he was practically asleep
and the rest of us were all sleeping. This meant that we never had a real family
life. The two of us, Fatima and I, being the oldest, we benefited from our father

14.8

Women at Abdellah Senhaji's funeral. Ghalia Moujahide is in white at the corner of the door, and Rabiaa Taibi in white in foreground.

Source: Aicha Senhaji.

a little bit. But all [the children] who came after us, no, no, they never [had a chance to be with him]. Because he traveled a lot, we only saw him once every two weeks or ten days, and then we would stay with him for about five minutes. He would say, "Come here next to me" and everything, and then, well, someone would come up [to him], and then there would be ten people, fifteen, a whole group of people, which meant that we didn't ever see him.

Then, as I told you, my mother, since his death, has begun to have a life that is a bit more stable. She has become more and more serene, and we take care of her. Before, it was too much. It was too much.

15

Zohra Torrichi and Rabiaa Taibi: Oujda

Oujda is the main city of Eastern Morocco, closer to Tlemcen and Oran in Algeria than to Fez, Rabat, and Casablanca in Morocco. It owes its prominence—its existence, really—to its location on the crossroads of two trade routes, one running between Western Morocco and Algeria, and the other between sub-Saharan Africa, the Mediterranean, and Europe. In 1912, when the French and Spanish protectorates were established in Morocco, Oujda ended up just inside the French zone, with the Spanish zone over the mountains to the northwest and the French colony of Algeria a few miles to the east. The city of Nador, just over the border in the Spanish zone, served as a refuge for resistance fighters from Oujda and as a base of operations for the Moroccan liberation army; and Oujda itself served as a base and refuge for members of the Algerian National Liberation Front (FLN) from the mid-fifties up until Algeria finally won its independence from France in 1962. In 1955–56, the French government was very concerned about the flourishing arms traffic which was supplying the Moroccan Liberation Army "rebels" and the Algerian FLN. Port cities in Spanish Morocco were the main points of entrance, after which some of the arms were smuggled to Oujda in the French zone and across the border into Algeria. Large quantities came from Egyptian Special Services: especially English "Enfield" and Italian "Stati" guns.[1]

Through the period of the protectorate, Oujda's population grew from six thousand five hundred to about eighty thousand—almost exactly the same growth rate as that of Casablanca—and significant numbers of Europeans and Algerians were added to the original mix of Moroccan Muslims and Jews.[2] These were years of rapid economic, demographic, and social change in Oujda, only the position of women was kept largely unchanged, even more than in most Moroccan cities. In Oujda, Moroccan Muslim girls didn't begin to go to school until very late in the protectorate period, and bourgeois women were very late in beginning to wear the djellaba instead of the haik, a move that scandalized some old men.[3] Even now, Oujda is much more conservative socially than other Moroccan cities: separation of the sexes is the rule even at informal parties, and while you see women walking through the streets on their way to work or school, you don't see them sitting in cafés or other public places.

Oujda had a long history of independence from the control of the sultan and his makhzen government, well before the French even entered the picture, and the protectorate policy of supporting the great caids and pashas only increased their power. In the last stages of the protectorate, many of the most prominent religious and political officials in Oujda supported the French and spoke in favor of the exile of the Moroccan Sultan. There was even a political party, the limonade *[soda] party of Oulad Kloufi, whose members refused to see the face of the exiled king in the moon. On the other hand, a massive anti-French uprising in Oujda on the sixteenth of August, 1953, established the city as a center of Moroccan nationalism and the resistance. A few days later, when the Moroccan king was sent into exile, Istiqlal leaders in Oujda were all emprisoned, "forty Moroccan militants were killed, and young Moroccan women were attacked by the French."*[4] *Women who lived through these events in Oujda told me of their experience:*

> *The city was surrounded; the machine-gun fire frightened the people. There were gunshots; we escaped; the walls were full of holes. We went up on the roof terrace; noone went out of the house. We couldn't have any lights because of the missiles that were flying overhead. . . . There was hunger, and the Americans came to help us. . . . Jewish neighbors helped us to hide from the French.*[5]

After World War II, an Algerian proletariat came to settle in Oujda in great numbers, and although Algerian Muslims never really assimilated with either the French or with Moroccan Muslims in Oujda, they did move gradually from a position of collaboration with the French colonists (1907–1942) to a position of opposition and collaboration with the Moroccan nationalist movement and resistance (after 1942).[6] *Thus Algerians living in Oujda collaborated with the Moroccan independence movement from the early forties until the king's return and independence in 1955–56, and then Moroccans in Oujda collaborated with the Algerian independence movement until Algeria won its independence in 1962. In Oujda, most women who fought in the Moroccan resistance went right on after independence to work with the FLN.*[7] *Oujdi women thus fought in the resistance for almost a full decade, first for Moroccan independence and then for Algerian independence, whereas in other Moroccan cities women only participated for two or three years.*

After the return of King Mohamed V in October 1955, many Algerian nationalists came to Oujda to take refuge; sick and wounded Algerians came to Oujda to be treated at the hospital. Rabiaa Taibi gave her blood to help wounded Algerians, and took care of them in her home while they were convalescing. Zohra Torrichi was raised by an Algerian family living in Oujda, and participated actively in the Algerian struggle for independence as well as in

15.1

Zohra Torrichi (1996).

Credit: Anne White.

the Moroccan resistance. Many of the inhabitants of Oujda took in young Algerian women who had fled their country. Some of these Algerian women stole other people's (Moroccan) husbands.[8]

Zohra Torrichi

Zohra Torrichi finally got her card in the summer of 1994. For some reason, perhaps because she was involved in the Algerian war and other missions until 1965, she didn't apply for the card until May 5, 1974, after the formation of the High Commission for Veterans of the Resistance. On October 4, 1977, her dossier was reviewed by the national commission, but they were not convinced by the evidence or the testimony of witnesses. One witness said that Zohra took care of partisans who were sick and wounded, but some others said that she didn't do anything in the resistance. The dossier was refused. On

October 5, 1982, a second commission took up Zohra's case again, on appeal. This time, the witnesses who had been called did not appear: They were called once, twice, and a third time, but none of them came to testify on Zohra's behalf before the commission, so the dossier was refused again. A third national appeals commission considered the dossier on May 15, 1984. This time, just one witness testified, but his testimony strongly supported Zohra's claim to be recognized as a veteran of the resistance.[9] The witness asserted that she had taken care of partisans, that she had given her own money for the cause, that on at least one occasion she had paid the doctor out of her own pocket, that she had hidden arms, that she had moved arms from one place to another, that she had hidden partisans who were being pursued, and that she had given them medical care. He swore to God that these were activities that he himself had witnessed, and that she deserved all possible recognition for her contributions to the resistance. The appeals commission was persuaded by this testimony and accepted the dossier. For some reason, it took another ten years for the national commission to confirm this decision and to issue Zohra's card recognizing her active participation in the resistance. Her card is dated July 19, 1994. While this was clearly an exceptional case, it was not the only one. As time goes by the national commission has tried to reexamine files to be sure that all the people currently registered deserve that recognition, and to review new applications and appeals according to very strict criteria before issuing new cards. A total of six women got their cards in 1994, including Zohra, and more than a hundred men.

I first met Zohra in Oujda, where she was living with her second husband, Captain Miloud, and a large household of children and grandchildren. They have a spacious second floor apartment, with a large salon, where we met, and an even larger, more formal salon that is used mainly by men. She is a very elegant woman, with fine features, rather shy when I first met her. Later I saw her again in her own apartment in Salé, where she showed me photos of herself from the sixties—she was clearly an extraordinarily beautiful young woman. I went to see Zohra in Oujda once more during the summer, when lots of children and grandchildren were visiting from France and Belgium, but my keenest memory is that of a meeting with Zohra in her apartment in Salé in November of 1996. Zohra was extremely tired and sad; she had come to Salé a few months earlier after her husband married a second wife, a much younger woman. At this time Captain Miloud was at least eighty, Zohra, seventy-two, and the new wife, about thirty-five. Another problem was that although she had finally received her card certifying that she participated in the resistance almost two years ago, Zohra had still not received any benefits from the commission. She remained the sole support for a daughter, who was repudiated by her husband twenty-three years ago, and none of her other children were offering to help, even though some of them were apparently doing quite well.

15.2

Zohra Torrichi as a young woman.

Source: Zohra Torrichi.

There were several points at which Zohra was reticent in telling me of her life and her participation in the resistance. She was born to Moroccan parents in Beni Mellal, but her Moroccan father died when she was quite young, and she was adopted by Algerian parents in Oujda. I never found out exactly why or how this happened; her brothers and sisters seem to have stayed with her mother in Beni Mellal. She was also reluctant to talk about her experience—now for the second time—of having her husband take a second wife. She worked with her first husband, a taxi driver, in the resistance in Oujda, and he encouraged her in this, but then he took a second wife. When he died in 1964, Zohra and the other wife divided the inheritance, and Zohra used her share to buy the apartment in Salé where she was now living. Her second husband had married a new, younger wife just a few months ago, and she was still shaken by the experience. She didn't seem to blame her husband; instead she almost blamed herself, saying rather sadly that she has gotten too old to take care of him. Other Moroccan women who know Zohra were sympathetic to her plight, under-standing how it must feel to have your husband take a second, much younger wife after thirty years of marriage, just when you yourself are getting old.

Over the course of several interviews, Zohra told me the story of her life and her participation in the resistance and the Algerian liberation war. Here she starts at the beginning.

We used to live in Beni Mellal when I was very young; then my father died and I went to Oujda. My father in Oujda—that is to say the father who adopted me—was a member of the Istiqlal Party, and used to work with Allal El Fassi. He was a great nationalist; he went to Tunisia and Algeria and he used to bring nationalist tracts home. He sent letters to Tunisia [in support of the Tunisian independence movement]. That's how I started being involved; I was brought up in this [atmosphere]; I followed the path of my father. When I went to school I used to hear talk about nationalism and my father's work, and so when I grew up I did the same kind of work that he did. I became involved in the Istiqlal Party. . . . Later, I was the secretary for Amina Barhiria in the women's association of the Istiqlal Party. I was intelligent, and people trusted me.

I studied Arabic and the Koran in the Koranic school, and then went to primary school from the age of seven until the age of thirteen; in fact I got my primary school certificate. Then I went to the ma'alma to learn other things, handicrafts and needlework. I got married at the age of sixteen.

My first husband and I fought in the resistance together. My husband had a taxi; he transported members of the resistance. Once during the resistance, one of the men betrayed us, and the police came to the house. Luckily my husband worked in transport and the police knew him. They asked after my husband, but he wasn't at home. Then they left, together with the traitor, but soon afterwards they came back. I knew enough to welcome them and to invite them in to have a coffee so that they would not suspect what I was doing. They said they appreciated the invitation, but they had to refuse since my husband was not at home. This time they left for good. And all the time they had been there, a wounded partisan was asleep in the house. Once the wounded man had recovered, we took him to Sidi Yahia [a village outside of Oujda] without anyone even knowing that he had been sick. Another wounded man came to my place to be taken care of, and I got the doctor to come and remove the bullet. Then he stayed in the house, which was empty. There was another wounded man from Berkane; I took care of him myself. And I also took care of a wounded man from another place; the hospital refused to take him in because he was wounded by a bullet.

In Nador, I helped financially. They told me that there was a man designated to take the money, but unfortunately this man was shot and badly wounded. A woman warned me about that. I went to see a doctor who worked with the resistance who was willing to take care of the wounded man. He asked me to bring the man to his clinic. Once the man arrived, I took him to the doctor's, and the doctor emptied out his clinic to take care of the wounded man. The man had been fired on and hit, and he had a fractured leg. After they released the wounded man from the clinic, I took him into my house and he stayed there for two months, convalescing. We put plaster on his leg, and I hid him in a small room. His wife and his two daughters were also in my house, all of them, and helped take care of him. The other partisans and friends came there to see him, and they wanted to take him home, but I refused for fear that our nationalism would be revealed.

We struggled, we got money together, gold to help members of the resistance. The day that the resistance succeeded [in its goal of bringing back the king and winning Moroccan independence], we went on to participate in the struggle for independence in Algeria. The woman I worked with in the Istiqlal Party, Amina Barhiria, was also ready to participate in the struggle for Algerian independence. My husband encouraged me in that, since my [adoptive] parents were of Algerian nationality. I collected a lot of money for Algeria. When we were about to finish our work here in Morocco, the Algerian resistance just started, and they asked me to work for them, so I went. When we finished in Morocco, we went over there, because things lasted much longer over there in Algeria; there they just started in 1957.

I used to collect money, organize meetings, go to people's houses to help. Because there was cooperation between Morocco and Algeria; the king gave us the opportunity to help our Algerian brothers. He used to tell us to help them, so I went to help over there. I used to organize meetings, and go to people's houses and ask people to give money and to help in the resistance. I told them, "You have to *participate*! You have to join in the fight against colonialism!" I worked with the FLN [National Liberation Front].

My first husband and I, we fought in the resistance together, but I still didn't have a card until very recently, because I made these sacrifices voluntarily. Mr. Senhaji [resistance leader Abdellah Senhaji] encouraged me to fill out the dossier in order to get a card. I filled out the dossier and my husband signed it, and since then I've waited for more than fifteen years to get the card. I helped

15.3

Certificate from the Frontier Command of the Algerian Republic. Text: "We, of the frontier command, attest by this certificate that the named Torrichi Zohra is one of the main compatriots in our organization in Oujda. By her participation at the heart of the ALN and the FLN, she was able to conduct psychological warfare among women in support of our revolution. We request that all civil and military authorities assist her and favor her in order to do everything possible to facilitate her activities.
Signed: The Commander of the Frontier."

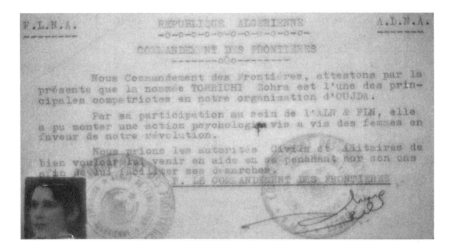

Source: Zohra Torrichi.

poor people, I took care of children and the wounded. My [first] husband married a second wife, and we divided the inheritance when he died. I sold the house and I divided the inheritance with the children. As for me, I bought an apartment in Salé with my share. Since I am sick, I need to get medical care in Rabat.

I didn't work directly with Rabiaa during the resistance; we worked separately. She used to work with people from Casablanca, whereas I worked at home then because I had young children. All the help I gave to the resistance was from my house. But when I was in the Istiqlal Party I used to do a lot of work, collect money and everything. . . . No, no, it wasn't because of my [first] husband that I stayed at home; he gave me all the freedom I needed. I told him, "I want to participate in the nationalist movement," and he said, "Do whatever you feel you are capable of. Of course we have to help our brothers, whether they are Moroccans or Algerians." This was my first husband. But Hajja Rabiaa wasn't married then and she didn't have children like me. That's why she did more work than I did. She went to Spain; in fact she escaped there.

15.4

Zohra Torrichi with her second husband, Captain Miloud (ca. 1965).

Source: Zohra Torrichi.

Zohra played an important role in arranging for the return of Abdellah Senhaji from Algeria in 1964–65. She worked as a sort of double agent, passing secret messages back and forth between Senhaji in Algeria and representatives of King Hassan II in Morocco. She went three times to Algeria to meet with Senhaji and convey the king's request that he return, until finally he agreed. The Moroccan government gave Zohra an agrément *for a large (intercity) taxi in recognition of her contribution, and in 1965, when Senhaji came back to Rabat, Aicha, Mina, and the children all stayed with Zohra and her new husband, Captain Miloud, in Oujda until Senhaji had rented a house in Rabat and gotten it ready for them.*

Now I've finally gotten my card from the Commission, but I haven't received anything, still nothing. I don't even have a pension. I asked for the sort of pension that they give to the disabled, but I have received nothing. Nothing! I only have the card. They must think that I can live on a card, as if I could live on a piece of paper, eat my card! It's ridiculous!

Now I am old; I am seventy-two years old. I couldn't even take care of my husband; he married another woman and they live in Oujda. I am here [in Salé] now, and I get financial support from nobody, neither my husband, nor the resistance, nor my children. God is the only provider. Even the first husband had another wife; I don't know why, but that's how things are. This is my own house from my first husband [from her share of the inheritance when he died]. After the resistance, I lived with my second husband [Captain Miloud] and took care of his children. I have ten children of my own: I had eight children from the first husband, four girls and four boys, and two more from the second husband. [My second husband] also has his own children [from a previous marriage]. When his first wife died, I was the one who took care of everybody. I had a lot of responsibility. Even now I still have a lot of responsibility. I've now been here [in Salé] for six months. My daughter lives with me. She isn't married, poor creature. She was married for just two years, and then she was repudiated and she hasn't married since then—it's been twenty-three years now. Moroccan women have no rights, nothing to protect them. Look at me! After all these years, I'm alone. Because I am old and cannot look after my husband, he has married another wife!

Rabiaa Taibi

All the women who know Rabiaa speak of her great courage and of her compassion, her depth of feeling. People who worked with her in the resistance, people in her neighborhood . . . everyone loves and trusts Rabiaa.

Rabiaa's house is on a small alley in an old, established neighborhood—it was in this same neighborhood, in a house just around the block, that she grew up; it was here that she lived in the period of the resistance. As in most

15.5

Rabiaa Taibi (1996).

Credit: Anne White.

traditional Moroccan houses, there is only a blank wall on the street, but inside,
the house opens up onto a central courtyard, once open to the sky but now
covered to keep out the rain. Coming in off the street, the house seems very quiet
and calm; in the heat of an Oujda summer it stays cool inside.

Straight ahead and on the right side as you enter, there are Moroccan-
style salons, on the left side there's a wall, two-stories high, faced with

15.6

Aicha Senhaji and Rabiaa Taibi (1996).

Credit: Anne White.

decorative tiling. Rabiaa spends much of her time in the central courtyard,
resting on a mattress along the wall or watching television. Guests are ushered
into the large salon facing the entrance, a long rectangular room, with
decorative tiling and banquettes lining all four walls, in the Moroccan style, and
several low tables for tea and meals. There are two small photos on the walls—
one of liberation army commander Abbess Messadi and one of nationalist
martyr Allal Ben Abdellah.[10]

Rabiaa is not in good health now—she has high blood pressure,
headaches, and some dizziness—but she still radiates warmth and energy,
especially when she smiles. In several old photos, she is photographed in
Western dress, wheeling a bicycle. She told me she stopped riding a bicycle
when she was thirty-five years old.

Rabiaa Taibi was born in 1931 in Oujda, one of eleven children—seven
girls and four boys—with just two younger sisters after her. Like many of the
women whose fathers died or left when they were still young, she describes

15.7

Rabiaa Taibi holding Khadija Senhaji (left) and Abbess's son.

Source: Rabiaa Taibi.

herself as an orphan, raised and educated by her mother alone. Although her father died when she was three, he is remembered as a man of exceptional courage who fought in the 1920–27 Rif war led by Abdelkrim El Khattabi.

Rabiaa herself was married rather late, at twenty-seven, and never had any children, something that still saddens her. In old photos she is often shown with babies in her arms or holding small children by the hand; she loves children, and has played an important part in the lives of friends' and neighbors' children. Just recently she adopted a young girl, and is sending her to school. For many years, Rabiaa used to take care of circumcision ceremonies for all the boys in the neighborhood, and have them in her house. Some of those boys are now grown up and married and have children of their own. Everyone in the neighborhood knows Rabiaa, and they are all ready to help if she needs anything.

Here is Rabiaa's story as she told it to me, bit by bit, over several sessions.

I lived in Oujda from the time I was little. My father died when I was three years old. We were seven girls. We learned to knit. I never went to school, not even to the Koranic school. I understand some French, but I didn't have any formal education. I was just taught needlework and things like that. People didn't think that school was important for girls.

When we were growing up, we found French colonialism. The husbands of my two older sisters participated in politics. Me, I was still young; I was just thirteen years old. We were seven girls in the family, but I was the only one who participated in the struggle for independence. I attended the meetings of the men, where they read tracts calling for the colonizers to be thrown out. We wanted our country to be free. The same thing was true [at the time] in Tunisia. We heard that all the Islamic countries sacrificed a ram for the Aid Kabir and that Tunisia sacrificed her children, that is to say that the French killed them. Me, I listened, and I was touched to the core when I heard that.

Me, I did embroidery. I gave my money [from selling embroidery], the little money I had, to help the Tunisians. My first real action was that I went and bought the first pistol and some cartridges, seven cartridges. My brothers-in-law loved me a lot, and they were astonished to see the pistol that I had bought. After that, they sent me to Casablanca. Often I was accompanied by a little girl so that the police wouldn't be suspicious of me. Each time I would wear different clothes—haik, djellaba, *roumi* [European clothes]. It was the husbands of my sisters who taught me how to do all that, at a farm where I took part in meetings. I also did embroidery and sewed to help the prisoners. They really appreciated me.

My sisters' husbands used to hold meetings in the house. They would send me across the border to Algeria to bring newspapers, and to bring other information from there. We didn't have newspapers here in Oujda. I used to

15.8

Rabiaa Taibi with Fatima Senhaji (left) and Zouhara Abbess.

Source: Rabiaa Taibi.

bring arms as well. [Algerian national liberation leader] Ben Bella was still very young at that time. I was very young too. When Mohamed V was sent into exile I was twenty-two.

I worked with the resistance fighters. The first time that I participated, I was sixteen years old. We held meetings in the house in secret, because we were always being pursued. There were some traitors. People trusted me. I used to go to Casa a lot. We would transmit the message by a sign, communicating by secret code. For instance, we would say, "I want to drink," and they would know what we were talking about.

When I was twenty-two years old, the king went into exile. I was ready to use weapons to fight against colonialism. I was courageous. I traveled between Casa and Oujda as a messenger, carrying arms to smuggle them to Berchid and to Bouzekoura, for example. I took care of communication between the different militants. I didn't let people know who I was, for fear of being arrested. In Oujda, I called myself Nora, in Casa I was Aicha. One time they did an investigation, and they captured a man. But they didn't find any evidence against me as a member of the resistance. I dressed in a man's djellaba; I disguised myself as a man, and I got away. They captured my mother to interrogate her. I was always on the run; I took refuge with some women.

I fought for independence in Oujda and in Casa. We made [handmade] bombs. There was someone in Oujda who was given the job of working with us, but this person was arrested by the police and he gave everything away. He had been with us in Oujda, when the group discussed the number of weapons and the number of Frenchmen and of traitors to be killed. Me, I got away, but the others were captured, because this person had betrayed us.

In 1953, I went with some men from the resistance to a movie theater in Casablanca which was frequented only by Frenchmen. We were in charge of setting off a bomb at the cinema. First we looked the place over, in order not to be captured. Then I went there all alone to set the bomb because the others were afraid. I went without eating in order to accomplish this mission and I was not afraid of death. Lots of Frenchmen were killed in the explosion.

I always worked with men; I didn't work with women. But I can tell you that from 1953 [when the king was exiled] to 1963 [after Algeria got its independence] women worked even harder than men. They were even more courageous. We sacrificed our lives for independence.

In Casa everyone liked me a lot, because I was a real militant. I cried at the exile of His Majesty. Everyone encouraged me in that. I loved my people and my king. I wanted our independence. I suffered a lot, because I could not deny my king. We loved the king a lot.

We worked for God and my country. Do you love your country or not? And its flag; it's the same thing. We are all human beings, but everyone defends his own country, his president, his home. My actions were not to take away the

15.9

Rabiaa Taibi, Salam Al Bachir, and Saadia Bouhaddou on a street in Casablanca (ca. 1954).

Source: Saadia Bouhaddou.

rights of others, but to get our own rights and our property and the wealth of our country, and especially our independence. No country would want to be colonized by another.

When I was working with the resistance, the police came looking for us. They had arrested one man and tortured him; he then pretended that he had become mentally deranged, so they sent him to an insane asylum. The resistance organization that I was working for gave me some money and food and sent me to visit him at the asylum. I went with two other people to visit him. He didn't know me at first, because he had never seen me before, but I used a secret code that he recognized and then he started talking to me. I told him that the members of the resistance wanted to help him get out of the country, but he said, "No, I want to stay here. But ask the partisans to give some money to the doctor and the chief administrator [who was Algerian] so that they can take care of me here." I went back to the organization and reported to them what he had told me. They gave me the money and they gave me some more food, and helped me to go back to the asylum. I gave a thousand dirhams [about $125] to the doctor and five hundred dirhams [about $60] to the chief administrator. They accepted the money and promised to keep him in the asylum and take care of him.

In what follows, Rabiaa tells her side of the story of the incident with Bouchaib El Ghazi in the train to Oujda, the same incident that Casablanca resistance fighter Saadia Bouhaddou told about in an earlier chapter.

I went back to Casablanca, and we were told that the police were looking for us. So they told me that I should go with them to Oujda so that we could go from there to the area of Gliba. When we got [close to Oujda on the train], the police arrested us. I denied everything. I told them I didn't know who anyone was. I had a gun hidden under my seat, and I also had a newspaper with a photograph of Mohamed V [in exile in Madagascar] on it, which they saw. They hit me to make me confess where I had gotten the paper from. In vain. Then they asked Bouchaib [El Ghazi], and he too denied everything. He had a gun, and he started using it to defend himself. There was a lot of shooting. Then he wanted to escape out of the window of the train, but somebody shot him here [in the chest] and here [in the stomach]. When we got there, the two of us were arrested. They also asked me about the newspaper; I said, "It's not mine, and anyway, I can't read Arabic or French." I said that some other people who had been on the train before must have forgotten the newspaper and left it behind when they got off. But then when they kept asking Si Bachir [Salam Al Bachir], he finally said that the newspaper was his. When I heard that, I told them that the newspaper was mine after all.

When we got to Oujda, I met this wonderful man named Krim. I gave him two hundred dirhams in gold, and I asked him to go to my mother and tell my mother that the man who Rabiaa was supposed to marry in Casablanca was here with her, and tell her that we were arrested, so that when the police asked her,

15.10

Rabiaa Taibi (in checked dress) at Bouchaib El Ghazi's funeral.
Standing next to Rabiaa is Bouchaib's mother.

Source: Rabiaa Taibi.

she would tell them: "We didn't want Rabiaa to marry in Casablanca and we asked her to come here with her fiancé for the wedding." My mother told all this to Si Mohamed Ramdani [another resistance fighter], and also told my sister's husband that Rabiaa and Si Bachir had been arrested. So they made great efforts and did everything they could to get us out of prison. There was a Jew in Oujda who had a café—his name was Ben Hammou; he was a great man who helped the resistance. They went to see him, and told him that "our daughter and her husband are in trouble; we don't want them to be tortured." So that Jew invited the police inspectors to the café and offered them free alcohol. When he asked them to let us go, they said they would, but that we had to find a place to stay, but somewhere else, not in our homes. Our relatives told them to just set us free and they would figure out what to do with us.

As soon as I was free, around six in the evening, they gave me a djellaba to wear, covered my hair, and took me away. They did the same thing with Bachir; they took him to the house of El Zaar. Later in the evening, the police came looking for me again—this time it was the police who had been sent from Casablanca. They had arrested Si Houcine [another partisan] in Casablanca, and

15.11

Rabiaa and an Algerian resistance fighter who convalesced at her home, with bicycles.

Source: Rabiaa Taibi.

he told them about us, and said that we all worked in Oujda. Nobody knew my real name; I was known as Nora here, but as Aicha over there. He told them that he only knew a woman by the name of Aicha, and that she used to take him to meet with Si Ramdani. Poor man, they tortured him [to make him talk].

So at midnight, there were two jeeps full of policemen. They stopped at my mother's house and took her with them. Houcine was at the police station when she got there; he was covered all over with blood and bruises. He told her, "Auntie Mina, I am Si Houcine." So she told him, "I know, you asked for my daughter's hand in marriage, but I didn't accept [your offer]." He understood what she was hinting at. Then the police went out and brought in Si Ahmed Ramdani, poor man. They had torn his skin and cut open his flesh so badly; it was terrible! They had kept asking him about me, and he kept denying everything. They brought his wife in too; she was very pregnant at that time. She went with my sister. Poor woman, she was tortured, and had blood all over her body. Then they brought their small child, their son, poor child. He didn't understand anything at all. So nobody revealed anything to the police. My mother told me afterward that she understood that I was in Spain because she heard the police repeat the only words she understood [in French]: "Rabiaa, Spain; Rabiaa, Spain." She was very happy for me. They arrested every woman wearing a djellaba, because they were told that I would be wearing a djellaba. Actually I was wearing old, torn clothes when I escaped. When I was taken to Spain I was in terrible shape, because the police had tortured me a lot. We stayed for about twenty-five days in Spain, until they brought back Mohamed V.

At that time I also went to Nador for just five months, and there I worked with Abbess and Senhaji in the Liberation Army. My house was the center where meetings took place, where the arms were hidden, and a rendezvous point in Nador. We worked out of Nador; we sent arms into the interior. That was where I met Mina [Senhaji] and Rita [Abbess].

After we got our independence in 1956, I did two extremely important jobs: I did more work for Morocco, and I worked in the hospital in Oujda. So I participated in the revolution in Algeria, and I also participated in the revolution in Palestine by giving money. I bought mattresses, clothes, and other things for the militants in Palestine. But I actually worked in Algeria. I have the certificates to prove it. I helped the Algerians and gave them arms. I had a lot of arms. I used to help the Algerian independence fighters. I stayed in Oujda, and worked with an office of the FLN that was here in Oujda. They trusted me and wanted me to work with them until they got their independence. I never actually went back to Algeria until after they got their freedom; I couldn't, because the police were after me everywhere. But I did a lot of work for the Algerians here in Oujda. The government asked us where the arms were [after the king's return, when the resistance and liberation army were supposed to turn over their weapons to the government]. We answered that we had given the arms to

15.12

Blood donor card of Rabiaa Taibi.

Source: Rabiaa Taibi.

Algeria after Morocco's independence. I gave my blood, not just once but many times, to help the militants in Algeria, and I worked at the hospital. Sometimes I took in wounded militants and took care of them at home until they got better.

We wore modern dress, but in order to work in the resistance we wore djellabas. I put on a djellaba to carry messages. After independence, I took off my veil, but then after I was married, I wore a veil from time to time. I was married at the age of twenty-seven years, after I returned from Spain. I continued with my work in the hospital even after I got married. But then my husband became sick; he needed help and I had to stop work. I had a lot of responsibility. He was sick for a long time, about four years. I stopped work in 1982, after I had worked for twenty-seven years in the hospital. Then I went into retirement, and my husband died. My husband has been dead for almost ten years now. Now I do nothing. That's life.

Hajja Zohra [Torrichi] just got her card [in 1994]; I have had mine for a long time. I was a woman who was trusted.

15.13

Rabiaa in djellaba, veil, and dark glasses.

Source: Rabiaa Taibi.

15.14

Rabiaa (about thirty-five years old) with her husband.

Source: Rabiaa Taibi.

IV

Conclusion

16

Conclusion

The Moroccan Women's Movement: New Generations

After the mid-1960s, the leadership of the women's movement passed out of the hands of the older generation of women who had participated in the independence movement, and younger generations took the lead. By this time—the late sixties and early seventies—a significant number of young women had succeeded in reaching the university; part of the large cohort of girls who had started their education on the eve of independence, when girls' access to education was rapidly expanding. These young women took part in student and Marxist political movements at the university, and when these movements developed into so active a political force that the government felt threatened and moved to crush them, women too were caught in the repression. Some women were put in prison, at least one was killed,[1] and others were sent into exile. It was in this period, for the first time in Morocco, that a Marxist feminist movement emerged, linking the cause of women to the class struggle.

In the mid-seventies, the two main political parties of the Left[2] formed a special section to help the parties to draw up a list of women's demands, to gather information on the status of women in Morocco, and to use the media to bring attention to women's issues. The parties also began some activities designed to link the two causes of women's emancipation and socialism. But because this movement came out of the parties, women's concerns tended to be marginalized and women's agenda postponed.[3]

Then, in 1981, the women's movement in Morocco took on a new dimension, with the founding of *8 mars*, an Arabic-language monthly newspaper named after the date of international women's day. *8 mars* was founded by Moroccan sociologist and feminist Latifa Jbabdi, together with some other women from the New Left movement.[4] Jbabdi was then not even thirty years old, but she was already a veteran of the Marxist feminist movement and had spent two and a half years in prison. In a recent interview, she talked about how she came to be involved in New Left politics.

As a little girl, whenever I had a heated argument with my father or did something disobedient, he would end up by calling me a Communist, a term which he, like many other people [at the time], thought of as an insult. What he didn't realize was that he was right; I had already begun to read Marxist writings as a very young child. When I was fourteen, I joined the Party of Liberation and Socialism, but shortly after that I left [the PLS] in order to get involved with the New Left movement, because I thought [the New Left] offered a stronger ideology and a program which answered the needs of the fight for democracy at that time.[5]

With *8 mars*, Latifa Jbabdi and her group wanted to address women's issues, and to provide a "women's vision" that had been lacking up until that point. This was a qualitative leap forward, as it represented the first time that there was a continuous feminist discourse generated by women. In *8 Mars*, for the first time, women were given a voice, a chance to speak for themselves directly, without mediation. Starting in 1988, a page on legal issues began discussion of women and the moudouana (Moroccan family law). Another page entitled, "If I could have a word," offered an opportunity for women who were illiterate to express themselves. A page on women in history tried to give a more accurate picture of Moroccan women's contributions in history; in this context, *8 mars* published an occasional series of interviews with women of the nationalist movement and armed resistance, recognizing them as the fore-mothers of the modern Moroccan women's movement. At the 1985 Nairobi conference to mark the end of the UN Decade of the Woman, *8 mars* was the only Arabic-language feminist paper represented; it later served as a model for similar papers in Tunisia and Senegal.

The Nairobi conference encouraged feminist organizations across the world, and especially those in the developing nations. In Morocco, the *8 mars* group grew into a political organization called the Women's Action Union (*Union d'action féminine* or UAF), which was the first political organization in Morocco to be established outside of one of the political parties, controlled by women, and taking women's emancipation as the first priority. The Democratic Association of Moroccan Women (*Association démocratique des femmes du Maroc*, or ADFM) has also been a relatively autonomous group, even though it is attached to the Progressive and Socialist Party (*Parti progressiste et socialiste*, or PPS). In the late eighties, the ADFM started a feminist paper, *Moroccan Woman* (*Nissa Al-Maghreb*), which published twenty-six issues; and in December, 1991, the ADFM took the lead in reactivating the Maghreb-Equality Committee, an organization linking the movements for women's rights in the three Maghrebi countries (Morocco, Tunisia, and Algeria).

At last count there were twenty-nine women's associations in Morocco, more than half of which were created since 1980.[6] Nineteen are based in Rabat, five in Casablanca, two in Marrakesh, and one each in Meknes and Oujda. Eight of these twenty-nine women's associations are purely social service organizations.

Women's groups in Morocco span a broad political spectrum. The National Union of Moroccan Women (UNFM) is sponsored by the Palace, and focuses on providing social services to women. The Istiqlal Party Women's Organization (OFI) still follows the Salafiya line of Allal Al Fassi in social issues, and focuses on integrating women into political life. Its stated aims are, "To educate women in the light of Islamic values, [and] to integrate women into the political, economic, social and cultural activities of the country."[7] Two out of twenty-four members of the Istiqlal Party central committee are women, a relatively large representation, and Latifa Bennani Smires, the president of the OFI, was elected in 1993 as one of the first two women to serve in the Moroccan parliament.

The major opposition parties to the Left of the Istiqlal are enthusiastic about promoting women's participation in political life, and see this as the primary task of the party women's associations.[8] On the other hand, they are reluctant to get involved with women's issues, especially with the issue of women's personal status within the family (reform of the moudouana). This reluctance to address women's issues runs right across the political spectrum. One party leader warns that "it is important not to make the question of women a pretext for division [within the party]." Even among women's associations, it has been easier to get a consensus on the necessity of integrating women into political life, and to organize women to raise money in support of the Palestinian *Intifada* or to provide relief for Iraq after the Gulf War. Only organizations outside of the political parties, such as the Moroccan Organization for Human Rights (OMDH)[9] and the previously mentioned UAF, have been willing to focus specifically on women's issues. Perhaps not surprisingly, women have played a large role in the OMDH: Women constituted 40 percent of the founding group of the organization, and five of the nineteen members of the central committee are women. Recently a separate OMDF (Moroccan Organization for Women's Rights) was founded.

On March 3, 1992,[10] in his address to the nation, King Hassan II promised a long-awaited reform of the Moroccan constitution. On the same day, the UAF launched what Moroccan feminist journalist Zakya Daoud calls "the most spectacular action ever undertaken by Moroccan women."[11] They drafted a petition demanding changes in the moudouana, setting themselves the ambitious goal of getting a million signatures, and sent a letter with the same demands to the president of the Moroccan parliament, the presidents of parliamentary groups, and the leaders of the political parties.

On March 8, 1992, I attended a meeting organized by the UAF to celebrate international women's day and to read and discuss their proposals for reform of the moudouana. The meeting was in the evening, held in an apartment building in downtown Rabat. In a crowd dominated by young women, I recognized some students from the university. The meeting started with the UAF leaders, sitting at a table at the front of the room, reading the letters that they had sent to leaders of the government and the parties demanding a review of the moudouana and certain changes that would make it more equitable to women. This went on for some time. Latifa Jbabdi (introduced earlier in this chapter), the president of the UAF, was the dominant figure at the speakers' table, reading the documents in a loud, clear voice. She is tall, with strong features and a commanding presence.

When the reading was over, the meeting was opened for discussion, and almost immediately the debate became heated, with people shouting and interrupting each other. There were several Islamic fundamentalists at the meeting, the men with beards and the women wearing the hijab. They were the ones who objected to the demands of the UAF, saying that it would be against Islam to abolish polygamy (and what would unmarried women do?) or to change divorce and inheritance laws. Others countered them saying that people were always saying that Islam wouldn't allow this or that, but they didn't think that was true; it wasn't Islam, it was traditional beliefs and practices that stood in the way. It seemed to me encouraging that young women, and some young men, were actively debating issues of the status of women that had always been beyond question before.

Several months later, on August 20,[12] the king specifically addressed the question of women. After an homage to "the Moroccan woman, wife, mother and daughter," the King said:

> I have heard the complaints on the subject of the moudouana or on its application. . . . That is a question that falls within my domain. . . . Moroccan woman, address yourself to me, write to the Royal Chambers. Women's associations, address your observations, your criticisms, your grievances, and [point out] whatever you believe is harmful to the Moroccan woman and her future to the King of Morocco, who, in His capacity as Commander of the Faithful, has the competence to apply and interpret religion.[13]

Undaunted by this patronizing response from the Palace, and the silence from the government and political parties, the UAF formed a coalition of women's groups to support their demand for reform of the moudouana, and, as they put it, "made a lot of noise." The king was forced to respond. At first he received some well-known women allied with the Palace and the Istiqlal Party, including Fatima Hassar and Aicha Terrab, at the Palace. Then he formed a commission of the oulemas, including other legal and religious authorities and one woman, a representative of the Palace. Under pressure from the OMDH, the commission was enlarged, including at least one more woman, journalist and writer Leila Abouzeid. The commission was instructed to review the moudouana—for the first time since it was originally drafted in 1957. In 1993, following the recommendations of the commission, some modest changes were made. Also in 1993, two women were elected to the Moroccan parliament: Baadia Skalli of the USFP, and Latifa Bennani Smires of the Istiqlal Party.

Feminism and Nationalism

If we compare the history of the Moroccan feminist and nationalist movements with histories of feminism and nationalism in other third world countries fighting to free themselves from Western colonial rule, we find many parallel and similar experiences.[14] In all these countries, traditional societies were transformed by capitalist economic development and the emergence of nationalism, and feminist movements were among the products of these economic and social changes.[15] Several countries experienced reform movements that called for educating upper class women and bringing them out of seclusion. And like the Salafiya Islamic reform movement in Morocco, most of these reform movements were socially conservative; they were intended to strengthen traditional family structures and thus to perpetuate the subordination of women in the family. In the same time period, rural-urban migration and economic pressures "emancipated" lower-class women, creating a new urban proletariat and bringing women out of their homes and into the industrial workforce.

Although individual women had been involved in the public debate that accompanied these early reform movements—in Morocco, Malika El Fassi began writing articles on girls' education in the mid-thirties—it was nationalism that got women *as a group* involved in political action. The nationalist movements brought women out of the traditional domestic sphere into the public and political sphere for the first time. But these same nationalist movements also placed real limits on the women's movements. These mixed messages about women's roles stemmed from the dual and sometimes contradictory motivations of the nationalist movements themselves. On the one hand the nationalists wanted to throw the colonizers out and to modernize their societies, drawing on European models, tasks that demanded the education and mobilization of women. On the other hand they wanted to assert a national identity that was separate and different from the colonizer, one based on their own distinctive history and culture. This led them to stress women's primary role in the home, at the center of the family, the guardian of tradition.

After independence was achieved, the nation state established, and women had won the right to vote, feminist movements generally faded away or were transformed into social welfare organizations sponsored by the government and directed by upper-class women. That is certainly what we see in the Moroccan case. After independence, most of the nationalist women who had been active in the women's associations of the parties took on leading roles in social welfare organizations under the patronage of the princesses. The roles of the king's daughters, the princesses, also changed. The Princess Lalla Aicha, who had been a symbol and leader of the women's movement, was now the honorary president of the Moroccan Society for the Protection of Children.

In none of these recently independent countries was there any organized movement that tried to question women's subordinate status within the family. The male political leaders, who had consciously mobilized women to participate in the struggle for independence, now just as consciously put them back into their accustomed place. In the decade after independence, women's consciousness and their visibility in the political arena had sunk to a very low level.[16]

This general pattern applies even to Egypt, a country where women's activity dated back to before World War I, giving rise to a feminist press, women's organizations, and demands for suffrage and other rights, as well as the participation of women of all classes in street demonstrations against the British. Even this multifaceted and rather autonomous feminist movement did not survive into the period after independence; Egyptian women didn't even get the vote until 1956, and family law remained very conservative. Egyptian feminist writer Nawal El Sadawi attributes this setback in the Egyptian feminist movement to its upperclass leadership and point of view:

> The movement was not representative of the overwhelming majority of toiling women, and its leadership ended, just as the political leadership did, by seeking accommodations with the British, the Palace and the reactionary forces in the country. The women's movement . . . kept away from an active involvement in the national and political life of the country, and limited its activities to charitable and social welfare work.[17]

In Algeria, women fought actively in the long and bitter struggle against French colonialism; several of these women are known and honored as heroines of the resistance. A socialist government took power after Algeria finally got its independence in 1962, but women's personal status continued to be governed by Islamic family law, with more or less the same provisions as the Moroccan moudouana, perpetuating women's subordination.

Since 1962 a very small number of Algerian feminists have tried to raise questions of women's rights and status within the family. And because there is still a powerful stigma attached to any "Western feminist" demands that threaten Algerian national identity—and because the women making the demands are especially vulnerable to criticism as members of a small French-educated elite—these feminists have always supported their claims by reference to the heroines of the Algerian resistance. Their argument is that women *deserve* equal rights *because* of the *moujahidats*, Algerian women warriors who participated as equals with men in the fight for independence.[18]

The problem with this argument is that the moujahidats themselves do not necessarily identify with this feminist elite or even with their demands for women's rights—what might be thought of as the "objective interests" of all women. Scholars who have interviewed some of these heroines of the Algerian resistance point out that even now they do not have a "feminist" political agenda.[19] Women's participation in the Algerian resistance was massive, militant—some even used arms—and often heroic. At least a few of these women are publicly acknowledged as moujahidats. But their political views were, and are, more or less the same as the views of men in their class and milieu.

Like most of the women who fought in the Moroccan resistance, the Algerian moujahidats speak of what they did in terms of patriotism, with Algerian independence as their goal. When sociologist Djamila Amrane, herself an Algerian resistance fighter, asked several moujahidats what independence meant to them, they spoke about the victory over French colonialism, the liberation of the country, a better life, with childcare centers and schools, the possibility for "every human being to flourish in his own country," and hopes that they would be peaceful and happy and that their children would have access to education and work.[20]

In Algeria there was nothing like the multi-faceted and autonomous feminist movement that developed in Egypt around the time of World War I. And because Algeria spent more than a century (1830–1962) as a French colony, *everything*—including all discussion of politics, society, and religion—revolved around the demands of nationalism and the struggle for independence. As we have seen, all of the nationalist movements in third world countries had mixed messages about the status of women. But in Algeria it went further than that. Nationalism effectively cut off any discussion or questioning of the basic ideology and structures of traditional society, and it was women who were assigned the heavy responsibility of keeping tradition alive, of saving the identity and soul of the community.

In Algeria this question of national identity was a question of life and death: the French had said there *was* no Algerian nation. According to the French, what had been Algeria was now a French province with a majority population of French-Muslims (i.e. the Algerians), "most of them under-developed, under-administered, under-employed, and under-fed," and a small, dynamic population of French origin (i.e., the French colonists). The French colonial administrators themselves saw the war that they were fighting in Algeria in ideological terms. A 1956 general directive to officers of the French military stationed in Algeria states this clearly:

The war that we are fighting in this country is a fight for the West, the
struggle of civilization against anarchy, of democracy against dictator-
ship. . . . *We are fighting for liberty!*[21]

The Algerians countered this smothering, obliterating French presence
with the ideology of nationalism, an ideology which stressed an Algerian
identity that was Islamic, Arabic, rooted in traditional customs—everything that
distinguished Algeria from the West. Arguing that the very existence of the
Algerian nation was at stake, the nationalists effectively stifled any debate about
Islam or tradition. After independence, this ideology of nationalism was
transmuted into an ideology of socialism, but a specifically Algerian form of
socialism, drawing on the Islamic notion of community, in which the interests of
the community were paramount. It was unpatriotic and thus forbidden to suggest
any conflict of interests between women and men or between different classes in
Algerian society. Any mention of individual rights or democracy was suspect as
stemming from Western, colonial influences.

Latifa Jbabdi draws some lessons for Morocco from the Algerian
experience, writing in the pages of *8 mars*:

Women have understood, after many experiences, that noone else will
take charge of their emancipation; it will depend on women themselves,
and it will depend on breaking down the political, ideological and social
differences among women that might prevent us from taking action. In
this we are translating the experience of the Algerian revolution and
learning one of its most valuable lessons: the participation of women in
the national struggle didn't suffice to liberate them as a sex; for that, they
would have had to lead their own struggle [focused on women's demands]
in parallel [to the national struggle].[22]

The women's movements in these two Islamic countries—Egypt and
Algeria—had significant advantages over the women's movement in Morocco.
In Egypt, the women's movement was well established, with a long history of
feminist writing and political activity. In Algeria, women resistance fighters
were recognized as national heroes—women warriors who came from a broad
cross-section of Algerian society. In Morocco, on the other hand, women got
access to education much later than in Egypt, and a modern women's movement
did not emerge until after 1930. Morocco did have its own long tradition of
moujahidats—the women in the Rif, the Sahara, and the Middle Atlas who
participated in jihads to drive out foreign invaders, starting at the end of the
fifteenth century—but women's participation in the urban armed resistance only
lasted for a few years, and has gone largely unrecognized. Considering all this, it
shouldn't surprise us to find that the elite Moroccan women's movement, like

that of Egypt, lost its combative edge shortly after independence, and that the women from the armed resistance went back into the domestic sphere. After all, the Moroccan nationalist movement was led by the king, in alliance with the oulema and bourgeois nationalist political leaders, and was profoundly conservative. The nationalists wanted to free Morocco from French control; they didn't want a social revolution.

Women's movements in Morocco and other countries seemed to fade away after independence, but this was only a temporary lull. Starting in the 1960s and 1970s, all of these countries, including Morocco, have experienced a new wave of feminist movements, and this time the women's movements are trying to reach across classes and raise questions of women's subordination within the family as well as economic and social issues affecting women. What is more, in doing this, they all more or less consciously draw on the memories and experiences of earlier feminist activity, including the women who fought in the nationalist movement and armed resistance.

What Did It All Mean?

The history of feminism and nationalism just outlined charts the course of political feminism within the framework of conventional history, an important first step in adding women back into history and bringing to light women's roles and contributions. With this new information, we can evaluate the significance of women's participation in achieving Moroccan independence. How much difference did women make?

In the political movement, especially in the period starting in 1944 when the Istiqlal and other nationalist parties focused on mass mobilization, the women's associations of the political parties played a critical role. Most importantly, they mobilized women by holding meetings to raise women's political consciousness and enlisting them in the nationalist cause. This is something that the men of the political parties would not have been able to do themselves, given the separation of women and men in the society at the time. Women also played an important role in raising money: for the parties, for the nationalist free schools, for the Palestinian and Algerian nationalist movements, and for other nationalist causes.

In the armed resistance too, women played roles that could not easily have been played by men. They were probably most valuable to the resistance as liaison, carrying arms and messages from one place to another, often over long distances and at considerable risk. Women also provided essential support services to the military and political organizations of the resistance (and after 1954, the liberation army in the Rif): collecting money, preparing food, washing and mending clothes, tending the sick and wounded, and sheltering those who were fleeing colonial forces.

By adding women back in, we can chart the stages of development of a visible, organized women's movement. Taking this view, the period after independence appears as a lull in the Moroccan women's movement, even a step backwards. Women from the armed resistance are back in domestic roles, and the old social order reasserts itself, unchanged, with women in a subordinate position in the family and marginal in the larger society. But adding women back into history is only the first step. This analysis does nothing to explain the dramatic changes in Moroccan women's lives from one generation to the next, or the resurgence of the women's movement starting in the early seventies. If we only recognize new waves of the women's movement once they are visible and organized, and if we only recognize social changes once they have occurred, we tend to overlook or underestimate the role that women's experience in the nationalist movement and armed resistance played in promoting social change. This is where the material of the oral histories is most valuable, because it enables us to study the complex and diffuse *process* of change in Moroccan society.[23] Oral history enables us to see the ways in which individual women were changed by their experience, sometimes in private, subtle ways, and to explore the connection between these individual changes and changes in the larger society.

The period after independence, which I have described as a lull in the growth of feminist consciousness and activity, is not viewed in that way by the nationalist women themselves. On the contrary, they seem to have been almost frenetically active in this period right after independence, and very much focused on getting women actively involved in "the struggle against under-development." The nationalist women also talk about how their education and work in the national movement affected the way they lived their lives, and the way they raised their children: They say they have tried to balance family and public responsibilities, and to raise girls and boys to be equal. Malika El Fassi's daughter Roqia commented that her mother had always encouraged her and her sisters to postpone getting married in order to pursue their education.[24]

In sum, the nationalist women are insisting that what may look like a lull in the women's movement was in fact a period of enormous social change, one in which they played an active role. When I asked questions about what happened to the women's movement after independence, why women disappeared from the political arena, and why they did not take up issues of women's personal status and family law, they told me that I was wrong; women did *not* disappear. But more importantly, they told me I was asking the wrong questions. The question really was how these women viewed their responsibilities in the public arena after independence, and what were their new roles and activities. After the struggle to win independence from France, there was an enormous job of nation-building to do—the struggle against underdevelopment—and these women did what was needed to contribute to that mission.

Women in the Resistance—Myth and Reality

When women tell stories about what they did in the armed resistance, they use narrative forms and archetypes of character and plot that are reminiscent of Moroccan folktales and legends of women warriors. Like all oral histories, these are myth-biographies, but in Morocco they are given additional strength and resonance by tapping into a long Islamic tradition of celebrating women's exceptional contributions in war. How then do we reconcile these positive images of women resistance fighters with the inequality between men and women in Moroccan society generally? French scholar Monique Gadant, in her work on women in the Algerian resistance, suggests that the Algerian government's mythologizing of the moujahidats was far from innocent.[25] At the same time that women were being celebrated for their exceptional heroism in war and work they were being denied equality with men. Women's "rights" were linked with hardship, self-sacrifice, and patriotism; while they were lauded as fighters and workers, they were still viewed as women, that is to say, as dependent beings—daughters, wives—who did not belong to themselves. Even now in Algeria, while women use the myth of the resistance heroine to legitimize demands for equal rights, men in power use the same myth to put limits on women's rights and participation.

While the Moroccan situation is not exactly comparable to Algeria (Moroccan moujahidats have been largely ignored by their government), in Morocco too the myth of the resistance heroine has been a double-edged sword for the moujahidats and other women of their social class. At independence, there were only two models of emancipated Moroccan women: women warriors and women workers. But the armed resistance and liberation army were being disbanded; there was no more need for women. As for work, there was massive unemployment in Moroccan cities, so that women were competing with men for scarce jobs. The women who participated in the resistance generally lacked skills and were illiterate and, thus, unlikely to find work.

Women spoke enthusiastically about the new, active roles they took on during the resistance, and about the more relaxed and egalitarian relations that prevailed between women and men. But men may not have felt so positively about these changes. As we see in the oral histories, a great many men were reluctant to take women into resistance cells to begin with, because of prejudices against women and the problem of having men and women working together in the same organization. After independence, these same men were quick to reestablish the status quo—separation of the sexes, traditional roles and dress for women, and the subordination of women in the family.

Under the exceptional circumstances of the resistance, young women moved around freely in the city streets and traveled by bus alone over long distances between cities, carrying arms and messages. They worked closely with men other than their husbands, and received men in their homes even while their husbands were away or in prison. After independence, when traditional standards of behavior were reimposed, women's participation in the resistance opened them up to gossip and suspicion. Upper-class nationalist women seem to have generally disregarded and even despised the lower-class women of the armed resistance, hinting that they were not respectable. Some women who fought in the resistance were also criticized, even ostracized, by their peers. Women told me that their husbands had told them not to visit a certain woman because she had had relations with men other than her husband while he was in prison during the resistance. There was even a question on some of the forms in women's dossiers at the Commission asking about "moral character." Needless to say, the same criticism was never leveled at men, even though many of them apparently "ran around" with women other than their wives.

Women who participated in the resistance feel that their contributions were important, even decisive, in bringing Mohamed V back from exile and winning Moroccan independence. While they did not necessarily expect a radical change in relations between men and women after independence, the hope for an improvement in their status as women was a large, if largely implicit, part of global aspirations for a different, better life once colonialism was gone.[26]

In the milieu of the armed resistance, the shantytowns and working class neighborhoods of the cities, the expansion of women's roles was only temporary, it only lasted for the duration, while women were needed. For these women, independence seems to have marked the end of a chapter in history: While resistance activities carved out more space for women, and enabled them to take on "men's roles," it turned out that these changes were not permanent. But what *was* permanent was the transformation in these women's consciousness, in their concept of themselves as women. It is clear that the experience of participating in the armed resistance was for them a transforming experience. They see themselves as strong, competent women who have taken on new roles, and have demonstrated that they are courageous and capable of anything. And this change in women's ideas mattered; it made a difference in how they lived their lives after independence and in how they raised their children. Eventually the transformation in women's consciousness provided much of the impetus and support for what we see in Morocco today: women's presence in the universities, the streets, and the workplace—virtually all realms except politics, where women are just beginning to make their way—and a new wave of feminist movements.

The women from the armed resistance don't talk much about the period since independence, but to conclude that they just went home and played no further role in the transformation of Moroccan society is too simple. In fact they did much more than that. To begin with, they all got through difficult economic times, when they had to struggle to survive. Ghalia Moujahide supported two small children, her parents, and an invalid brother, at a time when she found it hard to work because of injuries suffered during the resistance. Aicha and Mina Senhaji spent years in which they had to make ends meet for themselves, eleven (eventually fifteen) children, and three cousins with little or no regular income. Aicha was beaten by the police, kept her wits (and her husband's secrets) in answering their questions, managed to escape to Casa with five small children and live in hiding there for two months, without running water or electricity, and then got to Algeria to rejoin her husband. All of the women did manage to survive through that difficult period, and to take care of their children. Even in these difficult times they tried to insure that their children got an education, the girls as well as the boys.

Almost all of the women in the oral histories are recognized as veterans of the resistance. Most of them went through the long, arduous application process twice, once starting in 1959 when the government was first giving out the cards, and again after the High Commission for Veterans of the Resistance and Liberation Army was formed in 1974 and all the dossiers were reviewed. This was no easy matter even if everything went smoothly, and some of the women, in the second round especially, had to defend disputed claims. In spite of the difficulties, they asserted themselves and claimed their due as veterans of the resistance, demonstrating once again that they could hold their own with men.

In the forty-odd years since the resistance, these women have not been idle. Saadia Bouhaddou, who lived mostly with her husband in Algeria until 1974, now owns several small businesses including a café and a grocery store. After she and her Algerian husband were divorced in 1974 she married for a third time. Fatna Mansar married a man of her own choice after her husband died in a car accident shortly after independence. She worked with the UNFP, the major political party of the left, on its program for economic and social reform, and now, at home, she and her husband try to put into practice their ideas of more equality between men and women in the family.

The Truth: Stories and History

What is the truth of all the stories? What is their historical accuracy and significance?[27] Scholars in Morocco have told me how important it is (and how difficult) to find the truth about the resistance—what really happened and what women really did. They warn me that women will embellish their stories and exaggerate their accomplishments. Even the women themselves are concerned with that issue. The expression "I won't lie to you" occurs prominently throughout their narratives, and in private conversations they talk constantly about people who claim to have participated in the resistance but actually did nothing.

Italian oral historian Alessandro Portelli, discussing the relationship of memory and fact, starts with the observation that oral sources are not always fully reliable in point of fact.[28] People remembering and telling about an experienced event may get the story all wrong, sometimes even shifting the date, context and actors of a particular event. But then Portelli goes on to say that this "unreliability" of oral testimony is not its weakness but rather its strength, insofar as "errors, inventions, and myths lead us through and beyond facts to their meaning."[29]

For the women who participated in the resistance, what establishes the truth is often the story itself, and the details that are remembered. At a gathering of women who all worked under resistance leader Abdellah Senhaji, Halima Ben Moussa described what happened "the day when the police came to arrest [Hammou, her] husband."

> I went into the room where Hammou had left [Senhaji] when he went off to work. . . .When they had identified [Senhaji as a member of the resistance], he came to our place. He was stretched out and had fallen asleep, and me, I was preparing lunch. The police came. They asked me about my husband, and I told them he had gone to work. Then I woke [Senhaji] up from his bed, and I told him, "They came to arrest Hammou, and if they find you here you'll pay the price." He took his shoes and he left. He went to some other people's house. I joined him there right after. I went to this woman's house [gesturing to Ghalia Moujahide], she can tell you about it.[30]

Ghalia objects. "Sister, I don't remember you!" and "No, no, no! It was [Senhaji] who sent me to *your* place!" She gives her version of the story:

> Me, I remember everything. I can still see it in front of my eyes. Si Abdellah came to my place; the proof of it is that it was raining and I let him in, I lit up a brazier, I gave him almonds, and prepared some tea which I put down in front of him. He said to me, "Look, my girl, lock me in here and go out to see what's going on, because the police want to arrest me. Be careful and look around." I put on my brown djellaba, and I went out to walk around. I told him, "l'Haj Si Abdellah,[31] there is nothing going on." He told me, "Go to Hammou's house; do you know it?" I told him, "Yes, I know it." He told me, "Go ahead and find his wife, and you ask her whether they took anything away and whether [Hammou] has been arrested." I went to her place, and she told me, "Look, me, I didn't see anyone." She said to me, "Here is the pistol case that they found; they didn't take anything away." And I came back to Si Abdellah and he stayed day and night with me at my house.

Later, I went to Halima Ben Moussa's home to do an interview with her by herself.[32] She came back to her version of the story. The police had come to her house to find her husband, Hammou, and she had sent them away to where he worked.

> Suddenly, Senhaji came in [from the room where he had been sleeping, in her house]. I told him, "Abderrahmane!" He said to me, "Yes?" I told him, "You know, they came for Hammou." He asked me, "Where did he go?" I told him, "Look, they went down by the ocean." He took his shoes—may God curse the liar, and [he's dead while] I'm still alive!!—he held his shoes in his hands, and me, I looked at him from the terrace, and he ran away. He went to the house of Moujahide's wife, to Ghalia's.

In the dispute between Halima Ben Moussa and Ghalia Moujahide, it's not so much the event itself that matters. One woman at the meeting commented that "at this point it's all the same." In fact "the event itself" has no real meaning except in the context of a narrative about female heroes of the resistance, and it is the story, with all its lively details, that convinces us that we are hearing about something that actually happened, a "true" event.[33] In this case, the two women's narratives have such a strong evocative force that they have the capacity to generate two competing and equally compelling versions of the "truth."[34] Both women stick by their stories, so there is no way of determining what *in fact* happened—the historical truth.[35] What makes the incident matter is that it demonstrates that the great resistance leader Senhaji trusted [one of these two] women to help him when he was being pursued by the police, and that they were instrumental in saving him from arrest. The women's narratives enable us to go beyond the visible events, to understand what these events meant to the women themselves.

The Eye/I of the Observer

Since Edward Said wrote his classic study of *Orientalism*, it is no longer possible—if it ever was—for a "Westerner" to enter innocently into an encounter with the "Orient."[36] In fact, if we accept the premise that any Western view of the Orient is a fantasy, a view that seeks to dominate its object, then all communication between Western and Eastern cultures becomes fraught with difficulty, and finally impossible. There has also been a good deal of discussion recently among American scholars about feminist research, including feminist oral history.[37] While at first many women recording oral history thought that there could be a special, more equal relationship between women researchers and their women subjects than if the researcher were male, now it seems clear that such equality is usually illusory, especially when "first world" researchers are interviewing "third world" subjects. French anthropologist Monique Gadant[38] suggests that the idea of a "dialogue between women" taking the place of "research" is an illusion: in fact, the woman subject tells the woman anthropologist what she thinks the anthropologist wants to hear.[39] American oral historian Daphne Patai claims that it is virtually impossible for U.S. academics interviewing third-world women to conduct ethical (feminist) research.[40]

If I had known about the complexity of debates around "orientalism" and feminist oral history when I started, I might never have had the courage to interview these women or to proceed in writing the book. But I was already "doing" oral history before I stopped to learn about the theory and controversies that have developed around the discipline. I started this project as an interested and sympathetic listener, I liked and admired these women and I was fascinated with their stories. Being an older woman gave me some access to older women in Morocco. Being an outsider, a foreigner, made it possible for me to interview women of different classes, different levels of education, different political views—because I stood outside of the Moroccan social hierarchy and political landscape.

Moroccans have a strong, almost sacred tradition of hospitality. A few of the women met me in their offices, and the interviews were quite formal, but most of the interviews were in women's homes, where I was welcomed warmly and offered glasses of Moroccan mint tea and trays of pastries. As time went on, I was invited to more and more women's parties, tea parties, weddings, circumcisions, henna parties, family meals, and other gatherings. Over the course of six or seven years, I became friends with many of the women I interviewed. Still I remain an outsider, a guest/foreigner, in a sort of ambiguous inside/outside position.[41]

I am on both sides of the camera, inside and outside of the picture: American anthropologist Ruth Behar calls it perpetually balancing "on the border between the opposite tendencies to see women as not at all different from one another or as all too different," and warns that "to go too far in either direction is to end up *indifferent* to the lives of other women."[42] The Moroccan women who appear in this book are neither "just like us" nor entirely exotic and strange. Ultimately they speak for themselves, as individual Moroccan women who have lived remarkable lives, and as women who share with us a common humanity.

Appendix A: Notes on Methodology

In determining the scope of the project, I decided to focus on several cities in the north of Morocco which were centers of the national movement and armed resistance. Fez was an obvious choice as birthplace of the nationalist political movement and the Istiqlal Party, and Casablanca as the birthplace and heart of the armed resistance. The other cities that are included in the book are Tetuouan, in the Spanish zone; Oujda, on the Algerian border; Rabat, the capital city; and Salé, a more traditional city just across the river from Rabat.

The women who played leading roles in the nationalist political movement are well known in Morocco: only about twenty-five women are still surviving from that small elite, and I was able to interview most of them. The women who participated in the armed resistance form a much larger group—approximately three hundred are registered as veterans of the resistance—and are almost unknown. I interviewed about thirty women who are registered, and another thirty who were of the same milieu, with various degrees of involvement in the resistance, but who are not officially recognized as veterans. With each of these sixty women, I conducted anywhere from one to six recorded interviews, with each interview lasting anywhere from fifteen minutes (the length of time some women spoke at group interviews) to four hours. I was also able to consult the dossiers of women who were registered at the Commission for Veterans of the Resistance.

The interviews with nationalist women were all held in their homes, except for two (Zhor Lazraq and Fatima Hassar) which took place in their offices. Sometimes family members were present, and sometimes I brought a young woman student or research assistant with me to the interview. In any case, the "interview" was an extended monologue, without significant intervention by me or others. I started the interviews off with a very brief, general description of my project, saying that I was interested in the roles of women in Morocco in the 1940s an 1950s, and explained that I was going to incorporate some of the oral histories in a book. Then I asked the women to tell their own life stories. In first introducing my project to these women, I did not stress their participation in the nationalist movement, because I wanted to find out from them how important this participation was to their lives and to their sense of themselves.

With women from the armed resistance, how I introduced the project depended on the circumstances of the interview. In group meetings organized by the Commission on Veterans of the Resistance I explained that I was interested in women's roles and experience in the resistance; in individual interviews in women's homes, I asked them to talk about their lives. The women's narratives varied according to the setting. When women spoke at meetings organized by the Commission, their narratives had the quality of oral testimony, bearing witness, public performance. In Casablanca, the women at the meeting actually applauded at the end of each woman's narrative. I first met and interviewed other women at informal women's parties, where things sometimes become chaotic, with women shouting and interrupting. Here, emotions such as bitterness and anger, that were not part of the women's public narrative, began to emerge. And then I came back to interview some women several times in their homes, where they spoke more privately about difficult and unhappy childhoods, and answered questions I had about what they had told me in previous interviews.

I conducted all the interviews myself, and the English translations of interviews and texts that appear in the book are mine except where noted. Several different research assistants helped me with the translation/transcription of interview tapes. In writing up the oral histories, I have kept the written text as close to the original spoken language as possible. If some of the interviews with nationalist women seem impersonal, stiff, and formal, and some of the interviews with women from the armed resistance seem repetitious, that is how the women presented themselves. While I have edited the oral history texts to improve coherence and flow of the narrative, and inserted some explanatory comments, I tried to keep the balance and priorities of the women themselves in selecting what to include and what to leave out.

The women themselves had an opportunity to shape the oral history text directly at two points in the process. First, I gave them copies of the interview tapes so that they could review them and amend or expand on anything in a subsequent interview. Then once I had written the oral history chapters, I gave each woman her own oral history to review, to make corrections, additions, or other comments. Even though the text was in English, most of the women went to some lengths to find someone to translate it, and several made changes, additions, and corrections which are incorporated into the final text.

Appendix B: Chronology of Events Mentioned in the Oral Histories

The nationalist women in particular referred to major events in Moroccan and world history that had marked them: This chronology lists some of the outside events mentioned in the oral histories. The French (and Spanish) protectorate lasted from 1912 to 1956.

1909–13	Sidi Mohamed Ameziane's war of resistance against Spanish colonialism in the Rif.
March 30, 1912	Treaty of Fez establishing the French Protectorate
1912–36	Guerrilla warfare against the French in the Middle Atlas.
1920–26	**The Rif War.** Abdelkrim El Khatabi led this war against Spanish (and finally also French) colonialism.
November 18, 1927	Mohamed Ben Youssouf named Sultan, at the age of seventeen.
May 16, 1930	**The Berber Dahir.** An attempt by the French to establish different political and legal systems for Arab and Berber areas, to divide Moroccans and strengthen French control. It backfired, uniting Moroccans against the French, and marking the beginning of the political independence movement.
December, 1934	*Plan des réformes* submitted to French Residency by the nationalists, calling for the strict application of the terms of the Protectorate.
1934	General Guillaume completes "pacification" of the south of Morocco.
1937	French Residency represses the nationalist movement, putting its leaders in prison or sending them into exile. Nationalist leader Allal El Fassi is exiled to Gabon for nine years.
1936–39	Palestinian uprising.
1936–39	Spanish Civil War. Moroccan *goumiers* fight with Franco.
1939–45	World War II
1940–44	Vichy France, after French army defeated by the Germans.

1942	**Year of the American war/Year of the ration coupon.** Americans landed in North Africa (Operation Torch). It was also a year of famine, in which ration coupons were issued for essential supplies.
January 22, 1943	During the course of a meeting with Winston Churchill, General Charles de Gaulle, and General Giraud held at Anfa (an area close to the center of Casablanca), President Franklin D. Roosevelt invites King Mohamed V and his son Hassan for dinner (without any representatives of the French protectorate). Roosevelt assures Mohamed V of his support of the principles of the Atlantic Charter (1941), self-determination of peoples, and of Moroccan independence.
1943	Princess Lalla Aicha gets her primary school certificate.
January 11, 1944	**Independence Manifesto.** Nationalists in Fez make first demand for outright independence from France, and form the Istiqlal (Independence) Party.
November 18, 1944	Sultan invites Moroccan Jewish leaders to Fête du Trône celebrations to protest Vichy antisemitic laws and policies.
June 18, 1945	Mohamed V presented with the Order of Liberation by DeGaulle and marches in victory parade at his side.
1946	Allal El Fassi returns to Fez from exile in Gabon. Other nationalists return, liberty of press for nationalists. Erik Labonne appointed resident general.
1947	The "slaughter of Casa" or "slaughter of Derb El Kabir": Demonstrations in Casablanca bloodily suppressed. Preparation of the armed resistance begins in Casablanca.
April 11, 1947	Mohamed V gives a speech in Tangier breaking with the French. Princess Lalla Aicha gives a speech calling for the emancipation of women.
May, 1947	General Juin named Resident General, replacing Erik Labonne. Strongman Boniface is chief of the Casablanca region.
1948	**Jewish occupation of Palestine.** State of Israel is formed, and Jerusalem occupied. Moroccan women raise money to support Palestinians.
1949	Opening of a women's branch of the Qaraouine university.
1950	French arrest or exile Istiqlal Party members.
1952	**Ferhat Hachad, Tunisian trade union leader, assassinated by French** (December 7). On December 8, a

general strike among workers in Casablanca, bloodily suppressed. Nationalist and trade union leaders in cities all over Morocco arrested and put in prison or sent into exile. Istiqlal Party outlawed.

August 20, 1953   **French exile King Mohamed V.** Spontaneous mass demonstrations in cities all over Morocco. Armed resistance goes into action, targetting Moroccan traitors and collaborators.

December 24, 1953   On Christmas eve (to match the exile of the king on the eve of the *Aid Kabir*) a bomb explodes in the central market of Casablanca. After this, Abdellah Senhaji and other resistance leaders go north to create the liberation army.

November 1, 1954   Armed liberation war begins in Algeria.

August 20, 1955   Uprisings in Oued Zem, crushed brutally by General Duval and his troops.

October 2, 1955   First attacks by liberation army *maquis* on three French garrisons on the Moroccan-Algerian border, led by Abbèss Messadi.

November 6, 1955   Mohamed V signs La Celle–St. Cloud agreement with French foreign minister Antoine Pinay to put Mohamed V back on the throne and leading to Moroccan independence.

16 November, 1955   **Return of King Mohamed V.** The French government under Edgar Fauré decided to give way in Morocco in order to focus on holding on to Algeria—the first step is to bring the sultan home from exile. There is wild jubilation, crowds of people. Mohamed is dubbed "The Liberator", and women sing out: "With bombs and revolvers, we have won back our King!" Cries of "Vive le roi!" and "Vive l'Istiqlal!"

March 2, 1956   **Moroccan Independence**

May 14, 1956   Creation of *Forces armées royales* (FAR—Royal Armed Forces), under the command of Crown Prince Hassan.

June 25, 1956   Liberation army leader Abbèss Messadi assassinated in the Rif.

1957-59   *Moudouana* family law code issued, in stages.

January, 1958   French and Spanish forces (in concert with the Moroccan government) start Operation Hurricane (also called *Ecouvillon*, "Mop-up"). In February, 1958, 15,000 French and Spanish troops, supported by about 100

	planes, sweep across the desert and eliminate the Liberation Army of the South.
September, 1959	Mehdi Ben Barka breaks off from Istiqlal to form UNFP together with other Istiqlal Party "Young Turks."
1960	Earthquake in Agadir. February: Leaders of the resistance, liberation army, and UNFP are arrested, accused of plot to assassinate Crown Prince Hassan. Liberation army leaders put in prison.
May, 1960	Ibrahim (Istiqlal) government dismissed by Mohamed V.
February 26, 1961	Death of Mohamed V. Hassan II comes to the throne.
1962	Algeria gets its independence from France.
December 7, 1962	Approval of Moroccan Constitution by referendum.
May 17, 1963	Legislative elections. UNFP candidates do well; Ben Barka elected as representative from Rabat.
July 16, 1963	Repression of UNFP: Arrest and imprisonment of UNFP leaders. Ben Barka leaves for Europe.
1963	"War of the Sand": Fighting with Algeria over the Sahara begins.
March 23, 1965	Demonstrations by *lycée* (high school) students in Casablanca to protest restrictions on education. Police fire on the students, turning the demonstration into an uprising, and people from the shantytowns join the students. Oufkir leads a savage four-day repression, and then goes on to quell demonstrations in Rabat and Fez.
March 29, 1965	Royal pardon for political prisoners.
June 8, 1965	"State of Exception" declared. Hassan II suspends the government, and assumes both legislative and executive functions. This state of exception will last for five years.
October 29, 1965	Mehdi Ben Barka disappears (assassinated) in Paris.
June 5, 1967	Beginning of Six-Day War launched by Israel.
July 10, 1971	Attempt to depose/assassinate Hassan II at his birthday party at Skhirat, outside of Rabat, by M'Hamed Ababou and crack cadets from Ahermoumou.
August 16, 1972	Second assassination attempt: Airforce pilots from Kenitra base attempt to shoot down Hassan II's plane as he returns from European trip. This attempt planned by Oufkir (then Minister of Defense), who committed suicide (or was killed) shortly after.
May 10, 1973	Polisario (Front for an Independent Sahara) created. Receives arms from Libya and Algeria.
November 6, 1975	King Hassan II launches the Green March to reclaim the Spanish Sahara for Morocco. Men and women walk into

the Sahara armed only with a copy of the Koran and a photo of the king.

June, 1981   Popular uprisings in Casablanca, after announcements of increased prices for staple foods (after a year of drought in 1980-81), and failure of 85 percent of the students who took the baccalaureate exam. Revolt crushed by the army.

1993   Reform of the *moudouana*. The first two women elected to the Moroccan parliament.

Appendix C: Glossary of Moroccan Arabic and French Terms

Note on pronunciation: In transliterating Moroccan Arabic, I have spelled words phonetically, with the non-Arabic speaker/reader in mind. "Q" (as in *qadi*) is pronounced as a deeper and more emphatic "k" sound, in the back of the throat; "gh" (as in Ghalia) is pronounced like a French "r" (as in *rien*); "kh" (as in *khalif*) is pronounced like the German "ch" (as in *ach*). Two other sounds in Moroccan Arabic that don't exist in English are the *hamza* and the *ayn*. The *hamza* is a glottal stop, and is represented here by an apostrophe, as in *shari'a*. The *ayn* is a deep sound in the back of the throat which makes the surrounding vowels deeper too. I have represented it here by double vowels, as in *aalim*. I have left the name Aicha with its French phonetic spelling, because it is so widely used with that spelling in Morocco. The English phonetic spelling would be "Aisha." Arabic citations in the bibliography are in classical Arabic phonetic spelling.

A	Used as a prefix with *lalla* (madam) or *sidi* (mister) in addressing someone—*A sidi, A lalla*.
aalim	(f. *aalima*) A learned man (woman).
Abd	Servant/slave of . . . This is combined with one of the ninety-nine names of God to form given names for men in the Muslim world such as: Abdelkrim, Abdelkhalek, Abdelmajid.
agrément	This is a French word, which women in the armed resistance used to describe the licenses given to them by the Commission for Veterans of the Resistance to author- ize them to hire out a taxicab or truck to earn some money.
aid	festival, celebration. *Aid Kabir* is the "big festival" which commemorates Abraham's willingness to sacrifice his son by the ritual slaughter of a ram.
bab	gate, door. In Morocco, the old cities (*medinas*) were surrounded by a wall with four gates, each with a name, such as Bab Boujeloud in Fez.
bey'a	A written contract of allegiance, reaffirmed each time there was a change of Sultan, which specified the reciprocal

rights and responsibilities of the Sultan and the population. Each year there is a ceremony to renew the *bey'a*: Leaders from all the provinces come to the Palace to renew their pledge of allegiance to the King.

bismillah In the name of God. Said to mark (and bless) the beginning of a meal or a talk.

bled Countryside (as opposed to city). It can also be used to mean a person's place of origin.

caid The chief local government official, similar to a governor.

Carrières centrales "Central quarries," the name of the biggest shantytown in Casablanca. This neighborhood was fiercely nationalistic and royalist. In fact, when the Glaoui wanted to challenge King Mohamed V in the early fifties, they told everyone that the King had lost all his power; the only power he had left was his control of the Carrières centrales. This district was the site of the worst massacres (by Boniface and the police) on December 8, 1952.

dada Grandmother. Familiar term for an older woman servant or slave.

dahir A decree issued by the Moroccan government, signed by the Sultan. In May, 1930, although the Sultan was forced to sign the Berber *dahir*, everyone blamed it on the French residency.

dirham The current Moroccan currency. In 1995, a U.S. dollar was worth a little more than seven *dirhams*.

djellaba A long, hooded robe, worn outdoors. It was originally worn only by men, and there were even laws against women wearing the djellaba (instead of the *haik*) in Fez in the 1930s. The old-fashioned women's djellaba has a large hood, which is worn up, around the face, with a headscarf and face veil, and is usually in sober greys, browns, dark blue, or green. The modern djellaba, on the other hand, is in bright easter-egg colors and patterns, with a small, decorative hood. Men's djellabas are in white for religious and other special occasions, and otherwise in brown, grey, or other dark colors, or with stripes.

douar Village. Used alone, or together with the name of a village or city neighborhood.

Doustour Constitution. The *Doustour* Party, which was headed by Maati Bouabid, is the Constitutional Union in English (*Union Constitutionelle* in French).

eiwa	A phonetic rendering of the expression used to mark off pauses in the narrative of women who spoke Moroccan Arabic. It doesn't mean anything specific—it could be translated as "Oh yes," or "That's it."
Emir	(f. *Emira*) Prince (Princess).
fassi	(f. *fassiya*) Someone (or something) from Fez.
fqih	(f. *fqiha*) A man (or woman) religious scholar, often a Koranic school teacher.
galassa	Derives from the verb *to sit*. Used here to describe a woman who is specially hired for weddings to take care of the room in which the bride gets changed, and who also serves as the first person to testify that the bride was a virgin on her wedding night. In current usage, the *galassa* is the receptionist at the women's *hammam*, a woman who is in a position to know all the gossip of the neighborhood. There is a chapter on "l'Assise" in the novel *La nuit sacrée* by Tahar Benjelloun.
goumier	From the Arab word *goum*, meaning tribe. A French term to designate the African contingents of the French military.
Hbibti	Auntie. Familiar term for an older woman who is a member of the family or close friend.
Hadith	The collected sayings and doings of the Prophet Mohamed, a religious text second only to the Koran in its importance.
haik	A traditional garment for Moroccan women to wear when they go out of the house. It is made of a single large piece of cloth, usually white or brown, which is wrapped loosely around several times, so as to cover the wearer completely, with the cloth held in one hand so that only one eye is exposed. Women carrying weapons for the armed resistance often wore haiks because they could conceal the weapons in its voluminous folds.
Haj	(f. *Hajja*) Title and form of address for a man (or woman) who has made the pilgrimage to Mecca.
hamdoullah	Thanks be to God!
hammam	Moroccan turkish baths, separate for women and for men. For women in seclusion, an outing to the hammam was one of very few opportunities to get out of the house, and the hammam was a place where women exchanged information and gossip.
harem	Derives from the word for *forbidden*, and has taken on "orientalist" overtones, evoking sensuous, scantily clad

women enclosed in the women's quarters of a palace, guarded by eunuchs. Because of this, I avoid using the term. Fatima Mernissi (1994) uses it to refer to the space where women and children were secluded inside her house in Fez.

henna
Powder derived from a plant that dyes hair or skin a reddish color. Elaborate designs were drawn on women's hands and feet in henna at times of celebration—brides, for instance. Henna thus was a symbol of celebration and joy.

hijab
The Arabic word for *veil*. In Morocco, the traditional face veil, which covers all of the face below the eyes, is called a *litham*; *hijab* refers to the veil of Islamic fundamentalists which frames the face tightly like a Christian nun's habit; or sometimes even the whole outfit worn by Islamic fundamentalist women, leaving no part of the body exposed except for the hands and the face.

horra
(*medrassa horra*) *Horra* means free, and *medrassa horra*, free school. This is the term used to refer to the schools created by the nationalists starting in the late twenties, with a curriculum focused on the Arabic language and culture and nationalism. *Free* refers to freedom of thought and freedom from French control—the schools were independent (i.e. not state-supported), and charged tuition fees.

hshouma
Shameful. Also used as an interjection, meaning "Shame on you!"

ijtihad
Exegesis—an established method of going back to the original sources (the Koran, the tradition of the Prophet Mohammed and the first Khalifs, and the founders of the four schools) in order to interpret the text of the Koran to meet changing circumstances.

istiqlal
The Arabic word for independence. The main nationalist party, founded in 1944 in Fez, was named the Istiqlal Party.

jahiliya
Ignorance and heresy. The word refers to the dark ages before Islam.

jihad
War to defend Islam. Contrary to what many Western analysts have thought, the jihad is usually a *defensive* war, when the Muslim faithful rise up to defend their nation against attacks by (non-Muslim) foreigners that threaten the national territory and religion.

kaftan	A long, loose robe worn inside the house by men and women. Women's kaftans are usually belted; kaftans for weddings and other festive occasions usually have two layers, and can be made of elaborate, expensive material, worn with belts made of gold.
khalif	(f. *khalifa*) Successor (or follower). This word was originally used to designate the followers and successors of the Prophet Mohamed.
khol	black powder used as eye liner by women.
kif	A plant that when dried and smoked acts as a narcotic drug, similar to marijuana. It is cultivated in the Rif mountains.
kissariat	The stalls in a city market where dry goods and more expensive materials are sold. In Fez, it was the merchants of the kissariat who funded the nationalist movement; the French burnt it down in retaliation.
lalla	Form of address for women. Lalla Fatima means Ms. Fatima, but you can also use *lalla* alone, like Madam (but much less formal).
llatif	The Muslim prayer of mourning, which became a protest against French colonialism.
ma'allma	A woman who teaches girls embroidery and other artisanal work at her home. Defined by Roger Le Tourneau (1965), p. 194, as "a single woman, widowed or divorced, who was obliged to earn her living."
maghreb	The far west of the Muslim world, the North African Maghreb includes Morocco, Algeria, and Tunisia. It is a distinct region within the Arab world, and a zone of contact between the Middle East, Africa and Europe.
makhzen	The central government of Morocco under the Sultan.
maquis	French word for wild bushy land (in Corsica), used from 1941-44 to refer to the French underground resistance, and, by extension, to guerrilla and underground fighters generally.
marabout	A holy man representing a saint's cult.
medina	The name of the city to which Mohamed fled after having been driven out of Mecca. In Arabic generally it just means city, but here it is used to distinguish the old, walled Moroccan cities from the French-built *villes nouvelles* (new cities).
mellah	The word derives from the Arabic word for salt. It refers to the separate quarters in traditional Moroccan cities reserved for Jews.

moudouana	The Moroccan family law code, based on the *shari'a* and the Malekite rite of Islam, which are the most conservative interpretations of the Koran.
moujahid	(f. *moujahida*, f. pl. *moujahidat*) A fighter in a holy war (*jihad*). This term was especially used for Algerian resistance fighters.
Moulay	My Lord. A form of address used in Morocco for the princes and other prominent *shorfa*, together with their first names.
mouqqadam	A Moroccan local government official.
negafa	A woman hired at marriage ceremonies whose special function is to dress the bride.
ouallah	"In the name of God!" (an oath)
oulema	Plural of *aalim*; refers to the Moroccan council of religious elders. One of the responsibilities of the council was to choose the new sultan when there was a succession.
pasha	Originally a Turkish word, from the Ottoman empire. Traditional regional overlord, loosely subject to the authority of the central government.
qadi	Local government official.
riffi	(f. *riffia*) Someone (or something) from the Rif mountains, in the north of Morocco.
rial	There are 20 *rials* in a Moroccan *dirham*, which is currently equivalent to about 15 American cents. (*Rial* coins or bills do not actually exist, but people still sometimes calculate prices using *rials*.)
salafiya	Derives from the *salafs*, or great ancestors in Islamic tradition. An Islamic reform movement originating in Iran, Syria, and Egypt that influenced the Moroccan nationalists. In order to rebuild Muslim society, the first step was to fight against false traditions within the family.
serrtla	A set of seven gold bracelets.
shari'a	Islamic law, social law of divine origin.
sherif	(f. *sherifa*, pl. *shorfa*) A blood descendent of the Prophet Mohammed, recognized to have special powers.
shoura	An Islamic concept meaning consultation. The *hez'b shoura* is the Parti démocratique de l'indépendence (PDI—Democracy and Independence Party) created by M.H. Ouazzani in Fez after his return from exile in 1946. In this case, the sense of *shoura* is consultation with the people.

souk	Open-air markets, usually held weekly and named for the day of the week on which they are held.
tsabih	A special kind of necklace used at the end of prayer.
zaouiya	Saints' tombs, the centers of saints' cults and of religious brotherhoods.
zellig	Traditional mosaic tile, very elaborate and beautiful, used to decorate the inside walls of houses and public buildings.

Notes

Preface

1. *Medina* means "city" in Arabic, taken from the name of the city where Mohamed went when he was driven out of Mecca. It is used here, and in common usage in Morocco, to distinguish the old walled city from the *ville nouvelle*, the modern city built by the French.

2. The *djellaba* is a long hooded robe originally worn by men, but now worn by both men and women. See glossary definition.

3. *Hijab* means "veil" in Arabic. In Morocco, it refers to the veil worn by Islamic fundamentalists, which leaves only the face uncovered, unlike the traditional face veil (*litham*) which usually covers all of the face below the eyes.

4. Some works on the independence movement give a nod to Malika El Fassi as the only woman to sign the 1944 Independence Manifesto, but American scholar John Halstead (*Rebirth of a Nation*) unaccountably leaves her off of his otherwise complete list of signatories.

5. Geertz, *After the Fact*, p. 6.

6. A traditional Moroccan woman's dress, long and flowing, worn with a belt. Kaftans for parties and weddings can be quite elaborate, with two layers, and done in expensive materials.

7. See Michael M. J. Fischer, in Clifford and Marcus, eds., *Writing Culture*, p. 20.

8. When resistance and liberation army leader Abdellah Senhaji was asked how he felt about the thirtieth anniversary of the 1944 signing of the Independence Manifesto in Fez, he answered: "If we celebrate such an event, the events of 1944, I ask myself who will celebrate the anniversary of 1934, the liberation war in the Sahara led by the Ait Ba'amran, and [who will celebrate the war of] Abdelkrim [in the Rif] in 1926? These are the heroes! They didn't just ask for independence; they also actually participated in the fight for the country's independence. Alas, who will celebrate events such as those?" [Interview with Dr. Bihi in 1974, reprinted in a special commemorative issue of *Tahebti* (The Challenge), Action Party (*Parti de l'action*) paper, forty days after Senhaji's death on May 18, 1985.]

Chapter 1. Oral History in Morocco

1. Notably Benjelloun, *Approches du colonialisme espagnol* and *Le patriotisme marocain* (on the national movement in the Northern zone) and Zaki, *Résistance et Armée de Liberation marocain* (on the armed resistance and Liberation Army).

2. See Hall, "Leila Abouzeid's Year of the Elephant," for a discussion of this double rebellion in several autobiographical novels by Moroccan and Palestinian women.

3. In setting out to do an oral history project in Morocco, I was entering a field that in the last thirty years has been dominated by American anthropologists, an unusually large number of whom have done work in Morocco, including some who have focused on subjects that relate to this project: the interviewing process, life stories, and women. (The Selected Bibliography lists works by M. E. Coombs-Schilling, Vincent Crapanzano, Daisy Hilse Dwyer, Kevin Dwyer, Dale Eickelman, Clifford Geertz, Hildred Geertz, Henry Munson, Jr., Paul Rabinow, and Lawrence Rosen.) There are also growing numbers of Moroccan scholars, journalists, and novelists who write about women, producing an expanding body of ethnographic studies of women in rural areas, as well as work on women in contemporary Moroccan society, and some fiction. *Femmes et Politique*, by Moroccan journalists Latifa Akharbach and Narjis Rerhaye, has chapters on Malika Al Fassi, Rqia Lamrania, Zhor Zarqa and Fatima Hassar, whose oral histories appear in Part II of this book; and the feminist journal *8 mars* [in Arabic] has published a series of interviews with women from both the nationalist movement and the armed resistance (including Malika Al Fassi and Saadia Bouhaddou, who appear in this book). Leila Abouzeid's novel, *The Year of the Elephant*, has as its protagonist a woman who worked in the resistance with her husband.

4. See Hermansen, "The Female Hero in Islamic Religious Tradition." The three main categories of female hero that she identifies are: woman warrior, wife and mother, and spiritual virtuoso. This article deals primarily with written sources, but most of the female heros she mentions are also well known in Moroccan oral tradition.

5. Ibn Sa'd, *Kitab al-Tabaqat al-Kabir* VIII (Leiden: E.J. Brill, 1905–1940), p. 304, cited in Hermansen, op. cit., p. 118.

6. Hermansen, op. cit., p. 122. Hind was the wife of the Meccan leader Abu Sufyan, and later became a Muslim.

7. Mernissi, *The Veil and the Male Elite*, pp. 116–117.

8. The judge had to hear the case, which was so celebrated that the judge's own wife attended and the *khalif* sent an emissary to get periodic reports. Mernissi, op. cit., pp. 192–193.

9. The *Arabian Nights* (also called *1001 Nights*) in itself is a dramatic illustration of the power of narrative: Scheherazade actually keeps herself alive by telling stories.

10. Stivers, "Reflections on the Role of Personal Narrative," summarizes work on this; see especially p. 412.

11. Moroccan anthropologist Fatima Hajjarabi, in collecting life histories among rural women in the north of Morocco, noted certain recurring patterns and turning points. Hajjarabi, "Les souks féminins dans le Rif Central: Rareté des biens et profusion social." I also collected several life histories.

12. Although my interviews with nationalist women and with women from the armed resistance all occurred in the same time frame (between January, 1992 and November, 1996) and as a part of the same project, there turned out to be some differences in the process as well as in the end results—the oral histories presented in this book. These reflected the significant differences, as well as some similarities, between the two groups of women.

13. There were also much more extensive school systems for Moroccan Jews and for Berbers—evidence of the French discrimination against Arabs.

14. In the oral histories, all Europeans are referred to as "Christians"; only occasionally do the women differentiate among nationalities. They also sometimes refer to Jews, usually meaning Moroccan Jews.

15. The Moroccan women had their own rather negative stereotypes of the French, especially Frenchwomen. In all the interviews I conducted, there was only one French*woman* who played a significant role. She was portrayed as exceptionally lacking in courage, "trembling with fear" when she was told that her (Moroccan) husband had been captured by guerrillas and that they were coming after her next, and easily persuaded to get out on the next plane to France. (March 3, 1992 interview with Oum Keltoum El Khatib.)

16. See Weitz, "Mémoire et oubli: Women of the French Resistance" and *Celebrating Human Rights*.

17. Gadant, *Parcours d'une intellectuelle en Algérie* (p. 84) disputes this: "The presence of women [in the Algerian resistance] was tolerated only to the extent that they were relegated to 'feminine' tasks. The number of those who actually bore arms, if indeed that is a sign of emancipation, was virtually nil."

18. The *haik* is made of a single large piece of cloth, usually white or brown, which is wrapped loosely around several times so as to cover the wearer completely, with the cloth held in one hand so that only one eye is exposed.

19. Islamic family law gives the husband the right to divorce (or repudiate) his wife unilaterally, with no stated cause, sometimes without even notifying her in person.

20. Abouzeid, *The Year of the Elephant*, p. 1.

21. Interview with Aicha Terrab, May 12, 1992, Casablanca.

Chapter 2. Nationalism and Feminism in Moroccan History

1. Cagne, *Nation et nationalisme*; Abdellah Laroui, *Les origines sociales et culturelles du nationalisme* and *Esquisses historiques* (especially part IV, p. 123 foll.).

2. The monarchy was consolidated by his son, Idriss II, who established his capital in Fez. The mother of Idriss II was Kenza, a Berber woman, who was "clever and strong in raising and educating her son . . . [and thus enabled him] to establish the pillars of the Moroccan state." Thus the founding dynasty established a monarch whose ancestry was both Arab and Berber. (From Allal El Fassi 1953 speech to the Egyptian Social Party.)

3. Through Hassan, the elder son of Mohammed's daughter Fatima and her husband 'Ali.

4. In earlier periods of Moroccan history, the king was called the *sultan*. During the protectorate he was sometimes called sultan and sometimes king, and since independence he has been called king (and Morocco has been a constitutional monarchy with political parties and a parliament). The French used the terms *Sharifian Empire* and *Sultan* to keep the sultan's traditional prestige and religious function without allowing him modern political power.

5. This was especially true during the Merinide Dynasty (1248–1465), which took the city as its capital.

6. Except for a brief period in the third century when it became a part of Roman Mauritania, Morocco had never been under foreign rule.

7. Voltaire, in the eighteenth century, noted that "the Moors conquered all of Spain, while the Spanish have not been able to do more than harass the Moors. They have crossed the Atlantic and conquered a new world, but they haven't been able to avenge themselves five leagues from home." Voltaire, *Essais sur les moeurs* (Paris: Garnier, 1963), vol. 2, pp. 429–430.

8. Laroui, *Esquisses historiques*, pp. 63–79.

9. Algeria was a French "colony" from 1830 to 1962; Tunisia a "regency" from 1881 to 1956; and Morocco a "protectorate" from 1912 to 1956.

10. This was known as the "policy of the great *caids*." The French thus increasingly aligned themselves with the most reactionary forces in Morocco, in an effort to neutralize the growing influence of the nationalists and finally, to attack the sultan himself.

11. Janet Abu-Lughod, *Rabat: Apartheid*, uses this provocative term advisedly in describing colonial city planning in Rabat.

12. See Laroui, *Esquisses historiques*. When the French occupied Morocco, there was profound and rapid social change going on (much more change than in the realms of culture or the economy). The French blocked this change, and focused on economic

development. There had been some political and social reforms proposed by Moroccan elites, such as the reform constitution drafted in 1908 (largely in reaction to the 1906 Treaty of Algéciras) by the *Lisan el Maghreb* association of Moroccan notables, which mentioned specifically the necessity of primary school education for girls. But this reform constitution was never put into effect, and all such reforms became moot in 1912 when Morocco became a French protectorate.

13. Stewart, *The Economy of Morocco.*

14. See Laroui, *Esquisses historiques*, p. 50, on the *bey'a*, as well as the definition in the glossary.

15. Fatima Hajjarabi is doing a great deal of very interesting research on women's work in rural areas in the north of Morocco. She made a film (unfinished at the time of writing) which focuses on one young woman, chronicling the entire process of fetching firewood. See Hajjarabi, "Sauver la fôret ou sauver les femmes."

16. Mernissi, *Dreams of Trespass.* In this memoir of growing up in Fez in the forties, Mernissi shows the depth and details of the invisible feminism of the harem, expressed in women's talk and in a whole variety of subversive acts and rebellions.

17. Hajjarabi, "Les souks féminins du Rif Central; anthropologie de l'échange féminin."

18. Interview with Amina Leuh.

19. Although Morocco is officially an Islamic country, there is also a lively religious life centered around saints tombs (*zaouiya*). Women are heavily involved as participants in zaouiya, and there are some women saints.

20. From Allal El Fassi, 1953 speech to the Egyptian Social Party, at the invitation of the Egyptian Women's Party (unpublished, translated from the Arabic by Leila Abouzeid).

21. The section that follows is summarized or cited (as noted) from Mohamed Ben Azzouz Hakim and Mohamed Molato, "Moroccan Women and Armed Resistance in the North."

22. There was a common French view of "Muslim woman as servant or slave, condemned to forced labor, and implicitly, forced sex, by her husband." The other view of the Arab or Muslim woman was that she was "nothing but an *objet de luxe*, a sensual, indolent, bored creature, caged like a bird in the *harem*." Julia Clancy Smith, referring to the writings of General Daumas in Algeria, in "La femme Arabe" in Sonbol, *Women, the Family*, p. 56.

23. It's interesting that in a text showing the courage of women, women's dress still signifies weakness and cowardice.

24. Abdelkrim wanted to establish an independent Republic of the Rif, with himself as president, so the sultan and his makhzen government did not really support his cause. If the French had not come to the aid of the Spanish, Abdelkrim might very

well have driven the Spanish out. Many of the women I talked with told me that the Chinese Communist leader Mao Tse-tung knew of Abdelkrim and the Rif War, and that Mao himself credited Abdelkrim as the real originator of the people's liberation war and techniques of guerrilla warfare. This story about Mao Tse-tung is also cited in Latifa Jbabdi's article in *8 mars*.

25. Allal El Fassi, 1953 speech to the Egyptian Social Party. Latifa Jbabdi, "The Moroccan Women's Movement", Part 1, *8 mars* 56 (May, 1991) also has this story.

26. This is a theme that Monique Gadant stresses in her work on Algerian nationalism and women. Women, she says, were celebrated as warrior heroines and as workers, but at the same time they were categorized as women, that is to say as dependent beings who did not belong to themselves. *Parcours d'une intellectuelle*, pp. 135, 138, 225.

27. Bessis and Belhassen, *Femmes du Maghreb*, pp. 18–19.

28. Allal El Fassi, *Autocritique*.

29. Halstead, *Rebirth of a Nation*, p. 263.

30. Moroccan historian Fatima Harrak's unpublished masters thesis, *Réflexions sur l'apport de la Salafiya à l'évolution des femmes marocaines*, provides an excellent analysis and overview of (male) nationalist thought concerning women's issues, especially focusing on the influence of the Salafiya movement. The sections of this chapter on the Salafiya and on discussion of women's issues in the nationalist press summarize her much more extensive treatment of those subjects.

31. Perhaps Ahmed Balafrej, who used to sign his articles Ahmed Mansour, according to Halstead, *Rebirth of a Nation*, p. 209. *Maghreb*, no. 16 (Paris, 1933).

32. See Kumari Jayawardena, *Feminism and Nationalism in the Third World*, pp. 12–13, for parallels in other countries.

33. Halstead, *op. cit.*, p. 262. See Appendix D of that work, pp. 278-280, for a list of the "41 leading nationalists, 1921–44, and their education."

34. The section that follows summarizes information and analysis taken from Harrak, *Réflexions sur l'apport*.

Chapter 3. Colonialism, Conflict, and Independence

1. Interviews with Fatna Mansar (February 25, 1992) and Zhor Lazraq (March 5, 1992). The French countered this with talk of bringing progress and enlightenment to a backwards economy and society: "There is no 'colonialism' or French 'imperialism', just a human and moral work which is indispensable to the stability and security of the Western world." General Juin, 1949, quoted in Z. Lahlou-Alaoui, *D'Algéciras à Aix-les-Bains*, vol. 1, p. 31.

2. Malika El Fassi, March 12, 1992 interview, Rabat.

3. Thami Naamane, February 25, 1992 interview, Casablanca.

4. Dr. Mohamed Tazi, November 17, 1992 interview, Fez.

5. Moroccans referred to all black African troops as "the Senegalese," and felt that the French brought them into the Moroccan sections of the cities especially to terrorize the Moroccan population, brutally attacking civilians, even women and children.

6. Another informant (Mohamed Ben Abdeljalil, November 17, 1992 interview) told me that the youyous of Fassi women had such a powerful effect in encouraging the Moroccan fighters and striking terror into the hearts of the French military that the French forbade them, and that the French officer in charge used to say that women's youyous were more powerful than the canons of Napoleon in Egypt.

7. All citations of Haj Thami Naamane are from February 25, 1992 interview.

8. "Zerktouni, Hassan Laraychi, Slimane Laraychi who is still alive, Houcine Berrada, and me, Naamane Thami."

9. In an interview in Istiqlal Party paper *El Alam*, published on December 6, 1990 (French version published in *l'Opinion* on December 10, 1990).

10. Ibid.

11. Jbabdi, "The Moroccan Women's Movement," part 2.

12. Julien, *Le Maroc face aux impérialismes*, pp. 257–260; Témoignage Chrétien, *Le drame marocain.*

13. This "big festival" (contrasting with the "small festival" at the end of the month of Ramadan) commemorates Abraham's loyalty to God in his willingness to sacrifice his eldest son, Ismael (In the Christian tradition, it is the younger son, Isaac), with the ritual slaughter of a ram. It is held on a date in the Islamic calendar that corresponds to a different date each year in the Christian calendar.

14. The king was known as Mohamed, son of Youssef (Ben Youssef).

15. Interview with Amina Leuh March 18, 1994.

16. There were a few minor changes in the *moudouana* in 1993. The discussion here refers to the original code drafted just after independence except where noted. M. T. Essnoussi, *Code du statut personnel annoté*, first edition (French and Arabic). Rabat, n.d.

17. Cited in Moulay Rchid, *La condition de la femme*, p. 287, note 138.

18. Article 36, *Code.*

19. Article 35, *Code.*

20. Article 726, *Code.*

21. See Zhor Lazraq interview, Chapter 6.

22. *Libération: Spécial Mehdi Ben Barka* (29 October 1995), interview with his son Bachir Ben Barka, p. 14.

23. Ouardighi, *Al Malghrib, min harb arimal*, pp. 31–33.

24. Notably Waterbury, *The Commander of the Faithful*, and Perrault, *Notre ami le roi*. These books are both banned by the Moroccan government.

25. *Pasha* and *caid* are titles for traditional local government leaders. See glossary for full definitions.

26. Perrault, *Notre ami le roi*, p. 37.

27. "Operation Hurricane," started in January, 1958.

28. Except for Aicha and Mina Senhaji, who were implicated because their husband was an important leader of the resistance and liberation army.

29. This was an identification card issued by the government to certify active participation in the armed resistance or liberation army.

30. Interview in *8 mars*, December, 1983.

31. *Agrément* is a French word used by the women to describe the license given by the government which authorizes them to hire out a taxi or truck to earn some money.

32. Interview at Halima Ben Moussa's home in Rabat-Akkari on 5 June, 1993.

33. The Algerian example, where the resistance and women's participation lasted much longer, does not bear out this hope. Algerian women have been notably absent from public life since Algerian independence in 1962.

34. Interview with Khaddouj Zerktouni in *8 mars*, 1986, issue 31, p. 7.

35. It is only fair to note that when I commented to this effect in a meeting with the Women's Association of the Istiqlal Party, several of the women strenuously objected, and insisted that women have never been absent from public life, including political life. Nonetheless, to an outside observer, it looks as though this is a period in which women have a very low profile, unlike earlier and later periods.

36. The *Union nationale des femmes marocaines* was created in 1969 by King Hassan II, with his sister Lalla Aicha as honorary president.

37. "Especially at election time and in referendums and during the annual campaigns for charity." Jbabdi, "The Moroccan Women's Movement," part 2.

38. The UNFP and the Moroccan Communist party primarily; also the Moroccan Workers' Union (Union Marocain de Travail, or UMT).

39. See Jbabdi, op.cit.

Part II, Chapter 4. Fez and the Nationalist Women

1. The nationalist women came from the families of the great bourgeoisie, the religious aristocracy, or the traditional middle class of skilled artisans. The religious aristocracy, at the peak of the social hierarchy, was based either on heredity (the *shorfa*, or blood descendents of the Prophet) or on religious scholarship (the *oulema*, or council of religious elders and the *fqihs*, religious scholars and teachers). The urban middle class in this period had a core of traditional artisans, especially from the craftmen's guilds of Fez. Heavy taxes, a declining standard of living, and competition from manufactured products made them the most anticolonial segment of urban society, and they set the tone of the nationalist movement until the late 1940s. See Albert Ayache, *Le Maroc*, and Stephane Bernard, *Maroc, 1943–1956*, Vol 3.

2. Mernissi, *Dreams of Trespass*, pp. 165–66 footnote, and Gordon, *Slavery in the Arab World*.

3. In her memoir of growing up in Fez in the 1940s, Moroccan sociologist Mernissi includes several scenes describing the beginnings of a separation between Fatima's male cousin Samir's life and her own as they both approach puberty. One of the most vivid describes "the day that Samir was thrown out of the hammam because a woman noticed that he had 'a man's stare'." Mernissi, *Dreams of Trespass*, pp. 239–241.

4. Le Tourneau, *Vie quotidienne à Fez en 1900*, p. 196.

5. Hardy, *L'âme marocaine*, pp. 129, 139, 140, 145. Hardy was the general director of public instruction in the Fine Arts and Antiquities of Morocco.

6. Ibid., citing Si Kaddour ben Ghabrit, *La femme arabe dans l'Islam*, Conferences franco-marocaines (Paris: Plon-Nourrit, 1916).

7. Amina Leuh, March 18, 1994 interview.

8. Yvette Katan, *Oujda*, p. 293.

9. See Mernissi, *Dreams of Trespass*, pp. 127–128.

10. In Morocco, two themes of the neo-Salafiya dominate the discussion: the Islamic woman at the time of the great ancestors (the *salafs*), and the struggle against false traditions among women. There are also some articles on the education of girls. Margot Badran has noted fundamental differences between male- and female-generated discourses in Egypt. See Badran and Cooke, eds., *Opening the Gates*, p. xix.

11. J. and S. Lacouture, *Le Maroc à l'épreuve*, p. 320.

12. Madame Naamane, February 25, 1992 interview.

13. Interview with Aicha Terrab, May 12, 1992, Casablanca.

14. Interview with Dr. Mohamed Tazi, November 17, 1992, Fez.

15. French text of speech reprinted in *Le Matin du Sahara et de Maghreb*, April 10, 1992.

16. Interview with Malika El Fassi, March 12, 1992, Rabat-Souissi.

17. The women's association of the Reform Party in the northern, Spanish zone was started somewhat later, in 1947-48. Khadija Bennouna (Chapter 9) discusses this in some detail.

18. It was quite remarkable to use Moroccan Arabic in such a meeting. It symbolized the PDI women's efforts to reach out to women of all classes.

19. See glossary for a full definition of *galassa*.

20. Interview with Zahra Housseini Skalli, November 28, 1992, Fez.

21. Arab Mohamed Hassan Ouazzani, *Entretiens avec mon père*, pp. 49–51.

22. In this they were following the overall Communist Party strategy of first fighting against Naziism to achieve a victory of the proletariat in France, and only then exporting the Communist revolution to the colonized countries.

23. Mrs. Noufissa Mekouar was the wife of Ahmed Mekouar, a major leader and financier of the nationalist movement in Fez, the treasurer of the Istiqlal Party. The Mekouar house, one of the great houses of Fez, was a center for the nationalists, and the site of many women's gatherings presided over by Mrs. Mekouar.

24. Interview with Ftoma Skalli, Fez, December 10, 1992.

25. Harrak, *Reflexions sur l'apport de la Salafiya*, pp. 70–82.

26. *Risalat-al-Maghrib*, May 2, 1949.

27. *Risalat-al-Maghrib*, May 16, 1949.

28. *Al-Alam*, June 16, 1950.

29. *Al-Alam*, June 2 and June 30, 1950.

30. Hassar is the name of her husband's family, one of the great families of Salé, another traditional urban society in Morocco. Benslimane is a well-known Fassi family.

31. Zhor Lazraq's family were not prosperous, but because they were strongly nationalist she was able to get an education, including higher education at the Qaraouine.

32. There are important ways in which Rqia Lamrania is different from the other women. Her family was prosperous, but they were not one of the great bourgeois families of Morocco, and did not come from Fez or Tetouan. Most importantly, she did not get a formal education. Except for literacy classes in the 1950s, she had no schooling.

33. The National Party (not really a party, but a "mass"), was founded in 1925 in Fez. These same few leaders continued to dominate the movement in Fez up until the end of the 1940s.

34. In educating his daughters, most notably his eldest daughter, the Princess Lalla Aicha. In Leila Abouzeid's childhood memoirs, *Assirah a'datiya*, recently published in Arabic, her mother explains to her grandmother, who disapproved of girls going to school, that her husband (Leila's father) had insisted that his daughters go to school. Not only had he commanded his wife in this, but he himself had been commanded to send his daughters to school by King Mohamed V (because he was a nationalist).

35. Sondra Hale, "Feminist Process and Self-Criticism," (in Gluck and Patai, eds., *Women's Words*, p.132) uses these words to describe her frustrating experience interviewing Sudanese feminist Fatma Ahmed Ibrahim. This had some resonance for me when I looked back on my interviews with some of the nationalist women.

Chapter 5. Malika El Fassi

1. *8 mars*, April 1987. Translation by Leila Abouzeid.

2. "If people had read Mostapha Sadiq Rafiff's article, published in *Arrissala* magazine, they would have seen how an expert writes about a young man who was shot with six bullets by his foreign wife. A young Moroccan man also wrote about the subject in the paper *Al Umma* under the title, 'How our hopes are being dashed on the rock of Western civilization' because he saw the signs of this sickness in Morocco."

3. *8 mars*, April 1987.

4. After Sidi Allal Al Fassi was exiled to Gabon in 1937, Si Mohamed Al Yazidi, Haj Omar Ben Abdeljalil, Si Ahmed Mekouar, Si Abdelaziz Ben Driss, Haj Ahmed Balafrej and others continued to work in a restricted group. They weren't joined by some youth like (Mehdi) Ben Barka until 1943–44.

5. "There were five nationalist leaders in town: myself, Mohamed Bensouda, Abdelkabir Al Fassi [my brother], Mohamed Saadani, and Hassan Benchekroun."

6. Mohamed Ben Abdeljalil (November 17, 1992 interview in Fez) explained this in more detail: "The nationalist movement was remarkably successful in carrying the dead through the narrow streets of the medina and across the rooftop terraces, jumping thus from one house to another. In order to cross the streets by way of the terraces they used wooden planks, and in that way avoided the danger of being noticed or caught by the army that had laid siege to the medina of Fez. It was in this way that the bodies were taken from the Qaraouine mosque to the Mosque of the Dead in the Andalusian section of Fez. The distance between the two places is at least a thirty-minute walk, for someone who is completely healthy and fit. This was all done in the

middle of the darkest night. The French colonial authorities had decided to scatter these bodies; to bury them separately, in different places, so that the Fassi people wouldn't know the whys and wherefores of these deaths. However, the public will had decided otherwise: the nationalists infiltrated the mosque and transferred the dead from the Andalous mosque to Oued El Hrayki, which is now a cemetery to be found in Hay Echouhada [the area of the martyrs]. . . . They dug graves, and buried no less than thirty-one bodies, among which there were two women. One of these was named Kabour Mengad."

7. Women in mourning for their husbands not only wear white kaftans and head coverings, but also lots of additional white shawls wrapped all around them and around their faces.

8. At this point there were no women trained as teachers, and so a special exception had to be made, overriding the mores of the time to enable men to teach girls who were past puberty. This is why male teachers are cautioned to be beyond reproach in their dealings with female students.

9. The stereotypes that women are lazy and easily distracted, and that they can't be trusted.

10. In the French system *6ième* was equivalent to the American 8th grade, and *5ième* to 9th grade.

11. Dr. Abdelhadi Tazi, historian and director emeritus of the Institut universitaire de la recherche scientifique in Rabat. Dr. Tazi lived in Fez at the time, and taught Arabic in the women's section of the Qaraouine.

12. July 4, 1995 interview.

Chapter 6. Zhor Lazraq

1. Leila Messaoudi, quoted in Zakya Daoud, *Féminisme et politique au Maghreb*, p. 251.

2. She said of Abdelaziz Ben Driss, a nationalist leader she much admired, that "What was important to him was to do what it was his duty to do." It seems to me that might apply equally to Zhor Lazraq herself.

3. Known to most Americans as the founding of the State of Israel.

4. In 1993 the first two women were elected to the Moroccan parliament.

5. She is referring to Algerian support for the Polisario in the dispute over the former Spanish Sahara.

Chapter 7. Rqia Lamrania and Fatima Benslimane Hassar

1. Interview with Aboubakr El Kadiri, at his home in Salé, May 14, 1992.

2. As assistant to the treasurer of the Family Welfare Association, under Mme. Ghallab.

3. Her son said that he was 57; but his mother didn't want to reveal her age. In a subsequent interview, in June 1995, she said that she was 84.

4. *Rajab* is the month before *Chaban* in the Muslim calendar. The month after *Chaban* is *Ramadan*, the Muslim month of fasting.

5. The plural of *sharif*, descendents of the Prophet.

6. *Dada* is used for older women servants, something like "grandmother".

7. *Ghaif* and *b'gher* are different kinds of pancakes, traditionally prepared in Morocco for special occasions.

8. Muslims are meant to give one tenth of their money and property to charity.

9. This was a story that Malika El Fassi told her many years later.

10. It wasn't actually a university yet; they called it a *Institut Supérieure* (Institute of Higher Education).

Chapter 8. Oum Keltoum El Khatib

1. *Lalla* is a Moroccan form of address for women—Lalla Fatima would be Ms. Fatima. But it isn't really translatable here: *woman* sounds awkward and *madam* much too formal.

2. When Oum Keltoum El Khatib had read the English text [which she had translated into Arabic] for the chapter, she rewrote the whole chapter in Classical Arabic, keeping most of the same content, but changing drastically the style, tone, and language of the piece. We finally arrived at a compromise: I have made the cuts and additions that she requested, but I have kept the original (more colloquial, spoken) language. In this particular passage, her version was quite different from my translation of the original oral version, so I am including her new version here exactly as she wrote it (translated into English): "I still remember that my grandmother used to carry me on her shoulders and sing nationalist songs which women used to repeat, during the Rif war, to encourage men to fight better. Here is a sample in Moroccan dialect: 'Lalla, oh Lalla, the sound of guns is near the river. My brother, the one in the djellaba, has heard the guns near the river. Lalla, oh Lalla, we've sent help [soldiers], and with God's help may he come back safe.' This is how women used to sing songs and use them to exchange news or inform the warriors in the nearby area."

3. I was accompanied by Amina Fahim, a Moroccan friend and colleague.

4. Ramadan, the Muslim month of fasting, is a month in the Islamic calendar, which means that in the Christian calendar the dates of Ramadan shift. Each year Ramadan begins about two weeks earlier than it did in the previous year.

5. The prayer between the one at noon and the one in the evening.

6. The evening prayer before the last prayer of the day.

7. The American landing in Casablanca, "Operation Torch".

8. A number of the women I talked to, especially those from the nationalist movement, expressed this point of view. As far as I could tell, they were projecting onto the French the views of some Moroccan men, that if women came out of seclusion and got an education they might be a dangerous force.

9. Referring to the role of women in Fez. Women didn't actually use arms, as far as I know, but they did pose a dangerous threat to the French and their military by throwing rocks and boiling oil off the terraces, and shouting out youyous that, according to one source, were "more fearsome than all the armies of Napoleon."

10. Congratulations on the birth of a child.

11. At this point, in rewriting the chapter, Oum Keltoum added a section describing what other women did in the forties in Casablanca, especially the Amor sisters—Amina and Habiba—and Meriem Ben Della. One group of women bought a house and made it into a "House of Students" to house and feed students who came from a distance. On the second floor they opened a center to teach literacy and practical skills to women. Hajja Amina Amor and another woman started a "Center for the Poor" to provide general medical services and also facilities for women giving birth. Later, they started another center, "The Girl's Future," offering free primary schooling for girls and classes in needlework, crochet, and other skills; and then a daycare center called "Small World." "Although Hajja Amina got very sick—finally her legs were paralyzed—she continued all her activities and projects, and supervised many others, even when confined to a wheelchair, right up to the time of her death in 1994." Hajja Habiba, Hajja Amina's sister, got together with some other women, got land from the king, and built a center called "House of the Ma'allma" to offer courses in literacy and practical skills to girls; it was directed by Meriem Ben Della. After the king's exile, Hajja Habiba joined up with the resistance, transporting arms between Tangiers and Casa. "She was able to do this because she had a Spanish passport, and looked extremely elegant and beautiful dressed in European clothes. The police never suspected that she was a Moroccan." After independence, she created a "Center for the Children of Martyrs," and later she opened another center in Tangiers for the education of orphans. Meriem Ben Della created three daycare centers after independence, as well as an institute called *Taher Sebti*, which is still operating today, enrolling over eight hundred girls training to be nurses and governesses.

12. The surname *Roudani* just means that they came from Taroudannt. People were named according to the regions they came from. In any case, most of the resistance fighters didn't use their real names; they took new names for the resistance.

13. Ashes also keep things dry, so a revolver would be prevented from rusting.

14. Greetings. Literally, "Peace be with you."

15. Her husband added, "That baby was born while I was in prison, and died while I was still in prison. She brought me the baby to see while I was in prison, and in eight months she was dead."

Chapter 9. Amina Leuh and Khadija Bennouna

1. The Reform Party was the nationalist party in the north.

2. Specifically, 1936–1939. Moroccans, especially those from the Rif and the north of Morocco, fought with Franco's forces in the Spanish Civil War.

3. It was called "asphyxiating gas."

4. Leaders like Emir Chekib Arsalane, one of those leaders who was enthusiastic about the Moroccan cause.

5. It was called the Ahiya School, but it was just for boys.

6. Tangiers was an international city, which didn't belong to either the Spanish or the French zones. It had a lively diplomatic and cultural life.

7. *Medrassa Aasriya* (Modern School).

8. Al Hoceima is East of Tetouan. It is a major city of the Rif. Amina Leuh asked her mother to describe how and where she was born. "She described to me the place where I was born as a small village with a lot of almond trees. It was so abundant with almonds that people composed a song on this village: 'Let's go, Hmood, Let's go to Adooz/ You'll stay in the shadow/ And I will give you almonds.'" [Hmood is the name of the fiancé, and Adooz is the name of the village. The Arabic word for almonds is *looz*.]

9. Amina Leuh comments: "I personally believe that our being with the Spanish was beneficial. It helped us to open up to the outside world, so that we didn't remain enclosed in our world."

10. After independence, "I bid them farewell and left them there, because I had to follow my husband to Rabat, because he was working [in Rabat] in the Supreme Court."

11. Meaning that they were moving from the struggle for independence into the larger struggle against underdevelopment, to build the country.

12. "My husband was a teacher and a poet. He came to Rabat to work in the court; he had interests in law but also in literature. He is from the area of Rabat originally, but he went to the north because the French were particularly tough with the nationalists in 1938, so those who could not escape were taken to prison. He ran away to the north, and went back to Rabat after independence."

13. Mehdi Bennouna was the Moroccan representative at the United Nations in the late 1940's, making the case for UN support of Moroccan independence.

14. Torres was her mother's brother. He was the president of the Reform Party and the leader of the nationalist movement in the north.

15. The word she actually uses is *khalifa*, a word which is associated with the companions/successors of the Prophet Mohamed. "To mention their names: The president was Khadouj Rkainia, wife of Sidi Ahmed Ghaylen [who is one of the founders of the national movement]. We made her the president; she was the first lady in the city of Tetouan. I was her assistant. Oum Keltoum Torres, the sister of Abdelkhalek Torres, was the general secretary; her assistant was Khadiouj Lakhtibi, the wife of Abdellah Lakhtib."

16. At that time, he was in New York at the United Nations.

17. The Americans started getting rid of some Quonset huts where they housed their troops on the base at Kenitra. They gave them to the charity organization instead of throwing them away.

Part III, Chapter 10. Casablanca and the Woman of the Resistance

1. During the protectorate, a large-scale rural-urban migration caused the cities to grow faster than the population as a whole, and this growth was concentrated in the new cities along the Atlantic coast, especially Casablanca, and in Oujda on the border with Algeria. See Bernard, *Maroc*, vol. 3, pp. 87–91.

2. I found estimates of women who worked outside the home ranging from one in five to one in ten.

3. Men at that time said that women were one of the primary causes of unemployment, especially European and Jewish women. Adam, *Casablanca*, vol. 1, p. 447.

4. Montagne, *Naissance du prolétariat*, pp. 239–241; J. and S. Lacouture, *Le Maroc à l'épreuve*, p. 324.

5. Nelly Forget, "Femmes et professions," pp. 112, 118.

6. Adam, *Casablanca*, vol. 1, p. 447.

7. Katan, *Oujda*, p. 293.

8. Baron and Pirot, "La famille prolétarienne," pp. 26–54.

9. Repudiation, the most common form of divorce, was all the easier because most marriages in the proletariat were performed as *fatha* (a marriage concluded without the legal forms, in front of a few witnesses).

10. Adam, *Casablanca*, vol. 2, p. 747.

11. Ibid., vol. 1, p. 210. The same census showed only 2 percent of men in Casablanca who were widowed or divorced, and 2.2 percent in Morocco as a whole.

12. Ibid., vol. 2, pp. 741–742.

13. Baron, "Mariages et divorces à Casablanca," p. 42.

14. All of the women whose oral histories appear here, except Aicha and Mine Senhaji, have a current *Carte de Résistant* from the High Commission of Veterans of the Resistance and Liberation Army, which certifies their status as a veteran of the armed resistance.

15. Marie-Aimée Helie-Lucas, in Badran and Cooke, eds., *Opening the Gates*, pp. 105–106.

16. Italian oral historian Luisa Passerini points out that in ancient Greek, *mythos* and *istoria* had a shared meaning of discourse or narration, but with different implications. Myth implies project, plot, or tale, while history implies search, interrogation, and examination. Oral history lies somewhere between myth and history, with a complex relationship to both. Chapter 3 in Raphael Samuel and Paul Thompson, eds., *The myths we live by*, pp. 49 foll.

Chapter 11. Fatna Mansar

1. February 25, 1992. Thami Naamane was one of the five people who started building the organization of the armed resistance in 1947. Soumaya Naamane-Guessous is a professor of psychology at Ben Msik University in Casablanca. She has written a groundbreaking study of sexuality among young Moroccan women (*Au Dela de Toute Pudeur*, Casablanca: Editions eddif, 1991) and, most recently, a book on menopause and Islamic women. On April 16, 1994, I did a second interview with Fatna Mansar at her home in Casablanca. Material from both interviews is included here, but the shape of the narrative is that of the first interview.

2. Fatna was the first woman from the armed resistance that I met. Later I realized that of all the women of the armed resistance that I met, she was the most intellectual, including a good deal of analysis and commentary in her narrative.

3. She is referring to the 1936-1939 Palestinian uprising, not the (better-known) 1948–49 war.

4. What she says also has the sense of, "What is wrong with this woman?"

5. The old walled city of Casablanca, an area entirely populated by Moroccans, many of them poor.

6. Fatna and some of the other women of the armed resistance often referred to their husbands as "the man" (*rajel*) rather than "my husband" (*rajli*).

7. In this, Fatna was making the distinction between going out alone to women's meetings, which she had done earlier, and actually going to visit (stay with) another family without her husband, which she was doing for the first time in her life.

8. "We were Touria [Seqatte], Batoul Sbihi, Fatima Hassar, and Lalla Rqia Lamrania; two from Salé and the others from Rabat."

9. Translation by Leila Abouzeid.

10. Thami Naamane (and some other male resistance leaders) spoke in similar terms about hopes for the country after independence: "We wanted Morocco to have an economic policy, an agricultural policy, an interior policy, and a foreign policy. We had the means to make Morocco move forward in all these areas, and without needing anything from foreign countries. But in all the plots that people hatched regarding Morocco, it was always the French who were behind them. They were always plotting something that would benefit them, even up to the present time. There are still plots."

11. Here, at Fatna's request, I turned off the tape recorder while she discussed things that she did not want made public.

12. Bouabid and Ben Barka of the UNFP (which later became the USFP).

Chapter 12. Saadia Bouhaddou

1. The date was May 29, 1992.

2. Salam Al Bachir, who still lives in Casablanca.

3. See Chapter 15, Oujda.

4. Bouchaib had Sadiaa's poison pill, which she had given to him when they were cleaning out the house before her husband came home on leave.

5. Abbess Sbai.

6. In Islamic law, the husband can divorce his wife at will, and can also take her back at will within a certain period of time. But the third repudiation is final. This was what she was referring to when she said she finally got her divorce.

7. From a 1986 interview with Rachida Laouina (for her history BA thesis research), printed in the November 1986 issue of *8 mars*. Translation by Leila Abouzeid.

8. Lawyer and president of the Doustour Union, former Prime Minister.

Chapter 13. Ghalia Moujahide

1. It was March 9, 1992.

2. Reciting the beginning of the Muslim creed.

3. Cherqaoui was the head of Ghalia's resistance organization.

4. Akkari, where the revolt took place, is a poor neighborhood in Rabat, in the Cité Yacoub El Mansour district.

5. She was dressed in white because she was in mourning for her husband's death.

6. His name, *Djayji*, means the person who sells poultry.

7. There are 20 *rials* in a Moroccan *dirham*, which is currently equivalent to about 15 American cents.

8. The *mouqqadam* is a Moroccan local government official.

9. Ghalia's husband died in 1993.

Chapter 14. Aicha and Mina Senhaji

1. Mounaidil was a name given to Senhaji by King Mohamed V in recognition of his services. It means "resistance fighter."

2. The Senhaja are a powerful, rich tribe from the south who established the first great Berber dynasty, the Almoravids, under the leadership of Youssef Ben Tachfine, who established his capital in Marrakesh in 1062 and went on to conquer the north of Morocco and as far east as Algiers. Abdellah Senhaji and his family are descendents of Youssef Ben Tachfine and shorfa (descendents of the Prophet Mohamed).

3. Senhaji was about thirty-two years old (he was born in 1918) when he married Aicha.

4. Hajja Zohra, the wife of Commandant Miloudi, in Oujda, is also a friend of Aicha's and Mina's, and Rabiaa is also someone Saadia Bouhaddou knew during the resistance, as she used to travel back and forth between Oujda and Casablanca. But Saadia does not know the other women from the Senhaji networks in Casa/Rabat or Nador.

5. Zaim was his name in the resistance. Now he uses Fahim. His daughter is Amina Fahim.

6. See the Halima Ben Moussa–Ghalia Moujahide argument in Chapter 16.

7. Later I went to see Assila M'Barka and Halima Ben Moussa, the two who had been angriest, at their homes for individual interviews, and while they were still basically very angry and bitter, I began to understand better the roots of that anger (and they understood better what I was doing writing the book). Assila M'Barka was bitter that she had been denied the second card (in 1975 when they were reviewing dossiers,

she was weeded out). And Halima Ben Moussa felt that she and her husband had suffered greatly during the resistance and resented that now she and her children were still having a hard time just surviving (while others who didn't do as much were living well). Halima was denied her card at first, on the grounds that she had "only" been helping her husband. While she finally received it, on appeal, she is still bitter.

8. The date was June 28, 1995.

9. Two children of the neighbors were born with crippled legs, because the mother was so scared of the police while she was pregnant. In that period, lots of women had problems giving birth or children born crippled because of the difficult times.

10. Mina claimed that her daughter Khadija was born mute because she inhaled so much of cooking smoke and odors while she was pregnant, but Aicha said that Khadija fell on her head when she was eight months old, and that it was that accident that caused her to lose her speech. She also commented that if all the women who did a lot of cooking ended up having mute children there would be very few children in Morocco who were not born mute.

11. Mina originally said that she was sixteen, but Aicha corrected it to eighteen. This correction was important to Aicha (and her daughter Malika) because it means that Aicha is the younger of the two wives.

12. Abbess was killed in the Rif on June 25, 1956.

13. *H'bibti* means "Auntie." It is the term that Malika uses to refer to Mina, her father's second wife.

14. After Senhaji's death on September 17, 1985, King Hassan II told the governor of Rabat to take care of all arrangements and expenses for the funeral. He also directed that the two widows receive special pensions (what Aicha refers to here as a salary) for the rest of their lives, and that the families of the two wives each receive a villa and an *agrément* for a bus. The funeral and forty-day commemoration were indeed taken care of by the palace, and Senhaji's family received some money immediately after his death to pay hospital bills and to tide them over for a while. But the special pensions, the bus agréments and the villas that the king had promised them never materialized. There was no question that the king had given the directive, but the directive was never carried out. Finally Malika was the one who took on the job of actually getting what was given to them by the king. She worked on this from 1985 to 1989, and managed to get the special pensions. In 1995, she was back at work to get the bus agréments and villas.

15. This was a party created by veterans of the resistance and liberation army together with some younger intellectuals, including Dr. Zaki M'barek and Dr. Bihi. Malika continued in the party after her father's death; she was a counselor in the Parti de l'Action. They had even created a Party of the Moroccan Woman, but unfortunately it wasn't a success because it didn't have good leadership. But now the party isn't active anymore; there is still an office, but there isn't really a political party.

16. Abdellah Senhaji, *Al Tarak harakat al-Mugawama.*

17. In another conversation, Aicha and Malika said that Senhaji *never* talked to his family about what was going on. He tried to protect them from all of that.

Chapter 15. Zohra Torrichi and Rabiaa Taibi: Oujda

1. September 1955 Synthesis of conference of French military attachés. *Algérie —Affaires Politiques*, Cote 2131, dossier 3.

2. Yvette Katan, *Oujda, Une ville frontière du Maroc, 1907–1956* has an extensive analysis of the complex relations between the several distinct racial and religious groups in Oujda, focusing especially on Moroccan, Algerian, and French Jews.

3. In fact there was a law passed in Fez in 1937 which forbade women to wear the djellaba; this made the wearing of the djellaba a symbol of protest and women's emancipation; it also led to the substitution of Western heeled shoes for the traditional *belgha* and to carrying a European-style handbag. Paul Decroux, *Féminisme et Islam*, p. 11.

4. This is the only, rather elliptic, account I had of the French attacking, raping Moroccan women. Interview with Fatna Mezouar and Zineb Oumri, Oujda, April 1994.

5. Interview with Fatna Mezouar and Zineb Oumri, Oujda, April, 1994.

6. See Y. Katan, *Oujda*, part 3, section 2, Chapter 2, p. 359 foll. Algerian Muslims in Oujda found themselves in a situation where they didn't form a part of any other group: They couldn't assimilate with the French, who ultimately treated them as "natives"; they were not really foreigners; and yet they were also not assimilated with their Moroccan coreligionists, as they were just about a generation ahead of Moroccans in their access to French culture, education, and the liberal professions.

7. Even women who did not play active roles, who were just living in Oujda, told me that they experienced the Algerian war more than their own struggle against French colonialism.

8. Interview with Fatna Mezouar and Zineb Oumri, Oujda, April 1994.

9. Mohammed Moussaoui was the witness.

10. He was killed trying to assassinate Ben Arafa, the "false" sultan who had been imposed on Moroccans by the French when they exiled Mohamed V.

Part IV, Chapter 16. Conclusion

1. Saida El Mnebhi. Jbabdi, "The Moroccan Women's Movement," part 3.

2. The *Union socialiste des forces populaires* (USFP), the successor to the UNFP, and the *Parti progressiste populaire* (PPS), successor to the Moroccan Communist Party.

3. That is, postponed until after socialism was achieved. Jbabdi, *op. cit.* part 3.

4. Some of them from the women's section of the *Organisation de l'action démocratique populaire* (OADP), and some independent feminists.

5. Quoted in Akharbach and Rerhaye, *Femmes et politique*, pp. 101–102.

6. Belarbi, "Mouvements des femmes," p. 187.

7. Cited from an OFI information pamphlet published about 1990. See also Daoud, *Féminisme et politique*, p. 317.

8. The major opposition parties Left of the Istiqlal are the USFP and the PPS. See Daoud, *Feminisme et politique*, pp. 340–341.

9. Bessis and Belhassen, *Femmes du Maghreb*, p. 263.

10. The *Fête du Trône* [Celebration of the Monarchy], celebrated on the date that Hassan II acceded to the throne in 1961.

11. Daoud, *Féminisme et politique*, p. 333.

12. The date commemorates the exile of King Mohamed V and his family on August 20, 1953, and is called "The Celebration of the King and the People."

13. From King Hassan II's address, French version printed in *l'Opinion*, August 20, 1992.

14. Jayawardena, *Feminism and Nationalism in the Third World*, analyses and compares the histories of Turkey, Egypt, Iran, India, Sri Lanka, Indonesia, the Philippines, China, Vietnam, Korea, and Japan in this regard. The framework of this section and much of the information is based on her study.

15. Capitalism here is a shorthand to describe the opening up of traditional economies to incorporate them into the commercial, capitalist systems of the metropolis.

16. A somewhat similar retreat from expanded roles and rights for women occurred in the so-called developed countries (Europe and the United States) after World War II, contributing to the American "feminine mystique" that Betty Friedan chronicled in 1963. See Higonnet et al., eds., *Behind the Lines*, and Gluck, *Rosie the Riveter Revisited*.

17. Nawal El Sadawi, *The Hidden Face of Eve*, p. 176. Cited in Jayawardena, op. cit., p. 55.

18. Gadant, *Le nationalisme algérien et les femmes*, pp. 135 foll.

19. See Amrane, *Les femmes algériennes et la guerre*.

20. Ibid., pp. 270–71.

21. *Centre des Archives d'Outre-Mer*, Aix-en-Provence. Algérie—Affaires Politiques: cote 2131, dossier 3. General directive from Robert Lacoste to officers of the French military forces stationed in Algeria, May 19, 1956.

22. *8 mars* 56 (November 1991), part 3 of Jbabdi's series on the Moroccan women's movement.

23. See Gluck, *Rosie the Riveter Revisited*, pp. 259–60.

24. Even now, most Moroccan women do not continue their education after they are married; in that respect marriage still represents a definite shift in focus, from a woman's own development to her role as wife and mother.

25. Gadant, *Le nationalisme algérien*, pp. 137–38.

26. Gadant, *Parcours d'une intellectuelle*, p. 133, discusses the aspirations of Algerian women in similar terms.

27. Much of the material in this section is taken from Alison Baker, "History and Myth: Women's Stories of the Moroccan Resistance," in *Oral History Review* 22/1 (Summer 1995), pp. 29–49.

28. Portelli, *The Death of Luigi Trastulli*, pp. 1–2.

29. Ibid.

30. December 2, 1992 in Rabat.

31. *l'Haj Si* are honorific titles (*Haj* means someone who has been to Mecca), which Ghalia uses because she is younger than Senhaji. Halima Ben Moussa, who was born in 1916, is about the same age as Senhaji, and so just calls him by his name, without any honorific.

32. This interview was on June 5, 1993 in Rabat.

33. This is not so different from what eighteenth century English essayist Lord Kames writes about the evocative force of (fictional) narrative: "When events are related in a lively manner, and every circumstance appears as passing before us, we suffer not patiently the truth of the facts to be questioned." Lord Henry Home Kames (1761), p. 37. Cited in William Ray, *Story and History*, p. 2.

34. Ray, *Story and History*, p. 3. In discussing "narrative authority and social identity in the eighteenth century French and English novel," Ray comments that "the truth is always mediated by some motivation or agenda, and hence beyond perception in a pure state."

35. Both Abdellah Senhaji and Hammou Ben Moussa are dead. Even if they were alive, I doubt that they would remember this event or that it would have the same significance for them that it has for Ghalia Moujahide and Halima Ben Moussa.

36. Said, *Orientalism* suggests that "Western" views of the "Orient" have generally been fantasies seeking to dominate their object.

37. Gluck and Patai, eds., *Women's Words* gives a sampling of American scholars writing on the theory and practise of women's oral history.

38. Gadant, *Parcours d'une intellectuelle*, pp. 150–51.

39. Ibid. Gadant goes on to say that it is far better to stick with scholarly investigation and its principles, rather than to let these "disappear in sympathy and sisterhood, [as] the subject of the investigation merges with the anthropologist to such an extent that she has no other function than to listen to what her subject tells her."

40. In Gluck and Patai, eds., *Women's Words*, p. 137 foll.

41. See Gadant, *Parcours d'une intellectuelle*, p. 149. Gadant, as a young woman married to an Algerian, was potentially more of an insider and was thus more threatening. Being in my fifties, and a mother, gave me some commonality with the women I was interviewing, and also meant that I represented no threat, unlike a young woman who would threaten sexual competition with other women and all the chaos (*fitna*) associated with female sexuality.

42. Ruth Behar, *Translated Woman*, p. 301 and 34–36 footnotes.

Selected Bibliography

Books and Articles

Abouzeid, Leila. *The Year of the Elephant*. Austin: University of Texas Press, 1989.

———. *Assirah a'datiya*. (*Autobiography*.) Rabat: Self-published, 1995.

Abu-Lughod, Janet. *Rabat: Urban Apartheid in Morocco*. Princeton, NJ: Princeton University Press, 1980.

Abu-Lughod, Lila. *Writing Women's Worlds*. Berkeley: University of California Press, 1993.

Adam, André. "Naissance et développement d'une classe moyenne au Maroc." *Bulletin Economique et Social du Maroc* XIX, no. 68 (March, 1956) pp. 489–492.

———. *Casablanca: Essai sur la transformation de la société marocaine au contact de l'Occident*. Publications du Centre de Recherches sur l'Afrique Méditerranéene, Aix-en-Provence; Editions du Centre National de la Recherche Scientifique, Paris. [1968] 2 vols.

———. *Bibliographie critique de sociologie, d'ethnologie et de géographie humaine du Maroc*. Algiers, Mémoires du centre de recherches anthropologiques préhistoriques, XX. [1972] [Completed December, 1965]

Ahmed, Leila. *Women and Gender in Islam*. New Haven and London: Yale University Press, 1992.

Akharbach, Latifa, and Narjis Rerhaye. *Femmes et Politique*. Casablanca: Editions le fennec, 1992.

Amiti, Khadija. "Changement social et la situation de la femme au Maroc." *L'Avenir de la famille au moyen orient et en Afrique du nord*. Actes du Colloque, Tunis, 21–23 February, 1989. Cahier du CERES, Série Psychology No. 7, Tunis: December, 1990. pp. 107–125.

Amrane, Djamila. *Les femmes algériennes dans la guerre*. Paris: Editions Plon, 1991.

Aouchar, Amina. *La presse marocaine dans la lutte pour l'indépendance (1933–1956)*. Series: Sciences Humaines. Casablanca: Wallada, 1990.

Asad, Talal. *Anthropology and the Colonial Encounter*. London: Ithaca Press, 1975.

Asad, Talal, and John Dixon. "Translating Europe's Others." *Europe and Its Others.* Vol. 1. University of Essex, Colchester, 1985.

Ashford, Douglas E. *Political Change in Morocco.* Princeton: Princeton University Press, 1961.

Ayache, Albert. *Le Maroc. Bilan d'une colonisation.* Collection La Culture et les hommes. Paris: Editions sociales, 1956.

———. *Le mouvement syndical au Maroc.* 2 vols. Paris-Casablanca: L'Harmattan-Wallada, 1982–1990.

Badran, Margot, and Miriam Cooke, eds. *Opening the Gates: A Century of Arab Feminist Writing.* London: Virago Press, 1990.

Barkallil, Nadira. "La naissance et le développement du prolétariat féminin urbain." Mémoire d'études supéreures en sciences économiques, Université Mohammed V, Rabat, November, 1990. [unpublished thesis]

Baron, Anne-Marie. "Mariages et divorces à Casablanca." *Hesperis.* Paris: Institut des Hautes Etudes Marocaines de Rabat, XL, 1953.

Baron, Anne-Marie, and Henri Pirot. "La famille prolétarienne." *Cahiers des faits et idées.* No. 19. Rabat: 1955.

Behar, Ruth. *Translated Woman.* Boston: Beacon Press, 1993.

Belarbi, Aicha. "Mouvements des femmes au Maroc." *La société civile au Maroc.* Ed. N. Aoufi. Rabat: Smer, 1992. pp. 185–196.

Benaboud, M'Hammed. "Un document nouveau sur les événements sanglants de Tetouan [8 février, 1948]." *Revue d'Histoire Maghrebine.* Nos. 33, 34, pp. 197–212. Tunis: June, 1984.

Ben Jelloun, Tahar. *La nuit sacrée.* Paris: Editions du seuil, 1987.

Benjelloun, Abdelmajid. *Approches du colonialisme espagnol et du mouvement nationaliste marocain dans l'Ex-Maroc Khalifien.* Rabat: Editions Okad, 1988.

———. *Le patriotisme marocain face au protectorat espagnol.* Rabat: Editions Okad, 1993.

Benseddik, Fouad. *Syndicalisme et politique au Maroc, 1930–1956.* Paris: l'Harmattan, 1990.

Bernard, Stéphane. *Maroc, 1943–1956.* 3 vols. Brussels: Editions de l'Institut de Sociologie de l'Université Libre de Bruxelles, 1963.

Berque, Jacques. *Deux ans d'action artisanale à Fes.* Paris: 1940.

———. *Le Maghreb entre deux guerres. Collection Esprit Frontière ouverte,* Paris: Editions du Seuil, 1962.

Bessis, Sophie, and Souhayr Belhassen. *Femmes du Maghreb: L'Enjeu.* Moroccan edition: Casablanca: Editions Eddif, 1992.

Brown, Kenneth. *People of Salé: Tradition and Change in a Moroccan City, 1830–1930.* Manchester, UK: Manchester University Press, 1976.

Buttin, Paul. *Le drame du Maroc.* Paris: Editions du Cerf, 1955.

Cagne, Jacques. *Nation et nationalisme au Maroc.* Rabat: 1988.

Cerych, Ladislav. *Européens et Marocains, 1930–1956: sociologie d'une décolonisation.* Bruges: De Tempel (Collège d'Europe), 1964.

Chraibi, Driss. *Le passé simple.* Paris: Editions Denoel, 1954.

Clifford, James, and George E. Marcus, eds. *Writing Culture: The Poetics and Politics of Ethnography.* Berkeley: University of California Press, 1986.

Combs-Schilling, M.E. *Sacred Performances: Islam, Sexuality and Sacrifice.* New York: Columbia University Press, 1989.

Crapanzano, Vincent. *Tuhami: Portrait of a Moroccan.* Chicago: University of Chicago Press, 1980.

Daoud, Zakya. *Féminisme et politique au Maghreb.* Casablanca: Editions Eddif, 1993.

Davis, Susan S. *Patience and Power: Women's Lives in a Moroccan Village.* Rochester, VT: Schenkman Books, Inc. 1983.

Decroux, Paul. *Féminisme et Islam: la femme dans l'Islam moderne.* Casablanca: Gazette des tribunaux du Maroc, 1947.

Delanoe, Guy. *Mémoires historiques.* 3 vols. Paris: Editions l'Harmattan, 1988 (Vol. 1) and 1991 (Vols. 2,3).

Dwyer, Daisy Hilse. *Images and Self-Images: Male and Female in Morocco.* New York: Columbia University Press, 1978.

Dwyer, Kevin. *Moroccan Dialogues: Anthropology in Question.* Baltimore: Johns Hopkins University Press, 1982.

Eberhardt, Isabelle. *Notes de route.* Paris: 1923.

Eickelman, Dale F. *Moroccan Islam: Tradition and Society in a Pilgrimage Center.* Austin and London: University of Texas Press, 1978.

————. *Knowledge and Power in Morocco: The Education of a Twentieth Century Notable.* Princeton, NJ: Princeton University Press, 1980.

Fassi, Allal El, *An-Naqd ad-dati* (Autocritique). Beirut: Dar el-kechaf, 1952.

————. *The Independence Movement in Arab North Africa* (Al Harakat al-Istiqlaliyah fi al-Maghrib al'Arabi—Cairo, 1948). Translated by Hazem Zaki Nuseibeh. New York: American Council of Learned Societies, 1954. Reprint, New York: Octagon Books, 1970.

Fassi, Mohammed El, and Emile Dermenghem. *Nouveaux contes fassis*. 2nd ed. Paris: Editions d'Aujourd'hui, 1976.

Fernea, Elizabeth Warnock, and B.Q. Bezirgan, eds. *Middle Eastern Muslim Women Speak*. Austin: University of Texas Press, 1977.

Forget, Nellie. "Femmes et professions au Maroc. Attitudes à l'égard du travail professionel de la femme au Maroc." *Revue Internationale des Sciences Sociales* XIV, 1, (1962).

Foucauld, Vicomte Charles de. *Reconnaissance au Maroc*. 2 vols. Paris: 1888 (vol. 2 published in 1939). Reissued as one volume, Paris: Editions d'Aujourd'hui, 1985.

Frisch, Michael. *A Shared Authority*. Albany: State University of New York Press, 1990.

Gadant, Monique. *Parcours d'une intellectuelle en Algérie: Nationalisme et anti-colonialisme dans les sciences sociales*. Paris: l'Harmattan, 1995a.

————. *Le nationalisme algérien et les femmes*. Paris: l'Harmattan, 1995b.

Gaillard, Henri. *Une ville de l'Islam: Fes*. Paris: 1905.

Gaudio, Attilio. *Guerres et paix au Maroc [Reportages: 1950–1990]*. Paris: Editions Karthala, 1991.

Geertz, Clifford. *Islam Observed: Religious Development in Morocco and Indonesia*. New Haven: Yale University Press, 1968.

————. *After the Fact: Two Countries, Four Decades, One Anthropologist*. Cambridge, MA: Harvard University Press, 1995.

Geertz, Clifford, Hildred Geertz, Lawrence Rosen (and a photographic essay by Paul Hyman). *Meaning and Order in Moroccan Society: Three essays in cultural analysis*. Cambridge: Cambridge University Press, 1979.

Ghabrit, Si Kaddour ben. *La femme arabe dans l'Islam* (Conférences franco-marocaines). Paris: Plon-Nourrit, 1916.

Ghallab, Abdelkrim. *Tarikh al haraka al watania bi al Magrib* (History of the nationalist movement in Morocco). 2 vols. Rabat: Arissalah Press, 1987.

————. *Attatawur a'dasturi wa a'niyyabi bi al Magrib, 1908–1988* (Constitutional and parliamentary development in Morocco, 1908-1988). Casablanca: Matba'a annajah al jadida, 1988.

Gluck, Sherna Berger. *Rosie the Riveter Revisited: Women, the War and Social Change.* New York: Meridien, 1988.

Gluck, Sherna Berger, and Daphne Patai, eds. *Women's Words: The Feminist Practice of Oral History.* New York and London: Routledge, 1991.

Goichon, Amélie-Marie. "La femme de la moyenne bourgeoisie fasiya." *Revue des études Islamiques*, I. Paris: P. Geuthner, 1929.

Gordon, Murray. *Slavery in the Arab World.* New York: New Amsterdam Books, 1989.

Grele, Ronald J. *Envelopes of Sound: The Art of Oral History.* Chicago: Precedent Publishing, 1975.

Hajjarabi, Fatima. "Les souks féminins dans le Rif Central: Rareté des biens et profusion social." In *Femmes Partagées*, pp. 41–58. Casablanca: Le Fennec, 1988.

———. "Sauver le forêt ou sauver les femmes: la corvée de bois chez les Ghmara." In *Jbala - Histoire et Société. Etudes sur le Maroc du Nord Ouest*, pp. 373–94. Casablanca: CNRS and Wallada, 1991.

———. "Recherches sur les femmes rurales: Essai de bilan." In *Femmes rurales*, pp. 13–23. Casablanca: Le Fennec, 1996.

———. *Les souks féminins du Rif centrale: Anthropologie de l'échange féminin.* Unpublished Thesis. University Paris VII, 1987. Histoire et civilisation du monde musulman.

Hakim, Mohamed Ben Azzouz and Mohamed Molato. "Moroccan Women and Armed Resistance in the North of Morocco." Trans. from Arabic by Leila Abouzeid. In *Journal of the Ministry of Handicrafts and Social Affairs*. Rabat: 1991.

Hall, Michael. "Leila Abouzeid's Year of the Elephant: a Postcolonial Reading." *SPAN* (Journal of the South Pacific Association for Commonwealth Literature and Language Studies) 36 (October 1993): vol 2, pp. 377–384.

Halstead, John P. *Rebirth of a Nation. The Origins and Rise of Moroccan Nationalism 1912–1944.* Cambridge, MA: Harvard University Press, 1967.

Hardy, Georges. *L'âme marocaine d'après la littérature française.* Paris: Editions du Bulletin de l'enseignement publique du Maroc, April, 1926, No. 73. Librairie Emile Larose, 1926.

Harrak, Fatima. *Reflexions sur l'apport de la Salafiya à l'evolution des femmes marocaines, (1930–1955).* Unpublished Master's Thesis. University of Paris VIII, History Department, June, 1975.

Harris, Walter. *Morocco That Was.* Edinburgh and London: William Blackwood, 1921.

Hassan II. *Le défi.* A. Michel, 1976.

Helie-Lucas, Marie-Aimée. "Women, Nationalism and Religion in the Algerian Liberation Struggle." In M. Badran and M. Cooke, eds., *Opening the Gates*. London: Virago Press, 1990.

Hermansen, Marcia K. "The Female Hero in Islamic Religious Tradition." *The Annual Review of Women in World Religions*. Vol 2: *Heroic Women*, eds. Arvind Sarma and Katherine K. Young. Albany: SUNY Press, 1992. pp. 111–143.

Higonnet, Margaret R., Jane Jenson, Sonya Michel, and Margaret M. Weitz, eds. *Behind the Lines: Gender and the Two World Wars*. New Haven: Yale University Press, 1987.

Hijab, Nadia. *Womanpower*. Cambridge: Cambridge University Press, 1988.

Hoisington, William. *The Casablanca Connection: French Colonial Policy, 1936–1943*. Chapel Hill, NC: University of North Carolina Press, 1984.

Jayawardena, Kumari. *Feminism and Nationalism in the Third World*. London: Zed Books, Ltd., 1986.

Jbabdi, Latifa. "The Moroccan Women's Movement." *8 mars*. 3 parts: Issue nos. 56, 57, 58 (1991).

Julien, Charles-André. *Le Maroc face aux impérialismes, 1415–1956*. Paris: Editions Jeune Afrique, 1978.

Kadiri, Aboubakr al. *Difta'an a'n al mar'a al muslima* (In defense of the Muslim woman). Casablanca: Matba'a annajah al jadida, 1990.

Katan, Yvette. *Oujda, une ville frontière du Maroc (1907–1956)*. Rabat: Editions la porte, 1993.

Keddie, Nikki, and Beth Baron, eds. *Women in Middle Eastern History*. New Haven: Yale University Press, 1991.

Lacouture, Jean and Simonne. *Le Maroc à l'épreuve*. Paris: Seuil, 1958.

Lahlou-Alaoui, Zakia. *D'Algésiras à Aix-les-bains ou la guerre des mots*. 3 vols. Rabat: Editions Okad, 1991.

Landau, Rom. *Moroccan drama 1900–1955*. London and San Francisco: R. Hale, 1956.

———. "The Karaouine at Fez." *The Muslim World* 48, (1958). (Hartford, Conn.)

Laroui, Abdellah. *The Crisis of the Arab Intellectuals*. Berkeley: University of California Press, 1976.

———. *Les origines sociales et culturelles du nationalisme marocain 1830-1912*. Paris: Maspéro, 1977.

———. *Esquisses historiques*. Casablanca: Centre Culturel Arabe, 1992.

Lasskier, Michael M. *The Alliance Israélite Universelle and the Jewish Communities of Morocco: 1862–1962.* Albany: State University of New York Press, 1983.

Malti-Douglas, Fedwa. *Woman's Body, Woman's Word.* Princeton: Princeton University Press, 1991.

Mernissi, Fatima. *Le Maroc raconté par ses femmes.* Rabat: Societé marocaine des éditeurs réunis, 1984.

————. *The Veil and the Male Elite.* Translated by Mary Jo Lakeland. Reading, Mass: Addison Wesley Publishing Company, 1991a.

————. *Women and Islam.* Oxford: Blackwell, 1991b.

————. *Dreams of Trespass: Tales of a Harem Girlhood.* Reading, Mass: Addison-Wesley Publishing Company, 1994.

Montagne, Robert. *Naissance du prolétariat marocain: Enquête collective (1948–1950).* Series: Cahiers de l'Afrique et de l'Asie III. Paris: J. Peyronnet, 1951.

Moulay Rchid, Abderrazak. *La condition de la femme au Maroc.* Rabat: Editions de la Faculté des sciences juridiques économique et sociales de Rabat, 1985.

————. *La femme et la loi au Maroc.* Casablanca: Editions le fennec, 1991.

Munson, Henry, Jr. *The House of Si Abd Allah: The Oral History of a Moroccan Family.* New Haven and London: Yale University Press, 1984.

Ouardighi, Abderrahim. *La grande crise franco-marocaine 1952–1956.* Rabat: Editions Ouardighi, May, 1975.

————. *Al Maghrib, min harb arrimal ila halat khassa, 1963–1965.* (Morocco, from the war of the sands to the state of exception, 1963-1965). Chapter 3, "The political trials of the UNFP." pp. 31–33. N.p., July 5, 1986.

————. *Al muqawama al maghribiah didda al himaya al farancia, 1952–1956* (The Moroccan resistance against the French protectorate, 1952–1956) Rabat: Al Anbaa, n.d.

Ouazzani, lz Arab Mohamed Hassan. *Entretiens avec mon père: la lutte pour la démocratie et l'indépendence, 1946–1955.* Fès: Fondation M.H. Ouazzani, 1989.

Oved, Georges. *La gauche française et le nationalisme marocain, 1905–1955.* 2 vols. Paris: Editions l'Harmattan, 1984.

Perrault, Gilles. *Notre ami le roi.* Paris: Editions Gallimard, 1990.

Portelli, Alessandro. *The Death of Luigi Trastulli and Other Stories.* Albany: State University of New York Press, 1990.

Rabinow, Paul. *Reflections on Fieldwork in Morocco.* Berkeley and Los Angeles: University of California Press, 1977.

Ray, William. *Story and History: Narrative Authority and Social Identity in the Eighteenth Century French and English Novel.* Cambridge, MA and Oxford: Basil Blackwell, Inc., 1990.

Rézette, Robert. *Les partis politiques marocains.* Paris: Librairie Armand Colin, 1955.

Rosander, Eva Evers. *Women in a Borderland: Managing Muslim Identity where Morocco meets Spain.* Stockholm: Stockholm Studies in Social Anthropology 26, 1991.

Rosen, Lawrence. *Bargaining for Reality: The Construction of Social Relations in a Muslim Community.* Chicago: University of Chicago Press, 1984.

Sadawi, Nawal. *The Hidden Face of Eve: Women in the Arab World.* London: Zed Press, Ltd., 1980.

Said, Edward W. *Orientalism.* London: Routledge and Kegan, 1978.

———. *Culture and Imperialism.* New York: Alfred A. Knopf, 1991.

Samuel, Raphael and Paul Thomson [eds]. *The Myths We Live By.* London and New York: Routledge, 1990.

Senhaji, Abdellah. *Al Tarak harakat al-Muqawama wa Jaich a Tahrir al Maghribi min 1947 ila 1956* (Memoires: The History of the Resistance and the Moroccan Army of Liberation from 1947 to 1956). Mohamedia: Fedala, 1986-1987.

Sonbol, Amira El Azhary, ed. *Women, the Family, and Divorce Laws in Islamic History.* Syracuse, New York: Syracuse University Press, 1996.

Stewart, Charles R. *The Economy of Morocco, 1912–1962.* Cambridge, MA: Harvard Middle Eastern Monograph Series, 1967.

Stivers, Camilla. "Reflections on the Role of Personal Narrative in Social Science." *Signs* 18, no. 2 (Winter 1993). University of Chicago Press.

Témoignage Chrétien. *Le drame marocain devant la conscience chrétienne: les événements de Casablanca à travers la Presse Française du Maroc.* Paris: Cahiers du Témoinage Chrétien, 1953.

Tourneau, Roger le. *Fes avant le Protectorat: Etude économique et sociale d'une ville de l'Occident Musulman.* Casablanca: Publication de l'Institut des Hautes Etudes Marocaines [Rabat], XLV, 1949.

———. "Social Change in the Muslim Cities of North Africa." *The American Journal of Sociology.* Chicago: LX, May, 1955.

———. *Vie quotidienne à Fes en 1900.* Paris: Hachette, 1965.

Varde, Michel de la. *Casablanca: ville d'émeutes.* Paris: Givors, 1955.

Voinot, Capitaine L. *Oudjda et l'Amalat [Maroc]*. Extrait du Bulletin de la Societé de Géographie et d'Archéologie de la Province d'Oran, 1911-1912. Published in Oran, 1912.

Waterbury, John. *The Commander of the Faithful. The Moroccan Elite: a study of segmented politics*. London: Weidenfeld and Nicolson, 1970.

Weitz, Margaret Collins [ed]. *Celebrating Human Rights: Papers from the Bicentennial Symposium on Human Rights*. Boston: Suffolk University, 1990.

————. "Mémoire et oubli: Women of the French Resistance." *Contemporary French Civilization*. Vol. XVII, No, 1, Special Issue, Winter/Spring, 1994.

Zaki, M'barek. "Résistance et Armée de Libération marocain." Unpublished Doctoral Thesis. Université d'Aix-en-Provence: November, 1973.

————. "Résistance et Armée de Libération marocain." *Al Assass* 8 (February, 1978).

————. *Résistance et Armée de Libération: Portée politique, liquidation, 1953–1958*. Tangiers: E.T.E.I., 1987.

Periodicals and Archives

Al Maghrib [Arabic] Published in Salé 1937–1944, then in Rabat 1937, 1952 and after independence. Malika El Fassi articles in 1935 and 1943 issues.

Esprit Issues 1947–1955.
  "Les Evenements de Casablanca par la presse et les témoins." *Esprit*. February, 1953.

Al Alam [Arabic] and *l'Opinion* [French] Istiqlal Party papers, published in Rabat 1946–52 and then after independence.

Anoual [Arabic] OADP party paper. Series of articles on the resistance and the nationalist movement starting 28 February, 1992.

8 mars [Arabic] Interviews with women veterans of the national movement and armed resistance, and 3-part article by Latifa Jbabdi on the Moroccan women's movement.
  December, 1983 - Interview with widow of Allal Ben Abdellah.
  July, 1984 - Oumma Fatima, veteran of the resistance and mother of a political prisoner.
  November, 1986 - Saadia Bouhaddou interview.
  1986, issue 31, p. 7 - Khaddouj Zerktouni interview.
  1987 - Interview with Malika El Fassi.
  May, July and November issues, 1991 - 3-part series on the Moroccan Women's Movement by Latifa Jbabdi.

[*Solidarity*] [Arabic] Periodical published by the Moroccan Association for Human Rights [OMDH]. No. 7: April, 1990. Testimony of Oum Amina, veteran of the independence movement and the resistance.

Maroc-Europe Nos. 1–8. Rabat: Editions la Porte, 1991-1995.

Liberation: Spécial Mehdi Ben Barka [29 October, 1995]

Dossiers de l'Histoire du Maroc [monthly journal in French and Arabic, Publication Director, Professor M'barek Zaki], Nos. 1 [June, 1996] and 3 [August, 1996]

Archives de la France d'Outre-Mer, Aix-en-Provence
Archives du Gouvernement Général de l'Algérie - Série II, Soussérie 30-H-52.
Algérie - Affaires Politiques: cote 2131, dossier 3.

Index